Removed

HEALTH-RELATED COOKBOOKS:
A Bibliography

by
TIAN-CHU SHIH

The Scarecrow Press, Inc.
Metuchen, N.J., & London
1991

British Library Cataloguing-in-Publication data available

Library of Congress Cataloging-in-Publication Data

Shih, Tian-Chu, 1958-
 Health-related cookbooks : a bibliography / by Tian-Chu Shih.
  p. cm.
 Includes indexes.
 ISBN 0-8108-2513-9 (alk. paper)
  1. Diet therapy--Bibliography. 2. Cookery--Bibliography.
 I. Title.
 Z6665.D53S54 1991
 [RM216]
 016.6158'54--dc20   91-38133

With Tim

to

our loved ones,

the Shihs,

Su-Ying & Wen-Chi,

the Caldwells,

Tandra, Dondeena, & Maurice,

and

the Gerigs,

Dean, Selena, & Sonja

TABLE OF CONTENTS

CONTENTS

INTRODUCTION

A key in federal funding and scientific research especially during recent years has been to investigate the leading factors causing death. Thus the emphasis has been on prolonging human life. Although predisposed genetic combinations still play an important role in many lethal diseases, overwhelming evidence has been produced to link health and personal behavior. Some of the ties are smoking, drinking, exercising, wearing seat belts, and eating habits. Among these links, diet has great influence on our risk for several of the leading causes of death for Americans, notably, coronary heart disease, stroke, atherosclerosis, diabetes, and some types of cancer. These disorders together account for more than two-thirds of all deaths in the United States.

The worldwide trend toward healthier eating has spawned a burgeoning number of cookbooks published on health-related topics with deterrence and remedy as their focus. Among these subjects are prevention and treatment of cancer, coronary heart disease, and obesity; diabetes treatment; and various kinds of diets for longevity. However, despite the widespread and growing interest in health-related cookbooks, to date, there are no book-length bibliographies with the above scope listed in either *Books In Print* or *Forthcoming Books*.

This bibliography was created to fill this void and facilitate the locating of cookbooks on a specific health-related subject. Inclusion criteria are broad and include cookbooks published by vanity presses, commercial publishers, university presses, and the U.S. federal government regardless of distribution mechanisms, i.e., cookbooks range from free publications on meals for cancer patients to an expensive cookbook with color pictures. However, this bibliography includes only English-language books.

Comprehensiveness is almost impossible to achieve and has not been the main focus. All entries are unique. Each of the 1,092 listings appears in only one location. This placement was according to prevalent characteristics of the cookbook. To find other books of interest to the user, see the Detailed Chapter Outlines and the Diet Plan Locator Guide immediately following the Introduction.

In the creation of this book, my definition of health-related cookbooks encompasses
1. preventive or therapeutic diets, either specific for a certain illness, such as arthritis and renal diseases, or broad, such as low-salt and low-fat diets;
2. diets for pursuing longevity or improvement of general health, such as normal diets for children, macrobiotic and vegetarian diets.

To maintain a balance of cookbooks falling under the above categories, popular subjects (such as low-fat, low-cholesterol, and weight-reducing diets) are from 1980 to 1991, and for uncommon subjects, the inclusion date begins in 1970. This bibliography is targeted to assist health-conscious individuals, health-related offices, hospitals, and all types of libraries.

INTRODUCTION

Section I includes diets for specific diseases or disorders: cancer; coronary heart disease, hypertension, and cerebrovascular disease; diabetes mellitus; food intolerance; gastrointestinal diseases and disorders; muscular-skeletal diseases and disorders; oral and dental diseases and disorders; renal and kidney diseases and disorders; weight disorders-obesity; and other diseases and healing in general. Section II features diets for general health: life stages (pregnancy, infants and toddlers, children and teenagers, athletes, and the elderly); macrobiotic; natural foods; and vegetarian.

Within each chapter, cookbooks are further subdivided according to the individual diet plans: high-fiber, high-complex-carbohydrate, high-calcium, low-fat, low-cholesterol, low-calorie, and so on. Whenever possible, an annotation is provided. Each cookbook is given a number following a letter code designating a particular chapter. For example, the letter code "CA" in CA68 stands for cancer. This coding will be useful in the keyword index. It will become apparent, for example, which of the low-fat dietbooks are specifically designed for preventing coronary heart disease, or obesity. At the end of each chapter, a selected list of associations and foundations is given, with addresses and telephone numbers, when available.

To increase the access points of this book, as mentioned above, Detailed Chapter Outlines and a Diet Plan Locator Guide are provided immediately after the Introduction. The Diet Plan Locator Guide is a subject guide for locating specific diets. Under each diet plan in the Guide appear chapter name, subject headings within that chapter (pertaining to a particular diet plan), and dietbook codes under the subject heading. Three appendixes provide additional help following the Author, Title, and Keyword

Indexes, and References: Appendix 1, Directory of Selected Publishers; Appendix 2, Numbers of Deaths and Ranks of Selected Causes of Death, All Races, United States, 1985-88; and Appendix 3, 1990 Dietary Guidelines and Advice for Americans.

As a medical student favoring primary medicine, a preventive and holistic approach is my central interest. Food may not be the sole curing source but will assist in preventing and combating diseases. Dietary and nutritional information should be routinely disseminated at physicians' offices. Included in this bibliography are many health-related cookbooks, orthodox or not, even some that have received negative endorsements from the medical community. As a professional librarian of seven years, providing information without exercising individual censorship has been deeply rooted in me. All patients and their families have the right to know and to help select a personalized regimen with honest and complete background information provided. Such is the intent of this "book of books" in providing a wide selection of health-related cookbooks.

This bibliography is designed as a reference tool, not as a medical manual or a guide to self-treatment. Please seek competent medical advice in selecting treatment for illness or ailments before application of the dietary therapies listed in this book.

Tian-Chu Shih
College of Osteopathic Medicine
Michigan State University
East Lansing, Michigan, U.S.A.

DETAILED CHAPTER OUTLINES

CANCER (CA)

CORONARY HEART DISEASE, HYPERTENSION, AND CEREBROVASCULAR DISEASE (C)

DIABETES AND HYPOGLYCEMIA (D)

MUSCULAR-SKELETAL
DISEASES AND DISORDERS (MS)

ORAL AND DENTAL
DISEASES AND DISORDERS (OR)

RENAL AND KIDNEY
DISEASES AND DISORDERS (R)

WEIGHT DISORDERS - OBESITY (W)

HEALING IN GENERAL
AND
OTHER DISORDERS (H)

NATURAL INGREDIENTS (N)

In general N1-N36
With tofu, tempeh, and other soybean products N37-N52
Selected Associations and Foundations

VEGETARIAN DIET (V)

In general V1-V35
Fast & simple cuisine V36-V43
Festive cuisine V44-V51
From around the world V52-V57
From America, north and south V58-V60
From Asia V61-V77
From Europe V78-V86
From the Middle East V87-V88
With microwave oven V89-V91
With natural ingredients V92-V106
Yoga vegetarian diet V107-V111
Zen vegetarian diet V112-V114
Selected Association and Foundations

DIET PLAN LOCATOR GUIDE

under each diet plan, the word "in" is followed by the chapter name, then the subject headings within that chapter (pertaining to a particular diet plan), and the dietbook codes under the subject heading

CORN-FREE DIET
    in FOOD INTOLERANCE
        gluten-free milk-free egg-free <u>corn-free</u> diet F75-F83

EGG-FREE DIET
    in FOOD INTOLERANCE
        gluten-free milk-free <u>egg-free</u> diet F66-F83
        milk-free <u>egg-free</u> diet F94-F95

FISH AND SEAFOOD DIET
    in CORONARY HEART DISEASE...
        <u>fish and seafood</u> diet C17-C19

GLUTEN-FREE DIET
    in FOOD INTOLERANCE
        <u>gluten-free</u> diet F49-F84

HIGH-CARBOHYDRATE DIET
    in WEIGHT DISORDERS - OBESITY

SECTION I

DIETS

FOR SPECIFIC

DISEASES OR DISORDERS

CANCER (CA)

CANCER, also known as malignant neoplasm or tumors, is a group of conditions of uncontrolled cell growth originating in almost any tissue of the body. According to *Health, United States, 1990* (National Center for Health Statistics. Hyattsville, Maryland, 1991), cancer has been the second leading cause of death in the United States since 1985.

Complex interrelationships are now recognized between nutrition, physical activity, life-style, and development of various organsite cancers. The precise mechanisms underlying these connections as well as the nature of direct cause-effect relationships are the subjects of intense scientific investigation.

Although cancer's causal factors can be both environmental and genetic, besides external carcinogens such as cigarettes and alcohol, diet has been proven to be linked to cancer. The National Cancer Institute Dietary Guidelines state: reduce fat intake, increase fiber intake, include a variety of vegetables and fruits in the daily diet, avoid obesity, consume alcoholic beverages moderately, and minimize consumption of salt-cured, salt-pickled, and smoked foods.

Despite some inconsistencies in the data, animal studies reveal an effect of dietary fat on carcinogenesis and support fat's cancer-promoting role. International epidemiologic studies on humans have indicated a risk for breast, colon, and prostate cancers in correlation with total fat consumption.

In a large cohort study conducted by the American Cancer Society, the lowest overall cancer mortality was observed in men whose body weights ranged from 10 percent below to 20 percent above the average for their age and height. The lowest overall risk for women was seen in those whose weights ranged from 20 percent below to 10 percent above the average for their age and height. Nonsmoking males (who usually weigh more than smokers but have a lower cancer risk) showed a relationship between relative body weight and cancer death (that was nearly linear). In the United States, individuals greater than 40 percent overweight have mortality ratios (observed cancer deaths divided by expected cancer deaths) that are higher than those of average-weight individuals: 33 percent for men and 55 percent for women. In men, this relationship was statistically significant for cancer of the colon, rectum, and prostate, and in women, for cancer of the breast, uterus (cervix and endometrium), ovary, and gallbladder.

Dietary fiber includes components of plant materials that, when eaten, resist the action of human digestive enzymes. Carbohydrate and carbohydrate-like cellulose, hemicelluloses, lignin, gums, and pectins are some of the diverse chemical constituents of dietary fiber. High-fiber diets have not only been recommended for cancer prevention, especially colon cancer, but have also been touted as beneficial for individuals with coronary heart disease caused by extreme high cholesterol, diverticulosis, diabetes, and obesity. Major high-fiber food sources such as fruits, vegetables, whole grains, and legumes are also high in complex carbohydrates.

A large body of evidence suggests that foods high in vitamin A and carotenoids, cruciferous vegetables, and dark yellow-orange and green vegetables are protective against a variety of epithelial cancers such as those of the oral cavity, bladder, lung, and intestinal tract.

Despite some difficulties in distinguishing the cancer-producing effects of excessive alcohol intake from those of cigarette smoking, evidence suggests that a reduction in alcohol intake among the portion of a population that drinks most heavily would help to reduce the prevalence of cancers of the mouth, esophagus, pharynx, and perhaps other sites.

The following books include contemporary orthodox and unorthodox diets for cancer patients and cancer prevention. They are ranged by various types of diet plans such as high-fiber, high-fiber with whole grains, high-fiber with legumes, macrobiotic, and low-fat. Consult the Diet Plan Locator Guide and the Keyword Index for additional low-fat, high-fiber cookbooks included in other chapters.

PATIENT DIETS

IN GENERAL

CA1 Fishman, Joan and Anrod, Barbara. *Something's got to taste good: the cancer patient's cookbook.* Kansas City, MO: Andrews and McMeel, 1981.
ISBN: 0-8362-2103-6   222 p.
** high-protein and high-calorie recipes detailing calorie and protein content

CA2 King, Joy D. *Back to the bio-basics: a collection of recipes, menus, and diet information to aid alternative treatment of cancer/candida as recommended by cancer/candida treatment centers in Mexico.* U.S.A.: J.D. King, 1986.
ISBN: 0-9398-2500-7   288 p.
** presents recipes for treating candidiasis and cancer

CA3 Livingston-Wheeler, Virginia and Wheeler, Owen Webster. *Food alive--man alive: diet handbook for cancer and chronic diseases.* San Diego, CA: Livingston-Wheeler Medical Clinic, 1977.
ISBN: 0-9188-1605-X   221 p.

CA4 Rippon, Sadhya. *The Bristol recipe book: over 150 recipes from the Bristol Cancer Help kitchen.* London: Century Hutchinson Ltd., 1987.
ISBN: 0-7126-1518-0   150 p. illustrated
** vegetable recipes for cancer patients based on the

meals served to cancer patients in the Bristol Cancer Help Centre

CA5 Rosenbaum, Ernest H.; Stitt, Carol A.; Drasin, Harry; and Rosenbaum, Isadora R. *Health through nutrition: a comprehensive guide for cancer patients*. San Francisco, CA: Life, Mind, & Body, 1977.
ISBN: 0-9312-9003-1   120 p.
** dietary approach to common problems, sample menus and recipes for special diets: pureed, fat-restricted, bland, low-residue diets

CA6 Society for Cancer Research Staff. *Cookery book: from the Lukas Clinic for patients with cancer or precancerous conditions*. Translated by Anna R. Meuss. Hudson, NY: Anthroposophic Press, 1988.
ISBN: 0-8544-0716-2   72 p.

FOR CHEMOTHERAPY PATIENTS

CA7 Aker, Saundra N. and Lenssen, Polley. *A Guide to good nutrition during and after chemotherapy and radiation*. 3rd ed. Seattle, WA: Fred Hutchinson Cancer Research Center. Distributed by Clinical Nutrition Program, Division of Clinical Research, The Center, 1988.
147 p. illustrated
** preventing and controlling side-effects caused by chemotherapy and radiation, with high-calorie, high-protein, high-vitamin, and high-mineral recipes; includes lists of foods suggested to control specific reverse effects

associated with cancer treatments

CA8   American Cancer Society. *Nutrition: for patients receiving chemotherapy and radiation treatment*. Atlanta, GA: American Cancer Society, Inc., 1974. 65 p.
** high-protein and high-calorie recipes for beverages, snacks, desserts, and liquid feedings; suggestions on dealing with chewing problems and eat & taste appeal of food

CA9   *Eating hints: recipes and tips for better nutrition during cancer treatment*. Bethesda, MD: U.S. Dept. of Health, Education, and Welfare, Public Health Service, National Institutes of Health, National Cancer Institute, 1990. 86 p. illustrated, some color
** includes suggestions to combat specific side-effects caused by chemotherapy and radiation treatment; recipes are high in calories, protein, and vitamins; originally prepared by members of the Yale-New Haven Medical Center; can be obtained free from the National Cancer Information Hotline 1-800-422-6237 and is NIH publication no. 91-2079

CA10 Margie, Joyce Daly and Bloch, Abby S. *Nutrition and the cancer patient*. Radnor, PA: Chilton Book Co., 1983. ISBN: 0-8019-7120-9   269 p.
** recipes are high in calorie and protein; offers practical solutions for specific problems associated with chemotherapy and radiation treatment; special chapter on nutritional needs for children with cancer

FOR CANCER CHILDREN

CA11 Sherman, Mikie. *Feeding the sick child.* Bethesda, MD:
National Institutes of Health, 1978.
68 p.   illustrated
** designed for children with cancer

GRAPE THERAPY

CA12 Brandt, Johanna. *How to conquer cancer, naturally: the
grape cure.* Palm Springs, CA: Tree of Life Publications,
1989.
ISBN: 0-9308-5206-0
** a cookbook on the therapeutic use of grapes, revised
edition of *The grape cure*, 1928

LAETRILE THERAPY

CA13 Prince, Patricia; Gwyn, Sandra Prince; and Prince, Ellen
Beck; compilers. *The Contreras Clinic laetrile cookbook.*
Lott, TX: E.S.P., distributed by the Devin-Adair Co.,
1979.
ISBN: 0-8159-5221-X   247 p. illustrated
** features Ernesto Contreras Clinic's cancer therapy
recipes; applications of laetrile therapy

CA14 Salaman, Maureen Kennedy. *Nutrition, the cancer
answer.* Menlo Park, CA: Statford Pub., 1983.
ISBN: 0-9130-8700-9   309 p. illustrated

** contains recipes on the therapeutic use of laetrile

MACROBIOTIC DIET

CA15 France, Richard. *Healing naturally: the commonsense macrobiotic approach to cancer and other diseases.* 2nd rev. ed. Boulder, CO: Amaizeing Books, 1982.
139 p.   illustrated
** macrobiotic recipes included

CA16 Kushi, Aveline and Esko, Wendy. *Macrobiotic cancer prevention cookbook: recipes for the prevention & control of cancer.* Garden City Park, NY: Avery, 1988.
ISBN: 0-8952-9391-9   170 p. illustrated

CA17 Levin, Cecile Tovah. *Cooking for regeneration: macrobiotic relief from cancer, AIDS, and degenerative disease.* Tokyo: Japan Publications, distributed in USA through Harper and Row, 1988.
ISBN: 0-8704-0692-2   320 p. illustrated, color

CA18 Nussbaum, Elaine. *Recovery: from cancer to health through macrobiotics.* Tokyo: Japan Publications, 1986.
ISBN: 0-8704-0643-4   208 p.
** a macrobiotic diet book for cancer patients

PREVENTIVE DIETS

IN GENERAL

CA19 American Cancer Society, Florida Division, Inc. *The Good book of nutrition.* Nashville, TN: Favorite Recipes Press, 1987.
ISBN: 0-8719-7223-9   207 p. illustrated, color

CA20 Bohannon, Richard; Wuerthner, Terri P.; and Weinstock, Kathy Klett. *Food for life: the cancer prevention cookbook.* Chicago: Contemporary Books, 1986.
ISBN: 0-8092-5029-2   418 p.

CA21 Cross Cancer Institute. *Try it!: a cookbook for cancer.* Edmonton, AB: Cross Cancer Institute, 1984.
ISBN: 0-9691-6750-4   151 p. illustrated

CA22 De Winter, Jan. *How to avoid cancer.* Poole, Dorset: Javelin Books, distributed in USA through Sterling Pub. Co., 1985.
ISBN: 0-7137-1593-6   120 p.

CA23 Reingold, Carmel Berman. *The Lifelong anti-cancer diet.* New York: New American Library, 1982.
ISBN: 0-4511-2220-8   242 p.

CA24 Rivers, Jerry M. and Collins, Karen K. *Planning meals that lower cancer risk: a reference guide.* Washington, DC: The Institute, 1984.
88 p.   illustrated
** published by the American Institute for Cancer Research; section 1 includes food lists for liberal, moderate, and spare consumption; section 2, food patterns for basic diet, low-meat, high-dairy, lacto-ovo-vegetarian,

no legumes, no dark-green or yellow fruits and
vegetables, and no dairy; recipes are included in section
5, titled Practical Suggestions for Implementing Dietary
Guidelines

CA25 White, Kristin. *Diet and cancer*. Toronto, ON: Bantam
Books, 1984.
ISBN: 0-5532-4246-6   239 p.
** based on 1982 and 1983 reports by the National
Research Council's Committee on Diet, Nutrition, and
Cancer

HIGH-FIBER DIET

CA26 Adams, Ruth and Murray, Frank. *A Healthier you --
high fiber diet*. Atlanta, GA: Larchmont Books, 1986.
ISBN: 0-9159-6235-7   344 p.

CA27 Black, Maggie and Howard, Pat. *Eating naturally:
recipes for food with fibre*. London: Faber & Faber,
1980.
ISBN: 0-5711-1603-5   148 p.

CA28 Duff, Gail. *High-fibre cookery*. London: Hamlyn, 1984.
ISBN: 0-6002-0809-5   80 p.   illustrated, color

CA29 Edwards, Linda. *Baking for health: whole food baking
for better health*. Garden City Park, NY: Avery, 1988.
ISBN: 0-8952-9376-5   195 p.

CA30 Egan, Jeanette P. *Healthy high-fiber cooking.* Tucson, AZ: HP Books, 1987.
ISBN: 0-8958-6477-0   160 p. illustrated, color
** recipes for all types of dishes; calorie and fiber content provided for each recipe

CA31 Ellis, Audrey. *High fiber cookbook: over 250 fiber-rich recipes.* New York: Exeter Books, 1985.
ISBN: 0-6710-7720-1   192 p. illustrated, color

CA32 Fleetwood, Jenni; editor. *High fibre meals.* London: Octopus, 1986.
ISBN: 0-7064-2542-1   63 p.   illustrated, color

CA33 Forsythe, Elizabeth. *The High-fibre gourmet.* London: Pelham Books, 1983.
ISBN: 0-7207-1420-6   125 p. illustrated

CA34 Fraser, Margaret and Bishop-MacDonald, Helen. *The Total fibre book.* Toronto, ON: Grosvenor House, 1987.
ISBN: 0-9199-5929-6

CA35 Fredericks, Carlton. *Carlton Fredericks' High-fiber way to total health.* New York: Pocket Books, 1976.
ISBN: 0-6718-0269-0   208 p.

CA36 Groen, Elaine and Rubey, Jane. *Fabulous fiber cookery.* San Leandro, CA: Bristol, 1988.
ISBN: 0-9119-5487-2   187 p. illustrated, some color
** presents high-fiber recipes

CA37 Leach, Alison and Lewis, Jane. *High-fibre cookery.*
London: Octopus, 1986.
ISBN: 0-7064-2622-3   128 p. illustrated, some
color

CA38 Long, Ruth Yale. *Switchover!: the anti-cancer cooking
plan for today's parents and their children.* New
Canaan, CT: Keats Pub., 1984.
ISBN: 0-8798-3400-5   158 p.
** high-fiber recipes using natural foods including whole
grains, raw vegetables, fruits, nuts, and seeds

CA39 Prevention Magazine, editors of. *Fiber primer: how to
build a diet high in the health power of fiber.* Stamford,
CT: Longmeadow Press, 1991.
ISBN: 0-6814-1021-3

CA40 Rosenvall, Vernice; Miller, Mabel H.; and Flack, Dora D.
*The Classic wheat for man cookbook: more than 300
delicious and healthful ways to use stoneground whole
wheat flour.* New ed. Santa Barbara, CA: Woodbridge
Press Pub. Co., 1975.
ISBN: 0-9128-0016-X   229 p. illustrated

CA41 SerVaas, Cory; Turgeon, Charlotte; and Birmingham,
Frederic. *Fiber and bran better health cookbook.* New
York: Bonanza Books, distributed by Crown Publishers,
1981.
ISBN: 0-5173-6168-X   296 p. illustrated

CA42 Stanway, Andrew. *The High-fibre diet book: dietary*

fibre and your health: the essential handbook. 2nd ed.
London: Treasure Press, 1984.
ISBN: 1-8505-1007-5   279 p.
** previously published as *Taking the rough with the smooth*, 1976

CA43 Street, Myra. *The Fiber-plan cookbook.* Secaucus, NJ:
Chartwell, 1985.
ISBN: 0-8900-9863-8   128 p. illustrated, color

CA44 Taylor, Jenni; editor. *100 high fibre dishes.* London:
Octopus, 1984.
ISBN: 0-7064-2054-3   64 p.   illustrated, color

CA45 Tyler, Lorraine Dilworth; editor. *The Magic of wheat cookery.* Salt Lake City, UT: Magic Mill, 1975.
146 p.   illustrated, color

HIGH-FIBER
HIGH-LYSINE DIET

CA46 SerVaas, Cory and Turgeon, Charlotte Snyder. *The High lysine and fiber cancer prevention cookbook.* Old
Tappan, NJ: Fleming H. Revell Co., 1985.
ISBN: 0-8007-1436-9   122 p. illustrated

HIGH-FIBER
LOW-FAT DIET

CA47 Artaud-Wild, Sabine M.; editor. *Simply nutritious!: recipes and recommendations to reduce your risk of cancer.* rev. ed. Portland, OR: American Cancer Society, Oregon Division, 1986.
ISBN: 0-9617-1280-5   180 p.
** high-fiber and low-fat recipes from appetizers to desserts including foods rich in vitamins A and C and cruciferous vegetables; a revised edition of *Simply nutritious*, 1985

CA48 Dickerson, Sandra J. *The Power of prevention cookbook: a return to traditional healthy eating for the 21st century.* Washington, DC: Saville Books, 1991.
ISBN: 0-9296-9302-7
** low-fat and high-fiber recipes included

CA49 Gorbach, Sherwood L.; Zimmerman, David R.; and Woods, Margo. *The Doctors' anti-breast cancer diet.* New York: Simon and Schuster, 1984.
ISBN: 0-6714-9552-6   221 p.
** contains low-fat and high-fiber recipes to prevent and control breast cancer

CA50 Jones, Jeanne. *The Fabulous high-fiber diet: high-fiber, low-fat recipes: the gourmet approach to avoiding cancer and heart disease.* San Francisco, CA: 101 Productions, distributed by Scribner, 1985.
ISBN: 0-8928-6259-9   192 p. illustrated
** features high-fiber, low-fat, and low-calorie recipes

CA51 Koh, Frances M. *Creative Korean cooking: high-fiber,*

low-fat recipes. Minneapolis, MN: East-West Press, 1985.
ISBN: 0-9606-0901-6   148 p. illustrated
** recipes of appetizers, pancakes, soups, meat, seafood, rice, noodles, and sweets

CA52 Lindsay, Anne. *The American Cancer Society Cookbook: over 200 recipes reflecting the newest research on the simple nutritional guidelines that can reduce your risk of developing cancer*. rev. ed. New York: Hearst Books, 1988.
ISBN: 0-6880-7484-7   269 p. illustrated, some color
** high-fiber, low-fat, cruciferous vegetable recipes using ingredients from all four food groups; recipes provide caloric, fat, fiber, vitamin, and mineral contents; a revised edition of *Smart Cooking*

CA53 Orr, Suezanne Tangerose. *Cooking against cancer*. Springfield, IL: C.C. Thomas, 1984.
ISBN: 0-3980-5010-4   131 p.
** recipes follow the National Academy of Sciences dietary guidelines to reduce cancer risk, i.e., each recipe contains foods rich in beta-carotene and/or vitamin C; most recipes are low fat and many contain cruciferous vegetables or whole-grain products

HIGH-FIBER
VEGETARIAN DIET

CA54 Marshall, Janette. *Vegetarian high-fibre cooking*. New

York: Thorsons, 1987.
ISBN: 0-7225-1529-4   144 p. illustrated, some color
** vegetarian recipes including dairy products and eggs; each recipe provides fiber and caloric contents; originally published as *High-fibre cooking*, 1983

CA55 Westland, Pamela. *High-fibre vegetarian cookery.* London: Granada, 1983.
ISBN: 0-5860-5905-9   283 p.

HIGH-FIBER DIET
WITH BROWN RICE

CA56 Eno, David. *The Little brown rice book.* rev. and reset ed. New York: Thorsons, 1983.
ISBN: 0-7225-0854-9   56 p.   illustrated

CA57 Ishida, Eiwan. *Genmai, brown rice for better health.* Tokyo: Japan Publications, distributed in USA through Harper & Row, 1989.
ISBN: 0-8704-0781-3   220 p. illustrated
** a macrobiotic diet cookbook with brown rice

CA58 Pierce, Gail. *The Brown rice cookbook.* London: Paperback Division of W.H. Allen, 1985.
ISBN: 08637-90631   153 p.

CA59 Sams, Craig and Sams, Ann. *The Brown rice cookbook: a selection of delicious wholesome recipes.* Rochester,

VT: Healing Arts Press, 1988.
ISBN: 0-8928-1282-6   128 p. illustrated

HIGH-FIBER DIET
WITH WILD RICE

CA60 Anderson, Beth. *Wild rice for all seasons cookbook.*
Minneapolis, MN: B. Anderson, 1984.
ISBN: 0-9610-0300-6   173 p. illustrated

CA61 Cardiff, Cheryl. *Naturally wild rice: delicious, nutritious,
easy & elegant recipes.* LaRonge, SK: Naturally Wild
Pub., 1990.
ISBN: 0-9198-4581-9   62 p.

CA62 Ojakangas, Beatrice. *The Best of wild rice recipes.*
Cambridge, MN: Adventure Publications, 1989.
ISBN: 0-9348-6056-4   93 p.

CA63 One Thousand & Six Summit Avenue Society Staff.
*Wild rice, star of the north: 150 Minnesota recipes for a
gourmet grain.* New York: McGraw-Hill, 1986.
ISBN: 0-0700-2455-3   188 p.   illustrated

HIGH-FIBER DIET
WITH LEGUMES

CA64 Dixon, Pamela. *The Bean & lentil cookbook: colourful,
inexpensive and highly nutritious pulse recipes: includes*

sweet dishes. New York: Thorsons, 1982.
ISBN: 0-7225-0757-7   128 p. illustrated

CA65 Gregory, Patricia R. *Bean banquets, from Boston to Bombay: 200 international, high-fiber, vegetarian recipes.* Santa Barbara, CA: Woodbridge Press, 1984.
ISBN: 0-8800-7139-7   238 p. illustrated
** a high-fiber international vegetarian cookbook using beans, peas, and lentils

CA66 Norwak, Mary. *Grains, beans & pulses.* London: Bell & Hyman, 1985.
ISBN: 0-7135-2525-8   93 p. illustrated, some color

CA67 Scott, David. *Grains! beans! nuts!* London: Rider, 1980.
ISBN: 0-0914-1681-7   264 p. illustrated
** vegetarian cookery

CA68 Stone, Sally and Stone, Martin. *The Brilliant Bean: sophisticated recipes for the world's healthiest food.* New York: Bantam, 1988.
ISBN: 0-5533-4483-8   276 p.
** recipes of legumes from appetizers, salads, desserts, to main entrees.

HIGH-FIBER DIET
WITH WHOLE GRAINS

CA69 Arthur, Michael; Gaskin, Kathy; Kidder, Lew; and Marvel, Jean. *Uprisings: the whole grain bakers' book.* Rev. ed. Summertown, TN: Book Pub. Co., 1990. ISBN: 0-9139-9070-1   288 p. illustrated
** recipes, arranged by bakeries, collected from more than 30 cooperative whole-grain bakeries; from the 1980 Cooperative Whole Grain Educational Association Conference

CA70 Beck, Howard and Beck, Anna Ruth; compilers. *Whole wheat cookery: treasures from the Wheat Bin.* Halstead, KS: Wheat Bin, Inc., 1986.   165 p.

CA71 Better Homes and Gardens. *Better Homes and Gardens Cooking with whole grains.* Des Moines, IA: Meredith Corp., 1984.
ISBN: 0-6960-1315-0   96 p.   illustrated, some color
** recipes for breakfast, bread, main dishes, and desserts

CA72 Cole, Candia Lea. *Gourmet grains: main dishes made of nature.* Santa Barbara, CA: Woodbridge, 1991.
ISBN: 0-8800-7187-7
** a vegetarian cookbook

CA73 Conil, Christopher and Conil, Jean. *The Wholegrain oven.* London: Foulsham, 1986.
ISBN: 0-5720-1384-1   126 p.   illustrated, some color

CA74 Drachman, Linda and Rosman, Debra. *Great grains.*

New York: Simon & Schuster, 1991.
ISBN: 0-6717-2899-7   160 p.
** whole grain high-fiber recipes for wheat, corn, oats,
rice, barley, millet, rye, amaranth, buckwheat, and quinoa;
a part of *Feed your family right: low-fat low-salt reduced
calories series*

CA75 Fletcher, Janet Kessel. *Grain gastronomy: a cook's guide
to great grains from couscous to polenta.* Berkeley, CA:
Aris Books, 1988.
ISBN: 0-9431-8639-0   112 p. illustrated

CA76 Gelles, Carol. *The Complete whole grain cookbook: how
to buy, prepare & cook all high-fiber grains, including
over 400 recipes from soups to desserts.* New York: D.I.
Fine, 1989.
ISBN: 1-5561-1155-X   514 p.
** includes introduction to grain cooking and recipes for
wheat, rice, corn, barley, buckwheat, millet, oats, rye,
wild rice, amaranth, job's tears, quinoa, teff, triticale, and
breakfast cereal

CA77 Greene, Bert. *The Grains cookbook.* New York:
Workman Pub., 1988.
ISBN: 0-8948-0612-2   403 p. illustrated

CA78 Greene, Diana Scesny. *Whole grain baking.*
Trumansburg, NY: Crossing Press, 1984.
ISBN: 0-8959-4147-3   183 p. illustrated

CA79 Jacobs, Barbara and Jacobs, Leonard. *Cooking with*

seitan: delicious natural foods from whole grains.
Tokyo: Japan Publications, 1987.
ISBN: 0-8704-0637-X   240 p. illustrated
** a vegetarian cookbook using whole grains

CA80 Lambrecht, Helga. *Grains and fibres for optimum health.*
Winnipeg, MB: Gateway Pub. Co., 1986.
ISBN: 0-9193-8309-2   212 p. illustrated, some
color
** includes high-fiber recipes

CA81 Orton, Ellen and Orton, Vrest. *Cooking with wholegrains.* New York: Gramercy Pub. Co., distributed
by Crown Publishers, 1982.
ISBN: 0-5173-6834-X   64 p.
** a baking cookbook

CA82 Parsonage, Sally. *Wholegrains: cereals for essential fibre.* Nottingham, Nottinghamshire: Boots, 1985.
ISBN: 0-5720-1337-X   64 p. illustrated, some
color

CA83 Pitzer, Sara. *Whole grains: grow, harvest, and cook your own.* Charlotte, VT: Garden Way Pub., 1981.
ISBN: 0-8826-6251-1   169 p. illustrated

CA84 Polunin, Miriam. *The Wholemeal kitchen.*   New York,
New York: Thorsons, 1985.
ISBN: 0-7225-1194-9   127 p. illustrated, some
color

CA85 Ridgeway, Don. *The Healthy peasant gourmet: how to enjoy and thrive on a pennies-a-day diet based on whole seed and grain.* Palo Alto, CA: Earth Basics Press, 1983.
ISBN: 0-9103-6100-2   237 p. illustrated

CA86 Ridgway, Judy. *Cooking with nuts & cereals.* London: Century Publishing, 1985.
ISBN: 0-7126-0782-X   118 p. illustrated
** a vegetarian cookbook using nuts and cereals

CA87 Rodale Books; editors of. *The Good grains.* Emmaus, PA: Rodale Press, 1982.
ISBN: 0-8785-7391-7   96 p. illustrated

CA88 Saltzman, Joanne. *Amazing grains: creating vegetarian main dishes with whole grains.* Tiburon, CA: H.J. Kramer, 1990.
ISBN: 0-9158-1121-9   202 p. illustrated
** includes recipes for buckwheat, millet, oats, quinoa, rice, amaranth, job's tears, teff, and recipes for various sauces

CA89 Williamson, Darcy. *The All natural seed & grain cookbook.* Bend, OR: Maverick Publications, 1981.
ISBN: 0-8928-8068-6   153 p.
** using cereals and seeds in baking

LOW-FAT DIET

CA90 American Institute for Cancer Research. *An Ounce of*

prevention. Washington, DC: American Institute for Cancer Research, 1985-1986.
4 vols.   illustrated
** a low-fat cancer prevention and control cookbook based on AICR dietary guidelines; a part of *AICR cookbook series*; vol. 1: Spring, vol. 2: Summer, vol. 3: Fall, and vol. 4: Winter; each recipe includes fat and caloric contents

CA91 Merritt-Peralta Medical Center. Cancer Education and Prevention Center. *The Less fat cookbook: let's eat scrumptious, satisfying food and thrive.* Oakland, CA: Merritt-Peralta Medical Center, 1988. 1 vol.

SELECTED ASSOCIATIONS
AND FOUNDATIONS

American Cancer Society
National Office, 1599 Clifton Road, N.E., Atlanta, Georgia 30329
404-320-3333

Breast Cancer Advisory Center
P.O. Box 224, Kensington, Maryland 20895

Cancer Information Service
(funded by the National Cancer Institute)
NIH Building 31, Room 10A24, Bethesda, Maryland 20892
1-800-4-CANCER

Cooperative Whole Grain Education Association
c/o Wildflour Community Bakery
208 N. Fourth Avenue, Ann Arbor, Michigan 48104
313-994-0601

International Society Against Breast Cancer
26, rue de la Faisanderie, F-75116 Paris, France
1-47-047-032

Leukemia Society of America, Inc.
733 Third Avenue, New York, New York 10017
212-573-8484

Make Today Count
101 1/2 South Union Street, Alexandria, Virginia 22314
703-548-9674 or
703-548-9714

National Cancer Institute
Building 31, Room 10A24, Bethesda, Maryland 20892
1-800-4-CANCER

National Cancer Institute of Canada
77 Bloor Street W., Suite 1702, Toronto, Ontario, Canada M5S 3A1
416-961-7223

National Coalition for Cancer Survivorship
323 Eighth Street, S.W., Albuquerque, New Mexico 87102
505-764-9956

Task Force on Environmental Cancer and Heart and Lung Disease
Office of Health Research (RD-683)
Environmental Protection Agency
401 M Street, S.W., Washington, DC 20460
202-382-5900

World Federation for Cancer Care
44 Ladbroke Road, London W11 3NW, England
1-727-4808

Y-Me National Organization for Breast Cancer Information and Support
18220 Harwood Avenue, Homewood, Illinois 60430
708-799-8338

CORONARY HEART DISEASE, HYPERTENSION, AND CEREBROVASCULAR DISEASE (C)

CORONARY HEART DISEASE includes several cardiac disorders resulting from inadequate circulation of blood to local areas of heart muscle. This deficiency is nearly always a consequence of focal narrowing of the coronary arteries by atherosclerosis. The result of progressive narrowing of the vessels in our body may be angina pectoris, myocardial infarction (also known as heart attack), cerebrovascular diseases (such as stroke), or sudden death. Coronary heart disease has been the number-one killer in the United States since 1985. Of the half-million heart-attack deaths that occur annually, approximately 60 percent occur suddenly or outside of a hospital before treatment can be administered. Thus, much attention is directed at the prevention of coronary heart disease by identifying and modifying risk factors before clinical disease develops.

High blood cholesterol, hypertension (high blood pressure), and cigarette smoking are generally accepted to be responsible for the development of atherosclerosis, which causes heart attacks and strokes. Diet also plays an important role in the regulation of blood cholesterol levels and influences other risk factors for coronary heart disease as well. For millions of Americans, the most effective coronary heart disease preventive strategies are to avoid smoking cigarettes, to control high blood pressure, and to lower high blood cholesterol, especially the low-density-lipoprotein.

Cholesterol is a part of the normal cell membranes, performs necessary functions in the body, and is deposited in the lining of the arteries as atherosclerotic plaques. These deposits, if excessive, may obstruct the flow of blood. Hypercholesterolemia, very high serum cholesterol levels, can be caused by a diet that is high in cholesterol and saturated fat as well as by hypothyroidism, obstructive liver disease, nephrosis, porphyria, and dysproteinemia. Hypercholes-terolemia is also likely to be more severe in the genetically susceptible person.

Of the many dietary factors that have been studied, the strongest and most consistent villain is dietary fat. Clinical, epidemiologic, and animal research implicates (both the amount and nature of) dietary fats as important determinants of plasma cholesterol levels.

Saturated fatty acids were found to increase plasma cholesterol levels and arterial thrombosis while polyunsaturated vegetable oil tended to lower plasma cholesterol levels and decrease arterial clotting. Omega-3 fatty acid, a polyunsaturated fat found in many marine animals, may lessen chances of death from coronary heart disease.

Obesity is associated with many important coronary heart disease risk factors such as hypertension, low levels of high-density-lipoprotein, elevated plasma glucose levels, high blood cholesterol, and hypertriglyceridemia. This increases the risk for coronary heart disease. The connection of weight with coronary heart disease was strongest in those under age 50. Current evidence suggests that leanness and avoidance of weight gain before middle age are advisable goals in the prevention of coronary heart disease for most men and women.

Water-soluble fiber, as found in oat bran, guar gum, psyllium seeds, certain beans, and pectin, have been shown to have cholesterol-lessening effects in humans. Adding of fiber to high-carbohydrate diets has been reported to prevent high triglyceride levels. A high fiber intake is often associated with low-fat diets. The total effect may be additional benefits in cholesterol reduction.

HYPERTENSION, also known as high blood pressure, is a common chronic medical problem in the United States responsible for a major portion of cardiovascular diseases. By 1985, 77 percent of the public identified high blood pressure as the factor that most increases a person's chances of having a stroke, and 91 percent indicated that high blood pressure increases a person's chances of getting heart disease.

Blood pressure is regulated by a complex process involving the interactions of multiple factors that are not completely understood. Ultimately, the regulation of blood pressure reflects the interaction of cardiac output (the amount of blood the heart pumps per unit of time) and total peripheral resistance (the resistance to flow that blood encounters in the arteries and arterioles). Therefore, hypertension is an imbalance of the mechanism that affects either output or resistance, or both.

In over 95 percent of individuals with high blood pressure, the specific cause cannot be determined and sometimes may represent nonspecific disturbances in blood pressure regulation.

The control of hypertension is generally credited to a combination of improved detection and the use of antihypertensive medication. Currently, three nondrug methods are recommended as part of the treatment for established hypertension. They are weight control, alcohol restriction, and sodium restriction. These measures have also gained support as likely to aid in the prevention of high blood pressure, particularly for those at high risk.

Increased body weight is related to increased blood pressure and a fall in blood pressure can be expected with weight reduction. Weight loss is recommended for all overweight persons, particularly for those with hypertension. It has been suggested that control of obesity would eliminate hypertension in 48 percent of whites and 28 percent of blacks. Even when weight loss does not reduce blood pressure to normal, health risks may be reduced, and smaller doses of antihypertensive medication may be needed as a result.

Individuals who regularly consume large amounts of alcohol have higher blood pressure than people who abstain from alcohol or who drink only moderate amounts. This significant positive association was independent of age, relative body weight, exercise, and smoking status. Alcohol restriction in blood pressure control has proven to be of importance.

A direct relationship between decreased sodium consumption and lesser hypertension has been supported in some studies but not others. Investigators have been able to distinguish a salt-sensitive group, whose blood pressure falls in response to sodium restriction, and a salt-resistant group, whose blood pressure tends not to be influenced by changes in salt intake. However, it has not yet been possible to identify a way to consistently distinguish salt-sensitive from salt-resistant persons other than by measuring the blood pressure response itself.

Some population studies have shown both a positive relationship between sodium intake and blood pressure and an inverse relationship between potassium intake and blood pressure. In contrast to these findings, other studies showed no influence of potassium supplementation on high blood pressure. Because the duration of the majority of these studies has been only weeks or months, longer-term intervention studies have been recommended to evaluate the effects on blood pressure of both increased potassium and reduced sodium.

CEREBROVASCULAR DISEASE, or stroke, is the sudden loss of brain function caused by one of four vascular events: thrombosis or a blood clot in a cerebral artery; embolism or blockage of a cerebral artery by a circulating clot; stenosis or narrowing of a cerebral artery by atherosclerosis; or hemorrhage from rupture of a cerebral artery. These events deprive the flow of blood and oxygen and cause brain tissue death and irreversible damage to nerve tissue.

Persons at greatest risk for stroke are those with high blood pressure, diabetics, the obese, and smokers. These major risk factors for stroke are in part related to nutritional, dietary, and lifestyle factors. Diets low in sodium and alcohol, appropriate caloric intake and physical activity to achieve and maintain desirable body weight are recommended to prevent stroke and its related conditions.

Both orthodox as well as unorthodox cookbooks are included for coronary heart disease patients, high-blood pressure patients, and various contemporary preventive diets such as high-fiber, high-complex-carbohydrate, low-cholesterol, low-salt, and low-fat diets. For additional books covering the above topics included in other chapters, consult the Diet Plan Locator Guide and the Keyword Index.

PATIENT DIETS

HEART DISEASES

C1   Binggeli, Frances B. *Heart patient recipes*. New York:
      Vantage Press, 1989.
      ISBN: 0-5330-8068-1   102 p.

C2   Cooley, Denton A. and Moore, Carolyn E. *Eat smart for
      a healthy heart cookbook: from the Texas Heart Institute:
      conform to needs of patients with heart conditions: a
      renowned heart surgeon's plan for good eating, better
      nutrition, and increased longevity.* New York: Barron's,
      1987.
      ISBN: 0-8120-5745-7   386 p. illustrated, some
      color
      ** contains low-fat, low-calorie, low-salt recipes to
      prevent and control heart diseases as well as high blood
      pressure; each recipe provides nutritional information,
      exchange values, and calories; recipes are arranged in
      three main sections: luncheons, light dinners, and
      complete dinners

C3   Cousins, Eleanor. *Caring for the healing heart: an
      eating plan for recovery from heart attack.* New York:
      Avon, 1989.
      ISBN: 0-3930-2590-X   168 p.

C4   Defendorf, Virginia. *Cooking for a healthy heart: recipes
      for after-your-bypass.* Phoenix, AZ: Golden West

Publishers, 1991.
ISBN: 0-9148-4651-5
** contains low-cholesterol, low-salt, and sugar-free
recipes

C5 Hellerstein, Herman K. and Perry, Paul. *Healing your heart: a proven program for reversing heart disease without drugs or surgery.* New York: Simon and Schuster, 1990.
ISBN: 0-6716-8323-3   384 p.
** includes exercise therapy

C6 Keenan, Emma W. *Bypass patients' wellness diet: tasty recipes.* Virginia Beach, VA: Grunwald and Radcliff, 1986.
ISBN: 0-9151-3335-0

C7 Ornish, Dean. *Dr. Dean Ornish's Program for reversing heart disease: the only system scientifically proven to reverse heart disease without drugs or surgery.* New York: Random House, 1990.
ISBN: 0-3945-7562-5   631 p. illustrated
** a vegetarian cookbook including relaxation techniques

C8 Piscatella, Joseph C. *Don't eat your heart out cookbook: and cardiac patient's step-by-step guide to healthy cooking and eating in the real world: with over 400 recipes.* Boston, MA: G.K. Hall & Co., 1989.
ISBN: 0-8161-4746-9   500 p.
** low-cholesterol, low-fat, low-salt, and low-sugar recipes for prevention and control of cardiovascular diseases and weight control

PREVENTIVE DIETS

IN GENERAL

C9   Dept. of the Air Force, U.S. *Healthy heart shopping guide to better eating: guidelines, food groups, and meal plans for a healthier life style.* Washington, DC: Dept. of the Air Force, 1988.   50 p.   illustrated

C10   Jones, Jeanne. *Diet for a happy heart.* rev. ed. San Francisco, CA: 101 Productions, distributed by Ortho Information Services, 1988.
ISBN: 0-8972-1189-8   159 p. illustrated

C11   Langston, Nanda; Kindel, Beverly; and Miller, Regina. *From the heart: recipes from the Taste of Health restaurant.* Wichita, KS: Bio-Communications Press, 1989.
ISBN: 0-9423-3310-1   130 p. illustrated

C12   Lewis, Sylvan. *Heart watcher's complete diet & menu planner.* Hollywood, FL: F. Fell Publishers, 1989.
ISBN: 0-8119-0719-8   116 p.

C13   Nicholson, Susan and Jubera, Cynthia. *Save your heart with Susan: six easy steps to cooking delicious healthy meals in a microwave.* New York: Morrow, 1991.
ISBN: 0-6880-9016-8   360 p.

C14   Olivo, Rey and Dept. of the Air Force, U.S. *The Healthy heart cookbook: recipes.* 2nd ed. Langley Air Force Base, VA: Tactical Air Command, Medical Services, 1990. 98 p. illustrated

C15 Woodruff, Woody. *Cooking the Dutch oven way: with recipes for a healthy heart.* 2nd. Merrillville, IN: I C S Books, 1989.
ISBN: 0-9348-0251-3 160 p. illustrated

C16 Zugibe, Frederick T. *Fourteen days to a healthy heart.* New York: Macmillan, 1986.
ISBN: 0-0263-3610-3 273 p.
** includes recipes as well as exercise and relaxation therapy

FISH AND
SEAFOOD DIET

C17 Fletcher, Anne M. *Eat fish, live better: how to put more fish and Omega-3 fish oils into your diet for a longer, healthier life.* New York: Harper & Row, 1989.
ISBN: 0-0601-5833-6 378 p.

C18 Harsila, Janis and Hansen, Evie. *Seafood: a collection of heart-healthy recipes.* 2nd ed. newly rev. & expanded. Richmond Beach, WA: National Seafood Educators, 1990.
ISBN: 0-9616-4262-9 276 p. illustrated

C19 Morris, Edwin Lee. *Fish, fiber, and fitness: magic keys to a healthy, vigorous, happy life.* Corpus Christi, TX:

Helix Press, 1989.
ISBN: 0-9145-8705-6   154 p. illustrated

HIGH-COMPLEX-
CARBOHYDRATE DIET

C20   Fox, Arnold. *The Beverly Hills medical diet & long-life anti-stress program.* St. Louis Park, MN: Chain-Pinkham Books, 1981.
ISBN: 0-9389-4801-6   207 p.
** features recipes high in complex carbohydrates

HIGH-COMPLEX-CARBOHYDRATE
LOW-CHOLESTEROL DIET

C21   Gold, Robert and Rose-Gold, Kerry. *The Good fat diet.* New York: Bantam Books, 1987.
ISBN: 0-5530-5186-5   195 p.
** a weight-reducing fish cookbook including recipes that are low in cholesterol and high in complex carbohydrates

HIGH-FIBER LOW-CHOLESTEROL DIET

C22   Anderson, James W. *Dr. Anderson's Life-saving diet: the new high-fiber, low-cholesterol way to keep slim & stay healthy.* Tucson, AZ: The Body Press, 1986.
ISBN: 0-8958-6376-6   128 p. illustrated

HIGH-FIBER LOW-CHOLESTEROL
LOW-FAT DIET

C23   Mitchell, Patricia B. *Well, bless your heart: high fiber, low fat, low cholesterol recipes.* Chatham, VA: Mitchells, 1989.
vol. 1.   ISBN: 0-9251-1713-7; Breakfasts & Lunches, 37 p.
vol. 2.   ISBN: 0-9251-1714-5; Dinners, 38 p.

C24   Sunset Books and Sunset Magazine; editors of. *Sunset Light & healthy cook book.* Menlo Park, CA: Sunset Publishing Corp., 1990.
ISBN: 0-3760-2428-3   240 p. illustrated, color
** low-calorie, low-cholesterol, low-fat, and high-fiber recipes included

C25   Ulene, Art; editor. *Count out cholesterol cookbook: with 250 recipes, American Medical Association Campaign Against Cholesterol.* New York: A. A. Knopf, 1989.
ISBN: 0-3945-8194-6
** low-fat, low-cholesterol and high-fiber recipes are by Mary Ward, and additional recipes from *Eat right, eat well -- the Italian way* by Edward Giobbi and Richard Wolff; each recipe gives saturated fat, cholesterol, soluble fiber, and caloric content

HIGH-FIBER LOW-CHOLESTEROL
LOW-FAT LOW-SALT DIET

C26   MCG Foundation. *Cooking right for life: tasty recipes*

for your health. Nashville, TN: Favorite Recipes Press, 1990.
ISBN: 0-8719-7289-1
** contains recipes that are high-fiber, low-cholesterol, low-fat, and low-salt

HIGH-FIBER LOW-CHOLESTEROL LOW-FAT LOW-SUGAR DIET

C27   Allen, Francine. *Eating well in a busy world: well balanced, healthful meals for busy people who love to cook.* Berkeley, CA: Ten Speed Press, 1986.
ISBN: 0-8981-5163-5   128 p. illustrated
** recipes minimize the use of fats, oils, red meat, butter, cheese, eggs, and sugar; maximize the use of whole grains and fresh vegetables; a third of the menus feature chicken, a third fish, and a third vegetarian

HIGH-FIBER LOW-FAT DIET

C28   Longstaff, Roberta and Mann, Jim. *The Healthy heart diet book: enjoy delicious low-fat, high fibre recipes.* London: Dunitz, 1986.
ISBN: 0-9063-4897-8   125 p. illustrated, some color

HIGH-FIBER LOW-FAT VEGETARIAN DIET

C29 Wagner, Lindsay and Spade, Ariane. *The High road to health: a vegetarian cookbook.* New York: Prentice Hall Press, 1990.
ISBN: 0-1353-6129-X   287 p.
** high-fiber low-fat vegetarian recipes included

HIGH-FIBER DIET
WITH OATS

C30 Amsden, Pat. *Cooking with oat bran: recipes to live by.* Brentwood Bay, BC: AMS Publishers, 1989.
ISBN: 0-9694-3410-3   125 p.
** contains low-cholesterol recipes

C31 Baggett, Nancy and Glick, Ruth. *The Oat bran baking book: 85 delicious, low-fat low-cholesterol recipes.* Chicago: Contemporary, 1989.
ISBN: 0-8902-4289-3   128 p.
** includes recipes for bread, cakes, desserts, breakfast cereals, pancakes, and crackers

C32 Cadogan, Mary and Bond, Shirley. *The Oat cookbook.* London: Optima, 1987.
ISBN: 0-3561-5238-3   127 p. illustrated, some color

C33 Earnest, Barbara and Schlesinger, Sarah. *The Low-cholesterol oat plan: the revolutionary oat bran cookbook that can save your life with 300 delicious and innovative recipes for the new miracle food.* New York: Avon, 1988.

ISBN: 0-3807-0839-6   365 p.
** recipes for all types of dishes; provides percentage of recommended daily oat bran in each recipe

C34   Egan, Jeanette. *The Fast and easy oat bran cookbook: cholesterol reducing recipes for breakfast, lunch & dinner.* Los Angeles: Price Stern Sloan, Inc. (360 N. La Cienega Boulevard, Los Angeles, CA 90048), 1989. ISBN: 0-8958-6857-1   48 p.
** includes fiber, calorie, and cholesterol contents for each recipe

C35   Garden Way Publishing; editors of. *Cooking with oats, oat bran, oatmeal, and more.* Pownal, VT: Storey Communications, 1991. ISBN: 0-8826-6674-6

C36   Hinman, Bobbie. *Oat cuisine: over 200 delicious recipes to help you lower your cholesterol level.* Rocklin, CA: Prima Pub. & Communications, distributed by St. Martin's Press, 1989. ISBN: 1-5595-8003-8   289 p. illustrated
** offers recipes for breakfast, soup, main dishes, meatless dishes, and baking goods including calories and nutritive values (protein, fat, carbohydrate, cholesterol, fiber, and sodium)

C37   Jewell, Dina R. and Jewell, C. Thomas. *The Oat and wheat bran health plan: the delicious way to lower cholesterol, lose weight, live longer and feel better now.* New York: Bantam Books, 1989. ISBN: 0-5532-8212-3   279 p. illustrated

** contains high-fiber recipes

C38   Leahy, Linda Romanelli. *The Oat bran cookbook: reduce your cholesterol and your risk of heart attack with delicious easy-to-prepare recipes.* New York: Fawcett Gold Medal, 1989.
ISBN: 0-4491-4631-6   116 p.

C39   Marshall, Janette. *Eats with oats: the new soluble fibre cookbook.* London: W. Foulsham, 1986.
ISBN: 0-5720-1352-3   128 p. illustrated, color

C40   Maynard, Kitty and Maynard, Lucian. *The Oat bran cookbook.* Nashville, TN: Rutledge Hill Press, 1989.
ISBN: 1-5585-3016-9   160 p. illustrated
** provides recipes for beverages, salads, soups, entrees, and desserts; each recipe gives caloric measurement, percentage of calories from fat, and nutritive values (fat, fiber, cholesterol, and sodium)

C41   Ramp, Wilma; compiler. *Fantastic oatmeal recipes.* Iowa City, IA: Penfield Press, 1981.
ISBN: 0-9603-8583-5   60 p.

C42   Sperry, Shirley Lorenzani. *Oat bran recipes.* New Canaan, CT: Keats, 1989.
ISBN: 0-8798-3498-6   31 p. illustrated

C43   Westland, Pamela. *Oat cuisine.* Manchester, NH: Salem House, 1986.
ISBN: 0-8816-2167-6   96 p. illustrated, color

C44   Wilson, Josleen. *The Oat bran way.* New York: Berkley
Publishing Group, 1989.
ISBN: 0-4251-1809-6   158 p.
** low-cholesterol cookery using oat bran

LOW-CHOLESTEROL DIET

C45   Betz, Eleanor P.; Dolecek, Therese A.; Gernhofer, Niki
L.; Oppenheimer, Frances C.; and Skweres, Linda.
Holiday eating for a healthy heart. Chicago: Rush-
Presbyterian-St. Luke's Medical Center, Dept. of
Preventive Medicine, 1981.
** a low-cholesterol cookbook

C46   Betz, Eleanor P.; Dolecek, Therese A.; Gernhofer, Niki
L.; Oppenheimer, Frances C.; Skweres, Linda; and
Schoenberger, James A. *Summertime eating for a healthy
heart: cook-out camp-out eat-out the low cholesterol way.*
Chicago: Rush-Presbyterian-St. Luke's Medical Center,
Dept. of Preventive Medicine, 1981.
ISBN: 0-6863-1628-2   60 p.
** a low-cholesterol outdoor cookbook

C47   Cheraskin, Emanuel; Orenstein, Neil S.; and Miner, Paul
L. *Bio-nutrionics: lower your cholesterol in 30 days.*
New York, NY: Perigee Books, 1986.
ISBN: 0-3995-1268-3   176 p.
** low-cholesterol recipes as well as exercise routines are
included

C48   Columbia University. *Columbia University's Institute of*

Human Nutrition Diet and nutrition program for your heart. New York: Simon & Schuster, 1982.
ISBN: 0-6714-4357-7   128 p. illustrated
** low-cholesterol recipes prepared by the staff of the Institute of Human Nutrition, Columbia University--College of Physicians and Surgeons

C49   Cooper, Kenneth H. *Controlling cholesterol: Dr. Kenneth H. Cooper's preventive medicine program.* New York: Bantam Books, 1989.
ISBN: 0-5532-7775-8   395 p. illustrated
** includes exercise therapy and low-cholesterol recipes

C50   Cox, Peter and Brusseau, Peggy. *The Quick cholesterol clean-out.* London: Century, 1989.
ISBN: 0-7126-3087-2   176 p.

C51   *Diet for a healthy heart.* East Hanover, NJ: Nabisco Brands, 1985.
45 p.   illustrated, color
** contains low-cholesterol recipes

C52   Dujovne, Carlos A., et al. *A Change of heart: steps to healthy eating.* Kansas City, MO: Westport Publishers, 1990.
ISBN: 0-9337-0146-2   96 p.   illustrated
** features easy-to-follow meal plans, tips for meals eaten away from home, table of fat and cholesterol contents of foods, grocery guide, and recipes with nutritional analysis per serving

C53   Fisher, Hans and Boe, Eugene. *The Rutgers Guide to*

lowering your cholesterol: a common-sense approach.
New Brunswick, N J : Rutgers University Press, 1985.
ISBN: 0-8135-1135-6   218 p.

C54   *Good Housekeeping Eating for a healthy heart.* Headline, 1989.
ISBN: 0-7472-3278-4   248 p.
** provides low-cholesterol recipes

C55   Goor, Ron and Goor, Nancy. *Eater's choice: a food
lover's guide to lower cholesterol.* rev. ed. Boston:
Houghton Mifflin, 1989.
ISBN: 0-3955-0082-6   428 p. illustrated

C56   Grace, Vilma Janke. *Latin American and cholesterol
conscious cooking: enticing international recipes from
Latin America.* Washington, DC: Acropolis Books, 1979.
ISBN: 0-8749-1280-6   112 p. illustrated

C57   Hetherington, E. N. *The Healthful chef: a cookbook for
people who wish to lower their cholesterol and for people
with diabetes.* Danville, IL: The Healthful Chef, 1989.
ISBN: 0-9622-4542-9   165 p.

C58   Holst, Arleen and Willett, Sue. *Low cholesterol favorites
cookbook.* 3rd ed. Waverly, IA: G and R Pub. Co., 1989.
ISBN: 0-9621-5881-X   194 p.

C59   Hubbard, Mary and Robertson, Catherine. *Cholesterol
count down: enjoy eating while still controlling your
cholesterol.* San Diego, CA: Pegasus, 1989.
ISBN: 1-8778-9901-1

** a low-cholesterol diet book

C60   Jones, Jeanne. *The Mocha mix cook book.* City of
      Industry, CA: Presto Food Products, 1986. 130 p.
      ** presents low-cholesterol and milk-free recipes

C61   King, Mary Ellen and Van Meter, Carol. *Bless your*
      heart: low cholesterol cookbook. Williamson, WV:
      Green Valley Press, 1985.
      ISBN: 0-9320-4700-9

C62   Kowalski, Robert E. *The 8-week cholesterol cure*
      cookbook: more than 200 delicious recipes featuring the
      foods proven to lower cholesterol. New York: Perennial
      Library, 1990.
      ISBN: 0-0609-1689-3   341 p.
      ** recipes include calorie, fat, cholesterol, and sodium
      contents

C63   Kraus, Barbara. *The Barbara Kraus 30-day cholesterol*
      program: a diet and exercise plan for lowering your
      cholesterol. New York: Perigee Books, 1989.
      ISBN: 0-3995-1508-9   124 p.
      ** a low-cholesterol diet for hypercholesteremics
      including exercise

C64   Krimmel, Patricia T. and Krimmel, Edward A.
      Cholesterol lowering and controlling: 3 week plan
      handbook and cookbook. Bryn Mawr, PA: Franklin
      Publishers, 1990.
      ISBN: 0-9165-0303-8   256 p. illustrated

C65   Kwiterovich, Peter O. *Beyond cholesterol: the Johns Hopkins complete guide for avoiding heart disease.* Baltimore: Johns Hopkins University Press, 1989. ISBN: 0-8018-3828-2   395 p. illustrated

C66   Leviton, Roberta. *The Jewish low-cholesterol cookbook: a complete guide to the understanding, preparation and serving of food low in cholesterol and Kosher.* rev. ed. New York: New American Library, 1983. ISBN: 0-4522-5465-5   370 p.

C67   Longbottom, Lori. *Quick and easy recipes to lower your cholesterol.* New York: Avon, 1989. ISBN: 0-3807-5871-7   122 p.

C68   Ringrose, Helen. *Cooking for health: low cholesterol recipes for weight reduction and heart care.* London: Omega, 1984. ISBN: 0-9078-5314-5   207 p. illustrated, color

C69   Schlesinger, Sarah and Earnest, Barbara. *The Low-cholesterol olive oil cookbook: more than 200 recipes, the most delicious way to eat healthy food.* New York: Villard Books, 1990. ISBN: 0-3945-8074-5   307 p.

C70   Schneider, Ellie. *The Low-cholesterol kitchen cookbook.* Seattle, WA: Peanut Butter Pub., 1989. ISBN: 0-8971-6321-4   181 p. illustrated

C71   Seaver, Jeannette. *The Almost no cholesterol gourmet cookbook: more than 200 classic recipes to raise your*

spirits and lower your cholesterol. New York: Crown, 1990.
ISBN: 0-5175-7518-3   140 p. illustrated
** recipes for dinners, lunches, breakfasts, and finger foods; calories and nutritive values (cholesterol, fat, saturated fat, and sodium) provided

C72   Siegal, Terri J. *Low cholesterol desserts.* Freedom, CA: Crossing Press, 1990.
ISBN: 0-8959-4441-3   183 p. illustrated

C73   St. Francis Hospital, Milwaukee, WI. *Low cholesterol cookbook: sweet tooth pleasers.* Milwaukee, WI: St. Francis Hospital, 1987.   43 p.

C74   Tarr, Yvonne Young. *Low-cholesterol gourmet.* New York: Simon and Schuster, 1990.
ISBN: 0-6715-2321-X   239 p. illustrated

C75   Taylor, Barbara. *Cooking to your heart's content: a low-cholesterol cookbook for the ordinary kitchen.* Fayetteville and London: University of Arkansas Press, 1990.
ISBN: 1-5572-8128-9   121 p. illustrated
** includes suggested menu for one week, dinner party or special day menus, recipes from appetizers and desserts to main dishes with game

C76   Teng, Chao-Chao and Chen, Hsueh Hsia. *Low-cholesterol Chinese cuisine.* Translated by Heidi Dick. Taipei, Taiwan: Wei-Chuan Pub. Co., 1990.
ISBN: 0-9416-7647-1   124 p. illustrated, color

C77 Turner, Roger Newman. *Diets to help control cholesterol.* rev. format ed. New York: Thorsons, 1988. ISBN: 0-7225-1752-7   48 p.
** features cholesterol cutting recipes

C78 Wasserman, Debra and Stahler, Charles. *No cholesterol Passover recipes.* Baltimore, MD: Baltimore Vegetarians, distributed by Jewish Vegetarians of North America, 1986.
ISBN: 0-9314-1103-3   49 p. illustrated

C79 Wilson, Nedra P. and Wood, Susan, M. *Delicious ways to lower cholesterol.* Birmingham, AL: Oxmoor House, 1989.
ISBN: 0-8487-0777-X   240 p. illustrated, some color
** low-cholesterol recipes prepared with the registered dietitian faculty, Department of Nutrition Sciences, Schools of Medicine, Dentistry, and Health Related Professions, University of Alabama at Birmingham

LOW-CHOLESTEROL DIET
FOR CHILDREN

C80 Kowalski, Robert E. *Cholesterol and children: a parent's guide to giving children a future free of heart disease.* New York: Harper and Row, 1988.
ISBN: 0-0601-5907-3   302 p.
** on cholesterol conscious child-rearing

LOW-CHOLESTEROL
LOW-CARBOHYDRATE DIET

C81 Cantrell, Rose. *Creative low cholesterol and low
carbohydrate cooking.* New York: Weathervane Books,
1980.
127 p. illustrated

LOW-CHOLESTEROL
LOW-FAT DIET

C82 Becker, Gail L. *Heart smart: a plan for low-cholesterol
living: a step-by-step guide to reducing the risk of heart
disease: including 125 easy-to-prepare recipes.* rev. and
updated. New York: Simon and Schuster, 1987.
ISBN: 0-6716-4761-X   218 p. illustrated
** low-cholesterol low-fat recipes including nutritive
values; percentage of calories from fat, saturated fat,
monounsaturated fat, and polyunsaturated fat; ratio of
poly/saturated fat; and exchange values for weight control

C83 Better Homes and Gardens. *Better Homes and Gardens
Low-fat meals.* Des Moines, IA: Meredith, 1990.
ISBN: 0-6960-1889-6   128 p. illustrated, color
** low-cholesterol low-fat recipes for main dishes, side
dishes, and desserts with calories and nutritive values
(protein, carbohydrate, fat, cholesterol, sodium,
potassium, fat, saturated fat, monounsaturated fat, and
polyunsaturated fat)

C84 Bond, ClaraBeth Young, et al. *The Low fat, low*

cholesterol diet: what to eat and how to prepare it. new rev. ed. Garden City, NY: Doubleday, 1984.
ISBN: 0-3851-8879-X   512 p. illustrated
** recipes for all types of dishes including nutritive values and calories

C85   Crocker, Betty. *Betty Crocker's Low fat low cholesterol cookbook: a healthy approach to a healthy meal.* New York: Prentice Hall, 1991.
ISBN: 0-1308-4484-5   221 p. illustrated, color

C86   D'Agostino, Joanne. *Italian cooking for a healthy heart: low-fat, low-cholesterol gourmet dishes.* New York: Eagle Pub. Corp., 1989.
ISBN: 0-9319-3379-X   187 p. illustrated

C87   Elinsky, Stephen E. *Innovations in cooking: a revolutionary concept in food preparation.* West Chester, PA: Elins Laboratories, 1986.
72 leaves   illustrated
** features low-cholesterol and low-fat recipes using a steamer

C88   Fisher, Helen V. *Cookbook for the 90s.* Tucson, AZ: Fisher Books, 1990.
ISBN: 1-5556-1038-2   244 p. illustrated
** contains low-fat and low-cholesterol recipes

C89   Giobbi, Edward and Wolff, Richard. *Eat right, eat well--the Italian way.* New York: Knopf, 1985.
ISBN: 0-3945-3071-3   530 p. illustrated
** presents Italian recipes that are low-fat and low-

cholesterol; each recipe provides caloric content and nutritive values (cholesterol, fat, saturated fat, monounsaturated fat, polyunsaturated fat, protein, and carbohydrate)

C90 Griffin, Glen C. and Castelli, William P. *Good fat, bad fat: how to lower your cholesterol and beat the odds of a heart attack.* Tucson, AZ: Fisher Books, 1989.
ISBN: 1-5556-1013-7   316 p. illustrated
** low-fat and low-cholesterol recipes to prevent heart diseases

C91 Grundy, Scott M. and Winston, Mary; editors. *The American Heart Association's Low-fat, low-cholesterol cookbook: an essential guide for those concerned about their cholesterol levels.* New York: Random House, 1989.
ISBN: 1-5605-4032-X   340 p. illustrated
** recipes of foods from all four food groups and vegetarian dishes; also includes AHA and National Heart, Lung and Blood Institute diet step-one and step-two blood cholesterol lowering diet guidelines and menu plans; each recipe provides caloric content and nutritive values (protein, carbohydrate, fat, saturated fat, polyunsaturated fat, monounsaturated fat, cholesterol, and sodium)

C92 Hoxter, Gayle Shockey and Alexander, Kateri. *The Heartcare cookbook.* New York: Morrow, 1991.
ISBN: 0-6880-9258-6
** low-fat and low-cholesterol recipes

C93   Knight, Gerri. *Cookbook, "have a happy heart" recipes.*
Austin, TX: Barton, 1986.
ISBN: 0-9616-7020-7   259 p.
** contains low-fat and low-cholesterol recipes

C94   Lindsay, Anne. *The Low-cholesterol cuisine: gourmet
eating the low-cholesterol way with over 200 fast, easy
and great-tasting recipes for a healthy heart.* New York:
Hearst Books, 1989.
ISBN: 0-6880-8712-4   271 p.
** previously published as *The lighthearted cookbook*,
1988; each low-cholesterol, low-fat recipe provides
caloric content and nutritive values (fat, cholesterol,
sodium, protein, carbohydrate, fiber and vitamin C)

C95   Mills, Thomas; Mills, Arlene; and Henning, Cecilia.
*Healthy heart gourmet: timely nutritional guidelines and
gourmet quality, heart-safe recipes for healthier living.*
Jacksonville, FL: Mills, Thomas and Arlene, 1989.
ISBN: 0-9620-8960-5   256 p. illustrated
** a low-cholesterol and low-fat cookbook utilizing
natural foods

C96   Moore, Madeleine H. and Moore, James R., Jr. *Fats in
your diet: live a longer life: guide to lower saturated fat,
lower cholesterol: hints, quick cook recipes, nutritional
data.* Rockville, MD: MHM Pub., 1986.
ISBN: 0-9368-3300-9   148 p. illustrated
** tables of cholesterol and fat content of foods are
included

C97   Piscatella, Joseph C. *Controlling your fat tooth.* New

York: Workman, 1990.
ISBN: 0-8948-0431-6   526 p.
** includes low-cholesterol and low-fat recipes

C98   Prevention Magazine; editors of. *Reducing cholesterol; a heart-smart guide to low-fat eating.* Stamford, CT: Longmeadow Press, 1989.
ISBN: 0-6814-0718-2   87 p.   illustrated

C99   Roth, Harriet. *Harriet Roth's Cholesterol-control cookbook: over 250 low-fat recipes, over 100 menu plans.* New York: New American Library, 1989.
ISBN: 0-4530-0662-0   414 p. illustrated, some color
** recipes include caloric, and nutritive values (cholesterol, total fat, saturated fat, fiber, and sodium)

C100   SerVaas, Cory and Turgeon, Charlotte. *Health cookbook for family and friends: health recipes for all seasons, now taste-tempting, low-fat, and low-cholesterol recipes, healthful menus for Spring, Summer, Fall, and Winter, for just the family or for entertaining friends.* Indianapolis, IN: Saturday Evening Post Society, 1989.
ISBN: 0-8407-3135-3   106 p. illustrated

C101   Starke, Rodman D. and Winston, Mary; editors. *The American Heart Association cookbook.* 5th ed. New York: Times Books/Random House, 1991.
ISBN: 0-8129-1895-9
** contains low-cholesterol, low-fat recipes and is published by the American Heart Association

C102   Sunset Books and Sunset Magazine; editors of. *Low cholesterol cook book: wholesome, healthy, hearty and delicious.* Menlo Park, CA: Lane Pub. Co., 1990.
ISBN: 0-3760-2514-X   112 p. illustrated, color
** all recipes are low in fat and low in cholesterol; each recipe includes calories, content of fat, saturated fat, cholesterol, carbohydrate, protein, and sodium, and percentage of calories from carbohydrate, fat, and protein

C103   *A Taste for health: delicious low-fat, low-cholesterol recipes.* Iowa City, IA: Penfield Press, 1984.
ISBN: 0-9410-1664-1   88 p.   illustrated
** a weight-reduction diet book; revised edition of *Modified magic*, 1982.

C104   Underbakke, Gail. *Cardiac cuisine: a guide to healthy eating.* Madison, WI: University of Wisconsin Hospitals and Clinics, distributed through agreement by the University of Wisconsin Press, 1987.
ISBN: 0-2999-7064-7   115 p.
** designed to prevent and control heart diseases with low-fat and low-cholesterol recipes

C105   Zane, Polly. *The Jack Sprat cookbook, or good eating on a low-cholesterol, low-saturated-fat diet: over 600, new, easy-to-prepare recipes, tested and found well within the American Heart Association's rigid standards.* New York: Harper Colophon Books, 1980.
ISBN: 0-0609-0803-3   500 p.

LOW-CHOLESTEROL LOW-FAT
LOW-CALORIE DIET

C106 Harvey, Lee and Chambers, Helen. *Eat light and love it!: cholesterol control guide: low-calorie, low-fat recipes: microwave/conventional cooking instructions.* Ottawa, ON: H.C. Pub., 1988.
ISBN: 0-9692-3692-1   174 p. illustrated, color
** weight-loss cuisine for a healthy heart

C107 Melvin, Shelley and Stone, Marilyn. *Snack to your heart's content!: the low-fat, low-cholesterol, low-calorie quick and easy cookbook.* Gainesville, FL: Triad, 1990.
ISBN: 0-9374-0432-2   190 p. illustrated
** weight-reducing snack recipes using yogurt cheese

C108 Polak, Jeanne. *Fat and calorie controlled meals: palatable and prudent recipes.* Philadelphia, PA: George F. Stickley, 1982.
ISBN: 0-8931-3062-1   100 p.
** low-calorie, low-cholesterol, and low-fat recipes originally developed for use in the Multiple Risk Factor Intervention Trials(MRFIT) with diet guidelines set by the American Heart Association

C109 Stone, Marilyn; Melvin, Shelley; and Crawford, Charlie. *Not just cheesecake!: the low-fat, low-cholesterol, low-calorie great dessert cookbook.* Gainesville, FL: Triad Pub. Co., 1988.
ISBN: 0-9374-0429-2   142 p.

C110 Trieber, Rosalind H.; Sussman, Ann; and Brigham, Janet.

Life after schmaltz: heart-healthy Jewish holiday cooking.
Baltimore, MD: Trieber Associates, 1990.
193 p. illustrated
** contains low-calorie, low-fat, and low-cholesterol
recipes

LOW-CHOLESTEROL LOW-FAT
LOW-PROTEIN DIET

C111 Stafford, Julie. *Taste of life: 200 low cholesterol easy to make healthy life style recipes.* Long Beach, CA: Australian in Print, 1989.
ISBN: 0-7328-0009-9   147 p. illustrated
** low-fat and low-protein recipes using natural ingredients

LOW-CHOLESTEROL LOW-FAT
LOW-SALT DIET

C112 Adler, Bill and Harney, Heather. *The Anti-cancer, heart attack, stroke diet.* Nashville, TN: T. Nelson Publishers, 1991.
ISBN: 0-8407-7119-3   274 p.
** offers recipes that are low-salt, low-fat, and low-cholesterol

C113 Baker, Cherie. *Naturally delicious desserts: treat your family and friends to sweets the low-cholesterol, low-sodium, low-fat way!: from cookies to tarts to sherbets.* New York: Ballantine, 1985.

ISBN: 0-3453-0182-X   238 p.

C114   Carr, Donna Shaffer. *Quick and organized healthy cuisine for busy people.* Indianapolis, IN: Braes Corp., 1989.
ISBN: 0-9625-3380-7   216 p.
** includes weight-reducing recipes that are low-cholesterol, low-fat, and low-sodium

C115   Cavaiani, Mabel. *The Low cholesterol cuisine.* Chicago: Contemporary Books, 1981.
ISBN: 0-8092-5945-1   282 p.
** recipes are low-fat, low-salt, and low-cholesterol with suggestions for adapting to a low-sodium diet

C116   Domengeaux, Ray and Domengeaux, Jane. *Cooking up secrets the light way: low cholesterol, low sodium, and low fat menus and recipes.* New York: Vantage Press, 1989.
ISBN: 0-5330-8055-X   102 p.
** featuring Louisiana cuisine

C117   Dosti, Rose and Kidushim-Allen, Deborah. *Light style: the low fat, low cholesterol, low salt way to good food and good health.* rev. ed. San Francisco: HarperSanFrancisco, 1991.
ISBN: 0-0625-0241-7

C118   Jones, Suzanne S. *The Low-cholesterol food processor cookbook: 200 delectable recipes, low in cholesterol, sodium, and fat.* Garden City, NY: Doubleday, 1980.
ISBN: 0-3851-4745-7   210 p. illustrated

** recipes are low-cholesterol, low-fat, and low-salt

C119 Kruppa, Carole. *The Love your heart (low cholesterol) cookbook: 250 tempting recipes for a healthy heart.* Chicago, IL: Surrey Books, 1990.
ISBN: 0-9406-2512-1   278 p. illustrated
** includes low-cholesterol, low-fat, and low-salt recipes for all types of dishes with caloric, exchange, cholesterol, and fat values; also provides shopping, cooking suggestions and holiday menu

C120 McKinney, Judy; Cunningham, Joe H.; and Cunningham, Charles Casey. *I need help quick cookbook: family favorite recipes low in fat, cholesterol, and sodium.* Troup, TX: Health Saver Press, 1989.   1 vol.

C121 Morgan, Bessie C. *New directions in healthful cooking: a guide to low fat, low sodium, low cholesterol eating.* Pittsburgh, PA: DSK International, 1988.
ISBN: 0-9621-4500-9   80 p.   illustrated
** a cookbook using natural foods

C122 Pepin, Jacques, et al. *A Fare for the heart: a Cleveland Clinic cookbook: low sodium, low fat, low cholesterol.* Cleveland, OH: Clinitec, 1988.
ISBN: 0-9455-0400-4   100 p. illustrated

C123 Time-Life Books; editors of. *The Time-Life Book of elegant everyday cooking.* Alexandria, VA: Time-Life Books, 1990.
ISBN: 0-8094-9150-8
** recipes are low in fat, cholesterol and salt

LOW-CHOLESTEROL LOW-FAT
LOW-SALT LOW-CALORIE DIET

C124 DeBakey, Michael E.; Gotto, Antonio M., Jr.; Scott, Lynne W.; and Foreyt, John P. *The Living heart diet.* New York: Raven Press/Simon and Schuster,1986. ISBN: 0-6716-1998-5   397 p. illustrated ** low-cholesterol, low-calorie, low-sodium, and low-fat recipes; also includes menu planning

C125 Guste, Roy F. and the Ochsner Medical Institutions. *Louisiana light: low-fat, low-calorie, low-cholesterol, low-salt: cajun and creole cookery.* New York: Norton, 1990. ISBN: 0-3930-2714-7   297 p. illustrated

C126 Kafka, Barbara. *Microwave gourmet healthstyle cookbook: over 400 delicious recipes for vibrant health and great taste.* New York: W. Morrow, 1989. ISBN: 0-6880-7572-X   623 p. illustrated ** provides microwaveable recipes that are low-calorie, low-cholesterol, low-salt, and low-fat; each recipe provides nutritive values, calories, and vitamin and mineral content

C127 Wilson, Marie. *The Good-for-your-health all-Asian cookbook.* Rutland, VT: C.E. Tuttle, 1989. ISBN: 0-8048-1559-3   360 p. illustrated ** contains oriental recipes that are low-salt, low-fat, low-calorie, and low-cholesterol

LOW-CHOLESTEROL LOW-FAT
LOW-SALT LOW-SUGAR DIET

C128 Bennett, Cleaves M. and Newport, Cristine. *The Control your high blood pressure cookbook: created specially for high blood pressure sufferers, over 200 great-tasting, medically sound recipes: low in cholesterol, fat, sodium, and sugar; kitchen-tested, easy to prepare, including the latest medical developments in hypertension research.* Garden City, NY: Doubleday, 1987.
ISBN: 0-3581-9919-8   248 p.
** low-salt, low-cholesterol, low-fat, low-sugar recipes provided for all types of dishes

C129 Claiborne, Craig and Franey, Pierre. *Craig Claiborne's Gourmet diet: including 200 specially created, low-sodium, modified fat, modified cholesterol recipes.* New York: Random House, 1980.
ISBN: 0-8129-0914-3   258 p.
** includes low-cholesterol, low-salt, low-fat, and sugar-free recipes

C130 Fischer, Lynn and Brown, W. Virgil. *The Fischer/Brown Low cholesterol gourmet: the healthy heart guide: over 200 gourmet recipes - all low in fat, salt, and sugar!: all cholesterol tested, plus microwave directions: all absolutely delicious!* Washington, DC: Acropolis Books, 1988.
ISBN: 0-8749-1909-6   332 p. illustrated, color

C131 Hachfeld, Linda and Eykyn, Betsy. *Cooking a la heart cookbook.* Mankato, MN: Mankato Heart Health

Program Foundation, 1988.
ISBN: 0-9620-4710-4   450 p. illustrated
** recipes are high-fiber, high-calcium, low-cholesterol,
low-fat, low-sodium, low-sugar, and no-artificial
sweetener; each recipe provides calorie, fat, cholesterol,
fiber, sodium, and calcium content

C132 Prince, Francine. *Dieter's gourmet cookbook: delicious
low-fat, low-cholesterol cooking and baking recipes using
no sugar or salt!* New York: Simon and Schuster, 1986.
ISBN: 0-6716-2021-5   156 p. illustrated

C133 Prince, Francine. *Francine Prince's New diet for life
cookbook: with more than 150 delicious low-fat, low-salt,
low-cholesterol recipes.* New York: Perigee Books,
1990.
ISBN: 0-3995-1559-3   224 p.
** includes low-cholesterol, low-fat, low-salt, and sugar-
free recipes; also has a seven-day menu plan and holiday
meals

C134 Rose, Gloria. *Enjoying good health: gourmet foods made
with no fats, no oils, no sugar, or no salt added, over 200
recipes designed to help people who suffer from diabetes,
cancer, high cholesterol, hypertension, heart disease,
arthritis plus your questions answered by noted doctors.*
Los Angeles: Price Stern Sloan, 1989.
ISBN: 0-8958-6867-6   378 p.
** a weight-reducing diet; low-fat, low-cholesterol, and
low-salt recipes with nutritional breakdown

C135 Roth, Harriet. *Deliciously simple: quick-and-easy, low-*

sodium, low-fat, low-cholesterol, low-sugar meals: over 300 sensational recipes for great meals in minutes: includes a selection for microwave ovens. New York: New American Library, 1988.
ISBN: 0-4522-5984-3   403 p.
** recipes also high in fiber and provide caloric measurement and nutritive values for protein, fat, carbohydrate, fiber, cholesterol, and sodium

C136   Stern, Ellen Stock and Michaels, Jonathan. *The Good heart diet cookbook: no meat, no oil, no egg, no butter, no sugar, low salt: lose weight and reduce your cholesterol with these 200 tempting recipes.* New York: Warner Books, 1983.
ISBN: 0-4463-7547-0   236 p.

LOW-CHOLESTEROL LOW-FAT
LOW-SALT LOW-SUGAR
LOW-CALORIE DIET

C137   Becker, Gail L. and Hammock, Delia A. *Eat well, be well cookbook.* New York: Simon and Schuster, 1986.
ISBN: 0-6716-2895-X   214 p. illustrated
** contains low-cholesterol, low-salt, low-sugar, low-calorie, low-fat recipes and is published by the Metropolitan Life Insurance Company; recipes include caloric measure, nutritive values (protein, carbohydrate, cholesterol, fat, and sodium)

C138   Gilliard, Judy and Kirkpatrick, Joy. *The Guiltless gourmet: low in fat, cholesterol, salt, sugar, calories:*

recipes, menus, and nutrition information for the health conscious cook. Wayzata, NM: Diabetes Center, 1987. ISBN: 0-9377-2123-9   170 p. illustrated
** recipes are simple, inexpensive, low-calorie, low-fat, low-cholesterol, low-salt, and high-fiber; each recipe includes ADA exchange values, caloric content, and nutritive information (protein, carbohydrate, fat, cholesterol, sodium, and dietary fiber)

LOW-CHOLESTEROL LOW-FAT
LOW-SALT LOW-SUGAR
VEGETARIAN DIET

C139   Bienenfeld, Florence and Bienenfeld, Mickey. *The Vegetarian gourmet: over 200 low-fat, low-cholesterol, low-salt, sugar-free divine vegetarian entrees, soups, salads, and heavenly healthy wholegrain breads and desserts.* Beverly Hills, CA: Royal House Publishing Co., Inc., 1987.
ISBN: 0-9304-4048-X   184 p. illustrated

LOW-CHOLESTEROL LOW-FAT
LOW-SUGAR VEGETARIAN DIET

C140   Hoshijo, Kathy. *Kathy Cooks--vegetarian, low cholesterol.* New York: Simon and Schuster, 1989.
ISBN: 0-6716-7805-1   728 p. illustrated
** features vegetarian recipes that are low-fat, low-cholesterol, and sugar-free; originally published as *The art of dieting without dieting*, 1986.

LOW-CHOLESTEROL LOW-FAT
VEGETARIAN DIET

C141 Shriver, Brenda and Tinsley, Ann. *No red meat.* Tucson, AZ: Fisher Books, 1989.
ISBN: 1-5556-1021-8   313 p. illustrated
** a vegetarian cookbook with recipes low in fat and low in cholesterol

LOW-CHOLESTEROL
LOW-SALT DIET

C142 Rivkin, Jay; editor. *Quick 'n natural, no salt, low cholesterol cooking.* Sepulveda, CA: S.F.V.A.R. Press, 1988.   115 p. illustrated

C143 Tibbetts, Edith and Cadwell, Karin. *The Complete low-sodium low-cholesterol cookbook.* rev. ed. New York: Sterling Pub. Co., 1990.
ISBN: 0-8069-5852-9   318 p. illustrated
** recipes indicate sodium and caloric contents per serving; includes "The sodium and calorie content of fresh and convenience foods and seasonings" as an Appendix

LOW-CHOLESTEROL LOW-SALT
LOW-CALORIE DIET

C144 Brown, Ellen. *The Gourmet gazelle cookbook: delicious*

eating for a lifetime of good health. New York: Bantam, 1989.
ISBN: 0-5533-5309-8   333 p.
** recipes are low-calorie low-cholesterol and low-salt

C145   Jue, Daniel N. and Chew, Teresa. *Light and healthy Chinese cooking: the best of traditional Chinese cuisine made low in sodium, cholesterol, and calories.* Indianapolis: Bobbs-Merrill, 1984.
ISBN: 0-6725-2776-6   260 p.

LOW-CHOLESTEROL LOW-SALT LOW-SUGAR DIET

C146   Becker, Gail L. *Cooking for the health of it: wholesome meal preparations that conform with U.S.D.A. dietary guidelines.* Elmsford, NY: Benjamin Co., 1981.
ISBN: 0-8750-2090-9   159 p. illustrated, some color
** low-calorie, low-cholesterol, low-salt, and sugar-free recipes

C147   Lawton, Evelyn Jean. *Recipes for life.* Mississauga, ON: Lifestyle International, 1985.
ISBN: 0-9692-1823-0   268 p.
** includes recipes that are low in sodium, sugar, and cholesterol

C148   Schell, Merle. *Italian salt-free diet cookbook.* New York: New American Library, 1988.
ISBN: 0-4530-0568-3   367 p.

** low-salt, low-cholesterol, low-sugar, and low-calorie recipes listing calories, nutritive values, and sodium content; also includes a two-week diet plan with 500 mg sodium and 1200 calories daily

LOW-CHOLESTEROL VEGETARIAN DIET

C149 Stahler, Charles. *Healthy holidays: no-cholesterol vegetarian recipes*. Baltimore, MD: Baltimore Vegetarians, 1984.
79 p.   illustrated

C150 Victor, Steve. *The Lighthearted vegetarian gourmet cookbook*. Boise, ID: Pacific Press Pub. Assoc., 1988.
ISBN: 0-8163-0718-0   96 p.   illustrated

LOW-FAT DIET

C151 Blonder, Terry Joyce. *For goodness' sake: an eating well guide to creative low-fat cooking*. Charlotte, VT: Camden House, 1990.
ISBN: 0-9444-7508-6   192 p.
** low-fat recipes using chicken, fish, shellfish, grains, plus vegetarian recipes

C152 Mauder, Anny. *New low fat recipes: nutritional therapy for heart disease, weight control, digestive, gall bladder and pancreas disorders*. London: Foulsham, 1986.
ISBN: 0-5720-1335-3   160 p. illustrated

C153 Stillman, Joan. *Fast and low: easy recipes for low fat cuisine.* Boston: Little, Brown, 1985.
ISBN: 0-3168-1613-2   209 p.
** recipes include drinks, main dishes, and desserts

LOW-SALT DIET

C154 Ahrens, Prudence H. *Salt-free baking at home.* Minneapolis, MN: James D. Thueson, 1985.
ISBN: 0-9115-0619-5   165 p. illustrated

C155 Applebee, Jackie. *Salt-free cooking: recipes for eating well on a low-sodium diet.* New York: Thorsons, 1984.
ISBN: 0-7225-0846-8   128 p. illustrated

C156 Bagg, Elma W. *Cooking without a grain of salt: over 250 superb and nutritious recipes, plus valuable tips for dining with friends and in restaurants, at home and abroad.* New York: Bantam, 1964 (the 17th printing was in February, 1986)
ISBN: 0-5532-3418-8   206 p.

C157 Baltzell, Karin Bundesen and Parsley, Terry Martin. *Living without salt.* New York: Bantam Books, 1986.
ISBN: 0-5532-5722-6   284 p. illustrated
** hints for no-salt seasoning with herbs; recipes for appetizers, meatless main dishes, meat dishes, ethnic dishes, holiday cooking, desserts, canning, pickling, and preserving

C158 Barbour, Beverly. *Low salt diet and recipe book.* New

York: Simon and Schuster, 1985.
ISBN: 0-6715-5745-9   144 p.
** food sodium content tables are included

C159 Baum, Ruth and Baum, Hilary. *Lifespice salt-free cookbook: with guest recipes by Craig Claiborne, James Beard, Alfredo Viazze, Marion Cunningham, Barbara Kafka and others.* New York: Perigee Books, 1985.
ISBN: 0-3995-1093-1   191 p. illustrated
** recipes from soups to desserts including entertaining menu; each recipe indicates calories and sodium content

C160 Better Homes and Gardens. *Better Homes and Gardens Low-salt cooking.* Des Moines, IA: Meredith Corporation, 1983.
ISBN: 0-6960-1320-7   96 p. illustrated
** low-salt recipes to prevent and control heart diseases or high blood pressure; recipes include main dishes, side dishes, desserts, snacks, beverages, and homemade ingredients for salt-substitutes

C161 Bounds, Sarah. *No-salt cookery: wholesome recipes for low-sodium eating.* New York: Thorsons Publishers, 1984.
ISBN: 0-7225-0896-4   96 p. illustrated, some color
** salt-free recipes for high-blood pressure prevention; sodium and caloric contents included for each recipe

C162 Brenner, Eleanor P. *Gourmet cooking without salt: over 300 low-sodium recipes for people who love to eat well.* Garden City, NY: Doubleday, 1981.

ISBN: 0-3851-4821-6   432 p. illustrated

C163 Bruneau, Ida. *Condiments to the chef: cooking the low salt way.* New York: Forbes Publications, 1981. 133 p. illustrated, color

C164 Cadogan, Mary. *Low-salt cookery.* London: Panther, 1985.
ISBN: 0-5860-6487-7   222 p.

C165 Conason, Emil G. and Metz, Ella. *The Original salt-free diet cookbook.* revised and updated. New York, NY: Putnam Publishing Group, 1986.
ISBN: 0-3995-1231-4   174 p.
** menus and recipes for reduced sodium and/or reduced calorie diet for weight reduction as well as for hypertension; also includes salt-free diet menu for the diabetic

C166 *Cooking with herbs and spices; low-salt cookery: 100 healthy and delicious main dishes.* Tuscon, AZ: HP Books, 1986.
ISBN: 0-8958-6246-8   79 p.   illustrated, color

C167 Delahunty, Millie. *Microwave Cuisine cooks low-sodium.* Garden City, NY: Microwave Cuisine, 1985.
ISBN: 0-9322-4309-6   28 p.   illustrated
** a part of the *Microwave Cuisine cooks series*

C168 Failes, Janice McCall and Cawood, Frank W. *High blood pressure lowered naturally: the natural way to help control your blood pressure, with your doctor's*

permission, without using drugs. Peachtree City, GA: FC and A, 1989.
ISBN: 0-9150-9919-5   254 p.
** recipes and 14-day menu provided; introduction to high blood pressure; natural ways to lower high blood pressure: dietary factors, lifestyle, and little-known factors; relationship between prescription drugs and lowering blood pressure naturally

C169   Finch, Cindy and Sweetingham, Pat. *Salt: the role of sodium in your diet.* Nottingham, Nottinghamshire: Boots, 1985.
ISBN: 0-5720-1342-6   64 p.   illustrated, some color
** features low-salt recipes

C170   Greene, Audrey and Greene, Michael. *Audrey's Add no salt cookery.* Alhambra, CA: Greene Publications, 1982.
ISBN: 0-9608-8920-5

C171   Horsley, Janet. *Making do without salt.* Dorchester, Dorset: Prism Press, 1984.
ISBN: 0-9070-6161-3   112 p. illustrated

C172   Jacobs, George W. *Light-hearted cooking by George!* Woods Hole, MA: Cromlech Books, 1991.
ISBN: 0-9618-0595-1   173 p. illustrated
** a low-salt diet designed for a healthier heart

C173   James, Janet and Goulder, Lois. *The Dell Color-coded low-salt-living guide.* New York: Dell, 1980.
ISBN: 0-4401-7608-5   128 p.

** no-salt recipes included; color codes are used to indicate the sodium content level of supermarket goods, fast-food restaurant foods, salad bar items, and drugstore products

C174 Jones, Jeanne. *Secrets of salt-free cooking: a complete low-sodium cookbook.* San Francisco, CA: 101 Productions, distributed by Ortho Information Services, 1988.
ISBN: 0-8972-1175-8   192 p. illustrated
** includes diabetic exchange values, calories, and sodium content for each recipe

C175 Lloyd, Nancy D. *Salt-free recipes: to save your life!* Expanded, rev. and reset. New York: Thorsons, 1984.
ISBN: 0-7225-0963-4   112 p. illustrated

C176 *Low-salt cookery: 100 healthy and delicious main dishes.* Tucson, AZ: HP Books, 1986.
ISBN: 0-8958-6246-8   79 p.   illustrated, color

C177 MacGregor, Graham. *The Salt-free diet book: an appetizing way to help reduce high blood pressure.* New York: Arco Pub., 1985.
ISBN: 0-6680-5964-4   110 p. illustrated, some color

C178 Mayes, Kathleen. *The Sodium-watcher's guide: easy ways to cut salt and sodium.* Santa Barbara, CA: Pennant Books, 1984.
ISBN: 0-9152-0105-4   121 p.
** low-salt recipes and food sodium content tables

C179 Minear, Ralph E. *The Joy of living salt-free: a complete guide to breaking the salt habit forever and staying healthy while enjoying what you eat.* New York: Macmillan, 1984.
ISBN: 0-0258-5060-1   198 p.
** provides informative tips on locating hidden salt content, finding substitutions, shopping for salt-free products, and recipes for cooking the salt-free way

C180 Moore, Richard and Webb, George. *The K factor: reversing and preventing high blood pressure without drugs.* New York: Macmillan Pub. Co., 1986.
ISBN: 0-0258-6190-5   431 p. illustrated
** discusses the physiological effects of potassium (K) and includes low-sodium recipes to prevent and reverse high blood pressure

C181 Reader, Diane and Franz, Marion. *Pass the pepper please!: healthy meal planning for people on sodium restricted diets.* Wayzata, MN: International Diabetes Center, 1988.
ISBN: 0-9377-2117-4   66 p.   illustrated
** contains low-salt recipes for high-blood pressure patients and is a part of the *Wellness and nutrition library* series; includes introduction on hypertension and effects, sodium guide for foods in supermarket or fast foods, and suggestions for low-sodium cooking

C182 Ree. *Lemon twist: no salt added cookbook: zesty and zingy lemon recipes, garnishes, and menus.* Arcadia, CA: Nutrition Unlimited Publications, 1989.
ISBN: 0-9296-2200-6   204 p. illustrated

C183 Rodale Press; editors of. *No salt needed cookbook: featuring appetizers, soups, casseroles, salads, breads, and desserts.* Emmaus, PA: Rodale Press, 1982.
ISBN: 0-8785-7393-3   96 p.
** a part of *Rodale's High Health Cookbook Series*

C184 Rogers, Jean. *Cooking with the healthful herbs: over 300 no-salt ways to great taste and better health.* Emmaus, PA: Rodale Press, 1983.
ISBN: 0-8785-7449-2   278 p.

C185 Rowan, Robert L. *How to control high blood pressure without drugs.* New York: Scribner, 1986.
ISBN: 0-6841-8336-6   260 p.

C186 Salmon, Jenny. *Low-sodium cookbook.* London: Hamlyn, 1984.
ISBN: 0-6003-2407-9   128 p. illustrated, some color

C187 Schell, Merle. *Mexican salt-free diet cookbook.* New York: New American Library, 1986.
ISBN: 0-4530-0509-8   348 p.
** includes Mexican salt-free recipes for weight reduction

C188 Schell, Merle. *Tasting good: the international salt-free diet cookbook.* New York: New American Library, 1982.
ISBN: 0-4522-5364-0   412 p.

C189 Stephen, Marie-Joyce. *How to add spice to your life, without salt.* Winston-Salem, NC: Jordon Enterprises, 1983.

ISBN: 0-9612-2560-2   107 p. illustrated
** a cookbook of herbs and spices

C190   Stovel, Edith. *Salt-free herb cookery.* Pownal, Vt:
       Garden Way Publishing, 1985.
       ISBN: 0-8826-6342-9   31 p.   illustrated

C191   Weiss, Caroline E. and Uslander, Arlene S. *Creative
       cooking, low-sodium for hypertensives and families.*
       Chicago, IL: Budlong Press, 1983.
       132 p.   illustrated
       ** a companion book to *A doctor discusses hypertension
       (high blood pressure)*

C192   Wilson, Roger H. L. and Wilson, Nancy L. *Please pass
       the salt: a manual for low-salt eaters.* Philadelphia, PA:
       G.F. Stickley, 1983.   182 p.

LOW-SALT LOW-FAT DIET

C193   Gilliard, Judy and Kirkpatrick, Joy. *The Guiltless
       gourmet goes ethnic: Italian, French, Mexican, Spanish,
       and Cajun cuisine for the health conscious cook.*
       Minneapolis, MN: DCI Pub., 1990.
       ISBN: 0-9377-2168-9   219 p. illustrated
       ** international low-fat, low-salt, and low-calorie recipes
       providing ADA exchange values

C194   Oregon Health Sciences University. *The Best from the
       family heart kitchens: a guide to the alternative diet, low-
       fat, low-salt cookery.* Portland, OR: Oregon Health

Sciences University Bookstore, 1981.
152 p. illustrated

C195 Silverman, Goldie and Williams, Jacqueline. *The Quick and delicious low-fat low-salt cookbook.* New York: Perigee Books, 1986.
ISBN: 0-3995-1225-X   206 p. illustrated

C196 Starke, Rodman D. and Winston, Mary; editors. *American Heart Association low-salt cookbook: a complete guide to reducing sodium and fat in the diet.* New York, NY: Times Books, 1990.
ISBN: 0-8129-1852-5

C197 Williams, Lucy M. *Recipes for the heart: a nutrition guide for people with high blood pressure.* Bowling Green, OH: Sandridge Pub. Co., 1990.
ISBN: 0-9450-8041-7   192 p. illustrated
** a low-fat and low-salt cookbook for hypertension patients

LOW-SALT LOW-FAT
LOW-SUGAR DIET

C198 Ballantyne, Penny and Egan, Maureen. *Low salt, low sugar, low fat desserts.* San Leandro, CA: Bristol, 1988.
ISBN: 0-9119-5489-9   187 p. illustrated, some color

C199 Baskin, Rosemary M. *The Low sodium, sugar, fat cookbook.* Oneonta, NY: R.M. Baskin, 1984.

222 p.   illustrated

C200   Kallison, Jeri and Stoliar, Penny. *The Original no-no-no cookbook.* rev. ed. Shawnee Mission, KS: D and S Pub., 1985.
ISBN: 0-9615-9540-X   81 p.
** the three NOs are no fat, no salt, and no sugar

C201   Moore, C. Teresa Kennedy. *The Good life natural cooking from Teresa Kennedy Moore's kitchen: low fat, low sodium, low sweetener.* Abingdon, VA: C.T.K. Moore, 1982.
ISBN: 0-9153-0172-5   292 p.

C202   Reader's Digest. *Great recipes for good health.* Pleasantville, NY: Reader's Digest, 1988.
ISBN: 0-8957-7306-6   304 p. illustrated, color

C203   Schell, Merle. *Chinese salt-free diet cookbook: from soup to dessert, over 250 typically Chinese recipes - low in sodium, fat, sugar, calories, and without MSG.* New York: New American Library, 1985.
ISBN: 0-4530-0491-1   348 p.
** low-calorie, low-salt, low-fat, and low-sugar recipes with caloric, carbohydrate, fat, and sodium content

C204   Silverman, Goldie and Williams, Jacqueline. *No salt no sugar no fat cookbook: an easy, delicious approach to good health.* rev. San Leandro, CA: Bristol Publishing Enterprises, Inc., 1982.
ISBN: 0-9119-5465-1   150 p. illustrated
** recipes from all four food groups, especially legumes,

whole grains, and tofu

C205 Wedman, Betty. *Good nutrition for the family.* Hinsdale, IL: Nutrition Publications, 1985.
160 p.
** low-fat, low-salt, and low-sugar recipes include diabetic exchange and calories; provides menu planning for two-meal-a-day, lacto-ovo-vegetarian, and vegan diets

C206 Williams, Marcia Sabate. *More healthy cooking with no apologies.* Freedom, CA: Crossing Press, 1991.
ISBN: 0-8959-4452-9
** contains recipes that are free of sugar, free of salt, and low in fat

MACROBIOTIC DIET

C207 Kushi, Aveline. *Stress and hypertension: cooking for health.* Tokyo: Japan Publications, 1988.
ISBN: 0-8704-0679-5   191 p.
** a macrobiotic diet selected from the *Macrobiotic food and cooking series*

C208 Kushi, Michio and Jack, Alex. *Diet for a strong heart: Michio Kushi's macrobiotic dietary guidelines for the prevention of high blood pressure, heart attack, and stroke.* New York: St. Martin's Press, 1985.
ISBN: 0-3122-0998-3   532 p. illustrated

SELECTED ASSOCIATIONS
AND FOUNDATIONS

American Heart Association
National Office
7320 Greenville Avenue, Dallas, Texas 75231
214-373-6300

Arteriosclerosis, Hypertension, and Lipid Metabolism Advisory
Committee
Division of Heart and Vascular Diseases
National Heart, Lung, and Blood Institute
National Institutes of Health, Bethesda, Maryland 20892
301-496-1613

Canadian Cardiovascular Society
360 Victoria Avenue, Room 401, Westmount, Quebec, Canada
H3Z 2N4
514-482-3407

Cardiology Advisory Committee
Division of Heart and Vascular Diseases
National Heart, Lung, and Blood Institute
National Institutes of Health, Bethesda, Maryland 20892
301-496-2553

Citizens for the Treatment of High Blood Pressure for Public
Action on Cholesterol
888 17th Street, N.W. Suite 904, Washington, DC 20006
202-466-4553

International Stroke Clubs
(for stroke victims and families)
805 12th Street, Galveston, Texas 77550
409-762-1022

International Society for Heart Research
Department of Physiology
770 Bannatyne Avenue, University of Manitoba, Winnepeg,
Manitoba, Canada R3E 0W3
204-786-4336

National Heart, Lung, and Blood Institute
Public Inquiries and Reports Branch
Building 31, Room 4A21, National Institutes of Health,
Bethesda, Maryland 20205

National Hypertension Association
324 East 30th Street, New York, New York 10016
212-889-3557

National Institute of Hypertension Studies
Institute of Hypertension School of Research
13217 Livernois, Detroit, Michigan 48238
313-931-3427

National Stroke Association
300 East Hampden Avenue, Suite 240, Englewood, Colorado
80110
303-762-9922

DIABETES
AND
HYPOGLYCEMIA (D)

DIABETES MELLITUS or simply, diabetes, is characterized by hyperglycemia, a condition in which there is an elevated concentration of glucose in the blood. This metabolic abnormality is caused by insulin deficiency. Long-term complications of diabetes involve multiple organs, especially the eyes, kidneys, nerves, and blood vessels.

There are two types of diabetes mellitus. Type I diabetes, or juvenile-onset diabetes, is insulin-dependent due to an absolute insulin deficiency. Treatment for Type I diabetes usually requires a diet coordinated with an administered insulin dosage schedule, and regular physical exercise. At present, no method of preventing the development of Type I diabetes has been identified.

Dietary management of Type I diabetes includes quantity of calories, composition of diet, and distribution of calories throughout the day. Avoiding unnecessary caloric intake can effectively prevent or reduce obesity. In the composition of a diet, fat should comprise not more than 30% of the daily caloric allowance (low amounts of saturated fats and cholesterol reduce the risk of cardiovascular disease). Total carbohydrates, primarily fruits and starch, should comprise 50-65% of caloric allowance. Concentrated, refined carbohydrates should be discouraged because they induce wide swings in blood-sugar level. There is evidence that a high-fiber diet blunts postprandial (occurring after eating) glycemic excursions such as the above "swings."

Type II diabetes, or adult-onset diabetes, is noninsulin-dependent diabetes. It accounts for approximately 90 percent of all cases and affects at least 10 million Americans and usually appears in mid-life, most commonly among people who are overweight or obese. Genetic predisposition appears to play an important role in Type II as well as in Type I diabetes.

The three principal approaches to Type II diabetes management are diet, exercise, and treatment with oral antidiabetic agents, insulin, or other hypoglycemic agents. Since ancient times, diet has been recognized as a cornerstone of diabetes management, yet ideas about the most effective dietary treatment have varied widely throughout history. Recommended dietary carbohydrate composition for diabetes in 1550 B.C. was high, in 1797 was very low, in the 1930s was high again, from 1940 to 1970 was limited, and since 1971 to date it has been increased. The same kind of pendulum effect is obvious in the history of recommended dietary fat composition; high in 1797, low in 1931, moderate between 1940 and 1970, and reduced from 1971 to date. Since medical practices were first recorded, few physicians or researchers have agreed about the best approach to the nutritional therapy of diabetes. No specific dietary approach beyond caloric restriction and weight loss in the obese has proved more advantageous than another.

The dietary management of diabetes is the control of calories, protein, fat, and carbohydrates. The American Diabetes Association Task Force recommended a diet with 50 to 60 percent of total calories being carbohydrates. Not only do high-carbohydrate diets improve glucose tolerance and insulin sensitivity, but also the reduced fat, especially saturated fat, intake that accompanies a high-carbohydrate diet lowers cardiovascular risk.

Restriction of simple carbohydrates is recommended. Simple carbohydrates are defined as monosaccharides and disaccharides. Lactose, sucrose, and fructose are most prevalent as an inherent constituent of usual foods. The most widely used sweeteners, table sugar, corn syrup, and honey, are composed almost exclusively of sucrose and fructose.

Some studies have found that blood-glucose levels immediately following a meal are more influenced by soluble than by insoluble fibers and very high-carbohydrate, high-fiber diets improve glucose tolerance, lower insulin needs and blood-cholesterol levels. However, these benefits may be related more to the increased intake of complex carbohydrates than to fiber.

A calorie-restricted diet with low-saturated fat is generally recommended to avoid obesity, which causes insulin resistance. This diet also deters the acceleration of coronary heart disease. In Type II diabetics not taking hypoglycemic agents, caloric intake may be spread conveniently throughout the day. But for those taking insulin or oral hypoglycemic agents, caloric intake must be tailored to cover periods of peak pharmacologic action, as in Type I patients.

To aid meal planning, the American Diabetes Association and the American Dietetic Association developed an exchange system reflecting recommendations to restrict intake of calories, cholesterol, and saturated fat and to increase the intake of carbohydrates and fiber. In the exchange system, foods are divided into six basic groups called exchange groups. Each food item within a group contains approximately the same food value as any other food item in that group, allowing for exchange within groups and thus providing for variety in food choices, as well as food value control. The term "food exchanges" is used to refer to food choices or servings. The total number of exchanges per day depends on individual nutritional needs and is calculated by a clinical nutritionist or a dietitian.

HYPOGLYCEMIA is characterized as extremely low blood-sugar levels where blood sugar falls too low and /or too quickly and the brain cannot function properly. This can occur either after a fast (fasting hypoglycemia), or several hours after the consumption of a meal (reactive hypoglycemia). The causal factors are multifaceted and are not yet understood completely by the medical community. This condition can afflict a non-diabetic or a diabetic, whose postprandial plasma-glucose level drops too rapidly.

Where it would seem that to increase one's sugar intake is a solution for hypoglycemics, the opposite is true. When sugar or a refined food like white flour is eaten, too much insulin may be secreted by the pancreas, causing blood sugar to plunge rapidly. Eating more sugar temporarily increases blood sugar and makes the person feel better, but more insulin is secreted which in turn causes blood sugar to drop again. This becomes a "vicious cycle." The current recommended diet is low in refined and/or simple carbohydrates such as sugar (similiar to diabetics) while increasing intake of foods with low-glycemic indexes, primarily certain complex carbohydrates.

Following are selected contemporary diet therapies for diabetics and hypoglycemics. Consult the Diet Plan Locator Guide and the Keyword Index for additional low-sugar, high-fiber, low-calorie, and low-fat cookbooks included in other chapters.

IN GENERAL

D1   Algert, Susan; Grasse, Barbara; and Durning, Annie. *The UCSD Healthy diet for diabetes: a comprehensive nutritional guide and cookbook.* Boston: Houghton Mifflin, 1990.
ISBN: 0-3954-9477-X   373 p.
** from the University of California, San Diego, School of Medicine; Part 1 includes new nutritional information for diabetes such as weight control, exercise, meal planning, and monitoring and controlling blood glucoses; Part 2 contains recipes with an international flair from main entrees to desserts; each recipe lists calories, diabetic exchanges, and nutritive values (protein, fat, carbohydrate, fiber, cholesterol, sodium, and potassium)

D2   *American Diabetes Association--American Dietetic*

Association Family cookbook. rev. ed. New York:
Prentice-Hall, 1987.
ISBN: vol. 1: 0-1300-3915-2; vol. 2: 0-1300-3955-1; vol.
3: 0-1300-4145-9(for microwave also) illustrated
** recipes include ADA exchange values, calories, and a
nutritive breakdown (carbohydrate, protein, fat, sodium,
potassium, and fiber)

D3   American Dietetic Association and American Diabetes
Association. *Chinese American food practices, customs,
and holidays.* Chicago, IL: American Dietetic
Association; Alexandria, VA: American Diabetes
Association, 1990.
ISBN: 0-8809-1077-1
** developed by the Diabetes Care and Education
Dietetic Practice Group of the American Dietetic
Association and is a part of the *Ethnic and regional food
practices -- a series*

D4   Barbour, Pamela Gillispie. and Spivey, Norma Green.
*The Exchange cookbook: featuring dessert and casserole
recipes for diabetic and weight control programs.*
Atlanta, GA: G&G Pub. Co., 1982.
ISBN: 0-9610-0280-8   197 p. illustrated
** based on six major exchanges; all recipes include
caloric content and exchange equivalents

D5   Blanchard, Pat. *Basic menus and recipes for diabetics.*
Plaquemine, LA: Creole, 1989.
ISBN: 0-9264-2300-2   67 p.

D6   Bowen, Angela J. M. *The Diabetic gourmet.* rev. ed.
      New York: Barnes and Noble, 1981.
      ISBN: 0-0646-3526-0   193 p. illustrated
      ** recipes include caloric measurements, exchange
      values, and nutritive values (carbohydrate, protein, and
      fat)

D7   Brusseau, Peggy. *Healthy eating for diabetics.* London:
      Century, 1988.
      ISBN: 0-7126-2211-X   128 p.

D8   Budd, Martin. *Diets to help diabetes.* new rev. format
      ed. New York: Thorsons, distributed by Sterling Pub.
      Co., 1988.
      ISBN: 0-7225-1731-9   64 p.

D9   Calgary General Hospital. *Measure for measure and
      other "stirring" things.* Calgary, AB: Calgary General
      Hospital, 1984.
      ISBN: 0-9205-4500-9   174 p.
      ** diabetes recipes tested and recommended by the Dept.
      of Dietetics, Calgary General Hospital

D10   Canadian Diabetes Association and Ontario Dietetic
      Association. *Cookbook for diabetics and all the family.*
      2nd ed. Toronto, ON: Macmillan of Canada, 1981.
      ISBN: 0-7715-9550-6   169 p. illustrated

D11   Chantiles, Vilma Liacouras. *Diabetic cooking from
      around the world.* New York: Harper and Row, 1989.
      ISBN: 0-0601-6057-8   343 p.

** each recipe provides nutrient value, calories, exchange value; recipes arranged by types of dishes (appetizers, soup, fish, desserts, casseroles and others)

D12   Christy, Ann VonderHaar and Germann, Judy Dvorak. *Diabetes, recipes for health: a guide to healthy living featuring a cookbook with 242 recipes.* Bowie, MD: Robert J. Brady Co., 1983.
ISBN: 0-8930-3211-5   405 p. illustrated
** in cooperation with American Diabetes Association, Inc. and Metropolitan Medical Center of Minneapolis; includes a comprehensive diabetes self-care teaching program developed by the Metropolitan Medical Center of Minneapolis; each recipe includes exchange values, calories, and nutritive values

D13   Davidson, Barbara. *New diabetic cookery.* London: Octopus, 1986.
ISBN: 0-7064-2624-X   128 p. illustrated, color
** from the *Recipes for good health* series

D14   Farentinos, Bob; Fowler, Rosalind; Gowan, Peter; and Taylor, Mary. *Cooking with care: a feast of healthy recipes.* Denver, CO: American Diabetes Association, Denver Chapter, 1987.
ISBN: 0-9619-5820-0   96 p.   illustrated
** recipes using natural foods

D15   Finsand, Mary Jane. *Complete diabetic cookbook: delicious recipes for entrees, appetizers, desserts, snacks, elegant entertaining: featuring the all new and important*

ADA Exchange lists, and calorie and exchange values for fast foods by brand names and alcoholic beverages. New York: Sterling, 1980.
ISBN: 0-8069-8908-4   192 p.

D16 Finsand, Mary Jane. *Diabetic breakfast and brunch cookbook.* New York: Sterling, 1987.
ISBN: 0-8069-6432-4   160 p.
** recipes for beverages, fruits, cereals, eggs, main dishes, desserts with exchange, caloric, carbohydrate values

D17 Finsand, Mary Jane. *Diabetic gourmet cookbook.* New York: Sterling Pub. Co., 1986.
ISBN: 0-8069-6374-3   160 p.

D18 FitzGibbon, Theodora. *Good Housekeeping Good food for diabetics.* Terra Alta, WA: Headline, 1989.
ISBN: 0-7472-3280-6   243 p.

D19 Franz, Marion J. *Exchanges for all occasions: meeting the challenge of diabetes.* Minneapolis, MN: International Diabetes Center, Park Nicollet Medical Foundation, 1983.
210 p. illustrated
** includes expanded exchange lists, exchanges and guidelines for special occasions, guidelines for food purchasing and preparation, and sample menus for ethnic, holiday, lacto-ovo-vegetarian, and high-fiber high-carbohydrate diets

D20   Fredericks, Carlton. *Carlton Fredericks' New low blood sugar and you.* New York: Perigee Books, 1985.
ISBN: 0-3995-1087-7   253 p. illustrated
** for hypoglycemics

D21   Hall, Sue. *Diabetic cooking for one: balanced meals designed especially for the solo diabetic.* New York: Thorsons, 1987.
ISBN: 0-7225-1362-3   112 p. illustrated

D22   Hess, Mary Abbott and Middleton, Katharine. *The Art of cooking for the diabetic.* rev. ed. Chicago: Contemporary Books, 1988.
ISBN: 0-8092-4653-8   480 p.

D23   Hill, Novella S. and Dept. of the Air Force, U.S.A. *Recipes for the patient with diabetes.* Washington, DC: Dept. of the Air Force, Headquarters, U.S. Air Force, 1986.
40 p.   illustrated

D24   Huang, Elizabeth. *Healthful cooking: with recipes for patients with diabetes and /or renal disorders.* Taipei, Taiwan: Wei-Chuan Publishing Co., 1987.
ISBN: 0-9416-7617-X   115 p. illustrated, color
** provides low-calorie Chinese cuisine

D25   Jones, Jeanne. *More calculating cook: practical recipes for diabetics and dieters.* San Francisco: 101 Productions, distributed by Scribner, 1981.
ISBN: 0-8928-6184-3   192 p. illustrated

** low-calorie diabetes recipes with exchange values and caloric content

D26   Kahn, Ada P. *Diabetes control and the kosher diet.*
Skokie, IL: Wordscope Associates, 1984.
ISBN: 0-9301-2100-7   170 p. illustrated

D27   Kaplan, Dorothy J. *The Comprehensive diabetic
cookbook: a collection of wholesome and delicious
recipes incorporating the American Diabetes
Association's updated Exchange Lists for the Diabetic
Exchange diet.* rev. and updated. New York: Greenwich
House, 1984.
ISBN: 0-5174-4453-4   254 p.
** each recipe provides exchange values, carbohydrate,
protein, and fat content

D28   Kokoska, Vera. *A Cookbook for diabetics and their
families.* Little Rock, AR: Parkhurst/Little Rock, 1982.
ISBN: 0-9417-8002-3   98 p.

D29   Little, Billie and Ettinger, Victor G. *Gourmet recipes for
diabetics.* New York: Putnam, 1987.
ISBN: 0-3995-1279-9   223 p.
** ethnic recipes including French, Italian, Mexican,
European, and American dishes including main courses,
appetizers, soups, salads, desserts, and drinks; each recipe
provides calories and exchanges

D30   Lowry, Dianne. *Delicious delights for diabetics.* Hodder
and Stoughton, 1988.

ISBN: 0-3404-3130-X   170 p.

D31 Margie, Joyce Daly and Palumbo, P. J. *The Complete diabetic cookbook*. London: Grafton, 1987.
ISBN: 0-2461-2392-3   212 p.

D32 Marks, Betty. *Cooking for diabetes*. Los Angeles, CA: Price Stern Sloan, Inc., 1990.
ISBN: 0-8958-6640-4   256 p.

D33 Marks, Betty. *Light and easy diabetes cuisine*. Los Angeles, CA: HPBooks, 1990.
ISBN: 0-8958-6640-0   250 p.

D34 Marks, Betty and Schechter, Lucille Haley. *The International menu diabetic cookbook: 73 exciting menus from around the world featuring more than 300 low-fat, low-salt, high-fiber, sugarless recipes*. Chicago, IL: Contemporary Books, 1985.
ISBN: 0-8092-5390-9   364 p.
** recipes arranged by country of origin; each recipe includes nutritional values and diabetic exchanges

D35 Maynard, Kitty E.; Maynard, Lucian; and Duncan, Theodore G. *Cooking for diabetics: a complete guide to easy menu planning and enjoyable eating for healthy living*. Nashville, TN: Rutledge Hill Press, 1989.
ISBN: 1-5585-3000-2   229 p. illustrated, color

D36 Metcalfe, Jill. *Better cookery for diabetics: over 130 delicious and healthy recipes for diabetics, their families*

and friends to enjoy. London: British Diabetic Association, 1983.
206 p. illustrated, color

D37   Oexmann, Mary Jean. *TAG: a diabetic food system.* New York: W. Morrow, 1989.
ISBN: 0-6880-8458-3   190 p.
** includes food exchange lists and food sugar content tables

D38   Palumbo, P. J. and Margie, Joyce Daly. *The All-in-one diabetic cookbook.* New York: New American Library, 1989.
ISBN: 0-4522-6252-6
** with recipes for young cooks; previously published as *The complete diabetic cookbook,* 1987

D39   Park Nicollet Medical Foundation. International Diabetes Center. *Learning to live well with diabetes.*
Minneapolis: International Diabetes Center, Park Nicollet Medical Foundation, 1985.
392 p. illustrated, some color

D40   Pelican, Suzanne and Bachman-Carter, Karen. *Navajo food practices, customs, and holidays.* Chicago, IL: American Dietetic Association; Alexandria, VA: American Diabetes Association, 1991.
ISBN: 0-8809-1083-6
** developed by Diabetes Care and Education Dietetic Practice Group of the American Dietetic Association; part of the *Ethnic and regional food practices -- a series*

D41   Revell, Dorothy Tompkins. *Oriental cooking for the diabetic*. Tokyo: Japan Publications, distributed through New York: Harper and Row, 1981.
ISBN: 0-8704-0492-X   160 p.
** each recipe includes diabetic exchange values and calories

D42   Spicer, Kay. *Kay Spicer's Light and easy choices: food for fitness, nutrition and fun*. Toronto, ON: Grosvenor House Press, 1985.
ISBN: 0-9199-5920-2   216 p. illustrated, some color
** published for diabetics in cooperation with the Canadian Diabetes Association and the Juvenile Diabetes Foundation

D43   Stephens, John W. *Understanding diabetes*. 3rd ed. Beaverton, OR: Touchstone Press, 1987.
ISBN: 0-9115-1871-1   240 p.

D44   Strachan, Clarice Bowers. *The Diabetic's cookbook*. rev. ed. New York: McGraw-Hill, 1981.
ISBN: 0-2927-3212-0   303 p.

D45   Swanson Center for Nutrition. *Diet handbook*. Washington, DC: Dept. of Health, Education, and Welfare, 1980.
23 p. illustrated, color
** designed for diabetes in cooperation with Indian Health Service; supported by a subcontract with the National Diabetes Information Clearinghouse, National

Institute of Arthritis, Metabolism, and Digestive Diseases

D46   University of Alabama in Birmingham. Dept. of Dietetics.
All new cookbook for diabetics and their families.
Birmingham, AL: Oxmoor House, 1988.
ISBN: 0-8487-0750-8   234 p. illustrated
** developed by the Research Nutritionist of the General
Clinical Research Center, School of Medicine, and the
Registered Dieticians of the Department of Dietetics,
University of Alabama at Birmingham

D47   Whitaker, Julian M. *Reversing diabetes.* New York:
Warner Books, 1987.
ISBN: 0-4465-1304-0   389 p. illustrated
** presents recipes and exercise therapy

D48   Zats, Marjorie and Rubin, Karen. *The Elegant touch, a
cookbook for calorie conscious and diabetic people.*
Minneapolis, MN: Graphic World, 1980.
256 p.   illustrated
** includes low-calorie recipes for diabetes; prepared in
cooperation with Mount Sinai Hospital, Minneapolis, MN

FOR CHILD DIABETICS

D49   Babington, Caroline Hastings. *Cooking creatively for
your diabetic child: new recipes and menu suggestions to
help you plan tempting meals for your juvenile diabetic
and the entire family.* Garden City, NY: Doubleday,
1979.

ISBN: 0-3851-4809-7   224 p. illustrated
** based on six major exchanges; each recipe includes exchange equivalents; recipes are breakfast, school lunches, main dishes, desserts, and festive foods

D50   Briggs, Christy. *Dining with your diabetic child.* Salt Lake City, UT: Kerry and Christy Briggs, 1978.
79 p. illustrated
** includes recipes for soups, casseroles, salads, meats and canning; also includes menus for dinner and breakfast

D51   Hall, Sue. *Cooking for your diabetic child.* New York: Thorsons, 1988.
ISBN: 0-7225-1586-3   112 p.
** in collaboration with the British Diabetic Association

D52   Loring, Gloria. *Kids, food and diabetes.* Chicago, IL: Contemporary Books, 1986.
ISBN: 0-8092-4956-1   391 p.
** includes recipes for diabetics in children and adolescents

D53   Majors, Judith Soley. *Sugar free kids' cookery: easy calculated foods.* rev. ed. Milwaukie, OR: Apple Press, 1987.
ISBN: 0-9419-0501-2   128 p. illustrated
** approved by American Diabetes Association, Inc., Oregon Affiliate, Inc.; with recipes for beverages, breakfast, breads, sandwiches, dinner, and sweets with exchanges, calories, carbohydrate, protein, and fat contents

D54 Rossiter, Jane and Seddon, Rosemary. *The Diabetic kids' cookbook.* London: Optima, 1987.
ISBN: 0-3561-4913-7   127 p. illustrated, color
** from the *Positive health guide* series

FOR FESTIVE CUISINE

D55 Govindji, Azmina and Myers, Jill. *Diabetic entertaining: mouth-watering meals for the health conscious.* New York: Thorsons, 1990.
ISBN: 0-7225-2134-0   112 p.

D56 Wedman, Betty. *American Diabetes Association Holiday cookbook.* New York: Prentice Hall Press, 1986.
ISBN: 0-1302-4894-0   219 p. illustrated
** each recipe provides nutritional content, calories, and exchange value; includes holiday menus for diabetics, vegan diabetics, and lacto-ovo-vegetarian diabetics

D57 Wedman, Betty. *American Diabetes Association Special celebrations and parties cookbook.* New York: Prentice Hall Press, 1989.
ISBN: 0-1300-4219-6   243 p.
** includes menus and recipes from appetizers, desserts, vegetarian entrees, to picnic ideas; each recipe includes ADA exchange values, caloric and nutritive values (protein, carbohydrate, fat, cholesterol, sodium, and potassium)

WITH MICROWAVE OVEN

D58   Finsand, Mary Jane. *Diabetic microwave cookbook.*
New York: Sterling Pub. Co., 1989.
ISBN: 0-8069-6960-1   160 p.

D59   Hall, Sue. *The Diabetic's microwave cookbook: quick
and convenient meals for the busy diabetic.* New York:
Thorsons, 1986.
ISBN: 0-7225-1319-4   96 p.   illustrated
** published with the British Diabetic Association

D60   Majors, Judith Soley. *Sugar free ... microwavery:
calculated cookbook.* Milwaukie, OR: Apple Press, 1980.
ISBN: 0-9602-2383-5   168 p.   illustrated
** a cookbook for diabetics approved by the American
Diabetes Association, Inc., Oregon Affiliate, Inc.; recipes
based on the six major exchanges and all recipes provide
diabetic exchange equivalents and caloric contents

D61   Marks, Betty. *The Microwave diabetes cookbook.*
Chicago, IL: Surrey Books, 1991.
ISBN: 0-9406-2526-1   256 p.   illustrated

D62   McMaster, Catha and Empringham, Charlotte. *More
choice: the Canadian diabetic microwave cookbook.*
Toronto, ON: Macmillan of Canada, 1991.
ISBN: 0-7715-9432-1   221p.   illustrated

HIGH-FIBER DIET

D63 Anderson, James W. *The HCF guide book.* Lexington, KY: HCF Diabetes Foundation, 1987.
63 p. illustrated
** contains high-carbohydrate and high-fiber recipes

D64 Cavaiani, Mabel. *The High fiber cookbook for diabetics: high-carbohydrate recipes that provide the fiber most diabetics lack - actually helping control blood sugar.* New York, NY: Perigee Books, 1987.
ISBN: 0-3995-1335-3   208 p.
** each recipe includes nutritive values, food exchange values, and suggestions for modifications to suit the needs of a low-sodium or a low-cholesterol diet

D65 Finsand, Mary Jane. *Diabetic high fiber cookbook.* New York: Sterling Pub. Co., 1985.
ISBN: 0-8069-6228-3   160 p.
** recipes include exchanges and calories

D66 Krimmel, Patricia T. and Krimmel, Edward A. *The Low blood sugar cookbook: sugarless cooking for everyone: over 200 natural foods recipes.* Bryn Mawr, PA: Franklin Publishers, 1986.
ISBN: 0-9165-0301-1   191 p. illustrated
** high-fiber low-carbohydrate recipes for hypoglycemics, diabetics, and weight watchers

D67 Longstaff, Roberta and Mann, Jim. *The Diabetics' cookbook: delicious new recipes for entertaining and all*

the family: over 180 mouth-watering dishes for the high-fiber, low-calorie eating program. New York: Arco Pub., 1984.
ISBN: 0-6680-6148-0   122 p. illustrated, color
** each recipe includes calories and nutritive values (protein, fat, carbohydrate, and fiber)

D68   Metcalfe, Jill. *Cooking the new diabetic way: the high fibre calorie-conscious cookbook.* London: Ward Lock, 1983.
ISBN: 0-7063-4265-8   152 p. illustrated, color

HIGH-FIBER LOW-FAT
LOW-SUGAR DIET

D69   Cavaiani, Mabel. *The New diabetic cook book: 175 delicious recipes based on the American Diabetes Association's recent recommendations for a low-fat, low-sugar, low-cholesterol, low-salt, high-fiber diet.* Chicago, IL: Contemporary Books, 1989.
ISBN: 0-8092-4251-6   347 p.
** provides nutritive value, exchange value and indication for suitability of low-sodium diet; menu planning for special occasions; recipes for soup, salads, breads, desserts, beverages, canning, and freezing

D70   Mann, Jim and the Oxford Dietetic Group. *The Diabetic's diet book: a new high-fibre eating programme: recipes based on the Oxford diet plan for diabetics: control calorie intake, high-fiber, low-fat, low-refined*

sugar. New York: Arco, 1982.
ISBN: 0-6680-5339-9   123 p. illustrated, some
color
** recipes include calories and nutritive values
(carbohydrate, fiber, protein, and fat)

D71   Prince, Francine. *Francine Prince's Gourmet recipes for
diabetics and those on restricted diets: delicious low-cost,
low-fat, low-calorie recipes with no-sugar or salt--using
supermarket foods.* rev. and updated. New York: Simon
and Schuster, 1989.
ISBN: 0-6716-8368-3   223 p.
** low-fat and high-fiber recipes include ADA exchange
value, calories, nutritive contents (carbohydrate, fat,
protein, cholesterol, sodium, and potassium)

LOW-CARBOHYDRATE DIET

D72   Davis, Francyne. *The Low blood sugar cookbook.* rev.
ed. New York: Bantam Books, 1985.
ISBN: 0-5532-5085-X   229 p.
** includes low-carbohydrate recipes for the
hypoglycemic

D73   Revell, Dorothy Tompkins. *Hypoglycemia control
cookery: the feel better, eat better cookbook for people
with low blood sugar.* New York: Berkley, 1983.
ISBN: 0-4250-5734-8   192 p.
** recipes are low in sugar, carbohydrate, and milk, and
high in protein

LOW-FAT DIET

D74   Higa, Barbara W. *Desserts to lower your fat thermostat.*
Provo, UT: Vitality House International, 1988.
ISBN: 0-9125-4706-5   214 p. illustrated, some
color
** recipes for all types of desserts detailing RCU
(refined carbohydrate units), calories, percentage of fat,
diabetic exchange, and nutritive values (protein, fat,
carbohydrate, and sodium)

D75   Little, Billie. *Recipes for diabetics.* New York: Perigee
Books, 1990.
ISBN: 0-3995-1643-3   288 p.
** low-fat, low-cholesterol, and low-calorie recipes for
appetizers, soups, main dishes, desserts, canning, freezing,
jams, and jellies; instructions for converting to microwave
ovens; menu planning based on diabetic exchange lists;
recipes include calories and diabetic exchanges; includes
the latest exchange lists

D76   MacRae, Norma M. *How to have your cake and eat it,
too!: diet cooking for the whole family, diabetic,
hypoglycemic, low-cholesterol, low fat, low salt, low
calories.* rev. ed. Anchorage, AK: Alaska Northwest
Pub. Co., 1982.
ISBN: 0-8824-0226-9   308 p. illustrated

D77   Watson, Ann and Lousley, Sue. *The Diabetic's
international diet book: 150 delicious ethnic dishes for*

the diabetic diet. Tucson, AZ: Body Press, 1987.
ISBN: 0-8958-6466-5   128 p. illustrated, color
** low-fat recipes arranged by food categories; dishes
include Chinese, Japanese, Indonesian, Indian, Mexican,
and Middle Eastern cuisine; each recipe contains diabetic
exchanges

LOW-SUGAR DIET

D78   Gonshorowski, Addie. *The Sugar-less cookbook: no
sugar, no honey, no artificial sweeteners have been added
to the recipes.* 3rd rev. ed. Eugene, OR: Ad-Dee
Publishers, 1981.
ISBN: 0-9600-9826-7   100 p.

D79   Gonshorowski, Addie. *Sugarless desserts, jams, and
salads cookbook.* Eugene, OR: Ad-Dee Publishers, 1988.
150 p. illustrated

D80   Hine, Jacqui. *A Here's health guide to low-sugar
cooking: delicious dishes for a reduced-sugar diet.* New
York: Thorsons, 1987.
ISBN: 0-7225-1371-2   160 p. illustrated, some
color

D81   Horsley, Janet. *Sugar-free cookbook.* Dorchester,
Dorset: Prism Press, 1983.
ISBN: 0-9070-6149-4   96 p. illustrated

D82   Hum, Nellie G. *The Sugarless cookbook: cooking with*

the natural sweetness of fruit. Ottawa, ON: Hum Pub., 1987.
ISBN: 0-9198-4552-5   111 p. illustrated, color

D83   Kruppa, Carole. *The Free and Equal sweet tooth cookbook: 150 quick and delicious sugar-free recipes featuring the new, good tasting sweetener from the makers of NutraSweet brand sweetener.* Chicago, IL: Surrey Books, 1988.
ISBN: 0-9406-2507-5   159 p.
** low-calorie, with a sugar substitute, recipes for appetizers, soups, salads, entrees, vegetables, desserts, and beverages

D84   Lebrecht, Elbie. *Living without sugar.* Dobbs Ferry, NY: Grafton, 1989.
ISBN: 0-5862-0106-8   320 p.

D85   Majors, Judith Soley. *Sugar free: Hawaiian cookery.* Milwaukie, OR: Apple Press, 1987.
ISBN: 0-9602-2389-4

D86   Oxley, Veronica and Pinker, Jennifer. *The Sugar-free cookbook.* London: Omega, 1983.
ISBN: 0-9078-5311-0   128 p. illustrated, some color

D87   Stevens, Laura J. *The New way to sugar-free recipes: over 100 recipes using Equal brand sweetener.* Garden City, NY: Doubleday, 1984.
ISBN: 0-3851-9403-X   104 p.

D88   Weiss, Caroline   and Uslander, Arlene. *Creative cooking sugar free for diabetics and their families.* Chicago: Budlong Press, 1981.   181 p.

D89   Whalen, Freda. *Country cooking without sugar.* 2nd ed. Lake Charles, LA: F. Whalen, 1986.
174 p. illustrated
** sugar-free recipes for hypoglycemics and diabetics

D90   Wing, Natalie. *Sugar free: hints and recipes for meals free from added sucrose and other sugars.* Rotherham, South Yorkshire: Pawson, 1989.
ISBN: 0-9515-1410-5   64 p.

LOW-SUGAR CANNING

D91   MacRae, Norma M. *Canning and Preserving without sugar.* 2nd ed. Chester, CT: Globe Pequot Press, 1988.
ISBN: 0-8710-6724-2   230 p.
** includes USDA canning recommendations and diabetic exchange list from the American Diabetes Association

LOW-SUGAR DESSERTS

D92   Alimonti, Joan Mary. *52 sugar free desserts.* Pleasant Hill, CA: Quickline Publications, 1989.
ISBN: 0-9247-5300-5   121 p.

D93   Barkie, Karen E. *Fancy, sweet and sugarfree.* New

York: St. Martin's Press, 1985.
ISBN: 0-3122-8164-1   173 p.
** a dessert cookbook using fruits

D94   Barkie, Karen E. *Sweet and sugarfree: an all natural fruit-sweetened dessert cookbook.* New York: St. Martin's, 1982.
ISBN: 0-3127-8066-4   160 p.

D95   Bassler, Lynn and Raboff, Fran. *Virtuous desserts.* Freedom, CA: Crossing Press, 1989.
ISBN: 0-8959-4362-X   216 p. illustrated
** dessert recipes with sugar replacements: frozen apple juice concentrate, pureed dates, and dried fruits

D96   Buhr, Deborah. *The "I can't believe this has no sugar" cookbook: more than 100 sugar-free cholesterol-free dairy-free recipes for great-tasting cakes, cookies, pies, candies, breads, and muffins.* New York: St. Martin's, 1990.
ISBN: 0-3120-4330-9   153 p. illustrated
** low-fat recipes using only all-natural sweeteners with no additives

D97   Collier, Carole. *The Natural sugarless dessert cookbook.* New York: Walker, 1980.
ISBN: 0-8027-7161-0   180 p. illustrated

D98   Duval, Therese and Drouin, Renata. *Sweets without sugar.* Scarborough, ON: McGraw-Hill Ryerson, 1989.
ISBN: 0-0754-9884-7   135 p. illustrated, color

** sugar-free dessert recipes using fruits

D99   East West Journal; editors of. *Sweet and natural desserts: East West's best and most wholesome, sugar- and dairy-free treats.* Brookline, MA: East West Health Books, distributed by Talman, 1986.
ISBN: 0-9361-8405-1   120 p. illustrated

D100   Finsand, Mary Jane. *Diabetic candy, cookie and dessert cookbook.* New York: Sterling, 1982.
ISBN: 0-8069-7586-5   160 p.
** use of sugar replacements or sweeteners in candies, cookies, gelatin desserts, puddings, ice cream, crepes, pastries, pies, cakes, frostings, and toppings; recipes include calories and exchange values

D101   Finsand, Mary Jane. *Diabetic chocolate cookbook.* New York: Sterling, 1984.
ISBN: 0-8069-7900-3   160 p.

D102   Finsand, Mary Jane. *Diabetic snack and appetizer cookbook.* New York: Sterling Pub. Co., 1987.
ISBN: 0-8069-6560-6   160 p.
** recipes include frozen treats, soups, and sandwiches; a section on kids' stuff; lists exchanges, calories, and carbohydrate content

D103   Gerstenzang, Sharon M. Dregne. *Cook with me sugar free: favorite snacks, sweets, and desserts for children and grownups too.* New York: Simon and Schuster, 1983.

ISBN: 0-6714-6472-8   222 p. illustrated

D104   Hall, Sue. *Diabetic desserts.* New York: Thorsons,
       1989.
       ISBN: 0-7225-1653-3   112 p.
       ** sponsored by the British Diabetic Association

D105   Lebrecht, Elbie. *Sugar-free cakes and biscuits.* 2nd ed.
       Faber, 1989.
       ISBN: 0-5711-5418-2   150 p.

D106   Majors, Judith Soley. *Sugar free ... goodies.* Milwaukie,
       OR: Apple Press, 1987.
       ISBN: 0-9419-0500-4   159 p. illustrated
       ** designed for diabetes; approved by the American
       Diabetes Association, Inc., Hawaii Affiliate, Inc.; each
       recipe indicates exchange, caloric, carbohydrate, protein,
       and fat values

D107   Mayo, Patricia Terris. *The Sugarless baking book: the
       natural way to prepare America's favorite breads, pies,
       cakes, puddings, and desserts.* Boulder, CO: Shambhala
       Publications, distributed by Random House, 1983.
       ISBN: 0-8777-3227-2   116 p. illustrated
       ** features sugar-free recipes using natural ingredients

D108   Moe, Jeanne; Rubin, Karen; and Abrams, Sally. *The No
       sugar delicious dessert cookbook.* Berkeley, CA:
       Celestial Arts, 1984.
       ISBN: 0-8908-7402-6   121 p.

D109 Shandler, Nina and Shandler, Michael. *Holiday sweets without sugar*. New York: Rawson, Wade Publishers, 1981.
ISBN: 0-8925-6189-0   202 p.

D110 Spicer, Kay. *Light and easy choice desserts*. Toronto, ON: Grosvenor House, 1986.
ISBN: 0-9199-5928-8   175 p. illustrated, color
** contains low-calorie dessert recipes; published in cooperation with the Canadian Diabetes Association

D111 Suthering, Jane and Lousley, Sue. *Diabetic delights: cakes, biscuits and desserts*. London: Martin Dunitz, 1986.
ISBN: 0-9482-6907-3   125 p. illustrated, color

D112 Warrington, Janet. *Sweet and natural: desserts without sugar, honey, molasses, or artificial sweeteners*. Trumansburg, NY: Crossing Press, 1982.
ISBN: 0-8959-4072-8   143 p. illustrated
** a fruit cookbook

D113 Weber, Marcea. *Naturally sweet desserts: the sugar-free dessert cookbook* Garden City Park, NY: Avery Pub. Group, 1990.
ISBN: 0-8952-9443-5   248 p. illustrated, some color
** dessert recipes use natural ingredients and are free of sugar

MACROBIOTIC DIET

D114 Kushi, Aveline. *Diabetes and hypoglycemia: cooking for health.* Tokyo: Japan Publications, distributed in USA through Harper and Row, 1985.
ISBN: 0-8704-0617-5   160 p. illustrated
** focuses on a macrobiotic diet; part of the *Macrobiotic food and cooking series*

D115 Kushi, Michio. *Diabetes and hypoglycemia: a natural approach.* Tokyo: Japan Publications, distributed in USA by Kodansha International, 1985.
ISBN: 0-8704-0615-9   144 p. illustrated
** a macrobiotic diet cookbook and a companion volume to *Diabetes and hypoglycemia: cooking for health,* by Aveline Kushi, 1985

VEGETARIAN DIET

D116 Cousins, Margaret and Metcalfe, Jill. *Dieting the vegetarian way: the high-fiber, low-sugar, low-fat, whole food vegetarian cookbook, a guide for diabetics and those watching their weight.* New York: Thorsons, distributed in USA by Inner Traditions International, 1986.
ISBN: 0-7225-0887-5   188 p. illustrated
** recipes for soups, appetizers, quick meals, goodies, main dishes, and desserts; carbohydrates and caloric content given

D117 Mozzer, Patricia. *Vegetarian cooking for diabetics.* rev.

ed. Summertown, TN: Book Pub. Co., 1987.
ISBN: 0-9139-9047-7   144 p. illustrated, color
** includes conversions to a vegetarian diabetic exchange system

D118   Trupin, Judy. *A Concoctionist cookbook.* Buffalo, NY: White Pine Press, 1982.
ISBN: 0-9348-3432-6   59 p.   illustrated
** a vegetarian cookbook containing sugar-free recipes with natural ingredients

SELECTED ASSOCIATIONS
AND FOUNDATIONS

American Diabetes Association
National Service Center
P.O. Box 25757, 1660 Duke Street, Alexandria, Virginia 22314
703-549-1500

British Diabetic Association
10 Queen Anne St., London, England W1M 0BD

Canadian Diabetes Association
Suite 601, 123 Edward Street, Toronto, Ontario, Canada M5G
1E2

International Diabetes Center
P.O. Box 739, Wayzata, MN 55391

International Diabetes Federation
40, rue Washington, B-1050 Brussels, Belgium
2-647-4414

International Study Group of Diabetes in Children and
Adolescents
Department of Pediatrics
University Hospital, S-581 85 Linkoping, Sweden

Juvenile Diabetes Foundation
23 East 26th Street, New York, New York 10010

Juvenile Diabetes Foundation International
432 Park Ave. S., New York, New York 10016
1-800-223-1138

National Diabetes Advisory Board
1801 Rockville Pike, Suite 500, Rockville, Maryland 20852
301-496-6045

National Diabetes Information Clearinghouse
Box NDK, Bethesda, Maryland 20205

FOOD INTOLERANCE (F)

FOOD INTOLERANCE, also known as food allergy or food sensitivity, is adverse immunologic reactions in exposure to a food. It occurs more commonly in children and infants than adults. The human immune system usually protects the body against foreign substances; antigen-specific immune responses can sometimes produce adverse, even fatal, effects. Food is the largest antigenic challenge confronting our immune system. Food allergies are examples of the negative consequences of the immune function on the gastrointestinal tract, skin, lungs, and other organ systems. Symptoms can include acute abdominal pain, swelling, nausea, vomiting, rashes, vascular collapse, chronic itching, headache, tension, and fatigue. Eczema, asthma, and rhinitis are more common in children than in adults.

To distinguish a true allergic reaction from an intolerance due to a biochemical or psychologic disturbance, the specific food causing the reaction must be clearly identified, a proper diagnostic procedure followed, and the cessation of symptoms documented when the offensive food is eliminated. The most common food allergens are eggs, milk, wheat, peanuts, soybeans, chicken, fish, shellfish, and nuts.

The HYPERACTIVE CHILD SYNDROME, a childhood behavioral problem, is also termed Attention Deficit Hyperactivity Disorder. Through numerous unconfirmed reports, it has been linked to various foods and food constituents. The suspected allergens are artificial food colorings, flavorings, salicylate, sugar, caffeine, and food preservatives.

CELIAC SPRUE, also known as nontropical sprue or gluten-induced enteropathy, is a genetic-immunologic disorder resulting from an immunologic reaction to the gluten fraction of proteins from wheat, oats, rye, and barley. Its symptoms may be silent and its prevalence is uncertain, but it is thought to affect about 1 in 2,500 persons in the U.S. When patients with this disorder ingest gluten, the cells that line the small intestine undergo atrophy, causing malnutrition, stunting of growth, and anemia. Strict removal of gluten from the diet alleviates symptoms and restores the integrity of the intestinal mucosa.

Gluten-sensitive enteropathy should be considered a chronic disease that is controlled by diet. An asymptomatic state depends on the lifelong maintenance of a gluten-free diet. Although abstaining from these grains appears to be direct and simple, gluten-containing grains and products are a staple in Western diets. The widespread use of emulsifiers, thickeners, and other additives derived from gluten-containing grains in commercially processed foods further complicates the strict adherence to a gluten-free diet.

AN INSUFFICIENCY OF LACTASE, the enzyme responsible for the breakdown of lactose, or milk sugar, in the small intestine, can cause lactose intolerance. Many lactase-deficient individuals can consume modest amounts of lactose-containing foods with little difficulty. Some need to modify milk and milk products by addition of lactase, or the use of fermented products such as cheese or yogurt, permitting consumption of milk products. Others may require a milk-free diet.

IN GENERAL

F1   American Dietetic Association. *Food sensitivity: a resource including recipes.* Chicago: The American Dietetic Association, 1985.
      ISBN: 0-8809-1012-7   127 p.
      ** from the *Food sensitivity series* for persons suffering from food allergies

F2   Armstrong, Danila and Cant, Andrew. *The Allergy-free cookbook.* London: Octopus, 1986.
      ISBN: 0-7064-2621-5   128 p. illustrated, some color
      ** from the *Recipes for good health* series

F3   Breneman, James C. editor. *Handbook of food allergies.* New York: Dekker, 1987.
      ISBN: 0-8247-7558-9   297 p. illustrated
      ** from the *Immunology series*

F4   Buist, Robert. *Food intolerance: what it is and how to cope with it.* Bridport, Dorset: Prism Press, distributed in USA by Avery Pub. Group, 1984.
      ISBN: 0-9070-6168-0   238 p.

F5   Carter, Patricia. *An Allergy cookbook.* Henry, 1989.

ISBN: 0-8602-5423-2   120 p.

F6   Chiu, Beverly D. *How you too can outsmart your food allergies using the diversified rotation diet: complete workbook with food family charts and diary.* Vancouver, BC: Yellow Hat Press, 1987.
ISBN: 0-9219-3701-6   81 p.   illustrated

F7   Crook, William G. *Detecting your hidden allergies: foods you eat everyday can cause asthma, "sinus" headaches, fatigue, nervousness, digestive problems, arthritis ... and many other disorders.* Jackson, TN: Professional Books, 1988.
ISBN: 0-9334-7815-1   220 p. illustrated

F8   Daglish, Laurie; compiler. *The Allergy cookbook: foods for festive occasions.* Toronto, ON: Methuen, 1985.
ISBN: 0-4589-8230-X   156 p. illustrated
** published by the Allergy Information Association

F9   Dept. of Agriculture. Human Nutrition Information Service. *Cooking for people with food allergies.* Washington, DC: U.S. Dept. of Agriculture, 1988.
39 p.   illustrated

F10   Dong, Faye M. *All about food allergy.* Philadelphia, PA: G.F. Stickley Co., 1984.
ISBN: 0-8931-3040-0   210 p. illustrated

F11   Frazier, Claude Albee. *Coping with food allergy.* rev. ed. New York: Times Books, 1985.

ISBN: 0-8129-1149-0   322 p.

F12   Gislason, Stephen J. *Core program cooking: diet
revision cooking meal planning.* 2nd ed. Vancouver,
BC: PerSona Audiovisual Productions, 1990.
ISBN: 0-9694-1451-X   173 p. illustrated
** provides recipes for persons with food allergies; from
the *Nutritional medicine series*

F13   Golos, Natalie and Golbitz, Frances Golos. *If this is
Tuesday, it must be chicken, or How to rotate your food
for better health.* New Canaan, CT: Keats, 1983.
ISBN: 0-8798-3339-4   130 p.
** recipes to alleviate food allergies

F14   Gorham, Beth. *There is a way: an allergy and food
sensitivity cookbook.* Doaktown, NB: There is a Way
Pub., 1987.
110 p. illustrated

F15   Goulart, Frances Sheridan. *101 allergy-free desserts.*
New York: Simon and Schuster, 1983.
ISBN: 0-6714-5785-3   188 p.

F16   Greer, Rita. *Food allergy cookbook.* Twickenham,
London: Hamlyn, 1986.
ISBN: 0-6003-2606-3   128 p. illustrated, some
color
** a part of the *Hamlyn diet plan series*

F17   Jay, Terri and McCullough, June. *Exciting but safe*

recipes for celiacs and allergics. Port Angeles, WA: Rare Gem Publishing, 1989.
ISBN: 0-9299-2600-5   125 p. illustrated

F18   Johns, Stephanie Bernardo. *The Allergy guide to brand-name foods and food additives.* New York: New American Library, 1988.
ISBN: 0-4522-6059-0   256 p.

F19   Kaufmann, Doug A. and Skolnik, Racquel. *The Food sensitivity diet.* New York: Freundlich Books, 1984.
ISBN: 0-8819-1003-1   205 p.

F20   Lacey, Suzanne S. *The Allergic person's cookbook.* Springfield, IL: Thomas, 1981.
ISBN: 0-3980-4149-0   289 p.

F21   Lepinski, Martha Powers. *A Guide for the allergy cook.* Springfield, IL: Thomas, 1985.
ISBN: 0-3980-5108-9   221 p.

F22   Null, Gary and Feldman, Martin. *Good food, good mood: treating your hidden allergies.* New York: Dodd, Mead, 1988.
ISBN: 0-3960-8981-X   198 p.
** recipes for food-allergic persons

F23   Null, Gary. *The Complete guide to sensible eating: the egg project updated with new and expanded chapters on detoxification, homeopathy, herbs, and healing.* New York: Four Walls Eight Windows, 1990.

ISBN: 0-9414-2337-9   292 p. illustrated
** vegetarian recipes, rotary diversified diet, beginner's four-day rotation diet, vegetarian rotation diet and 28-day exercise plans included for food allergies and weight reduction; revised edition of *The egg project*, 1987.

F24   Postley, John E. and Barton, Janet M. *The Allergy discovery diet: a rotation diet for discovering your allergies to food.* New York: Doubleday, 1990.
ISBN: 0-3852-4682-X   369 p.

F25   Rascon, Bonnie and Levy, Judith. *Feasting on an allergy diet.* Sacramento, CA: Cuissential Arts, 1985.
ISBN: 0-9615-1364-0   224 p. illustrated

F26   Rudoff, Carol. *The Allergy cookie jar.* Menlo Park, CA: Prologue Publications, 1985.
ISBN: 0-9300-4814-8   116 p. illustrated

F27   Rudoff, Carol. *Main courses for the microwave-convection oven.* Menlo Park, CA: Allergy Publications Group, 1986.
ISBN: 0-9616-7080-0   116 p. illustrated
** prepared for food-allergic persons; published by the American Allergy Association

F28   Rudoff, James David. *The Creative cookie.* Menlo Park, CA: Allergy Publications Group, 1987.
ISBN: 0-9616-7088-6   100 p.

F29   Service, Denise H. *Dee Dee's Allergy delights: a*

121

cookbook for multiple food allergies. Collierville, TN: Fundcraft Pub., 1988.   50 p.

F30   Stevens, Laura J. *The Complete book of allergy control.* New York: Macmillan, 1983. ISBN: 0-0261-4450-6   341 p.

F31   Stone, Carolyn and Beima, Jan. *The Allergy survival guide and cookbook: to your good health.* Rolling Meadows, IL: C. C. and Co. Publishing, 1988.   251 p.

F32   Swanson, Elaine Beckett. *The Total harvest diet.* rev. and expanded ed. Sunland, CA: Fraser Products Co., 1986. ISBN: 0-9333-7900-5 ** contains weight-reducing recipes for persons with food allergies

F33   Yoder, Eileen Rhude. *Allergy-free cooking: how to survive the elimination diet and eat happily ever after.* Reading, MA: Addison-Wesley, 1987. ISBN: 0-2010-9797-4   211 p. ** elimination-diet recipes (without common allergens) included; each recipe indicates which of the allergens the recipe has omitted

FOR ALLERGIC CHILDREN

F34   Hartung, Shirley. *Cookies naturally: for children of all ages!* rev. ed. Kitchener, ON: S. Hartung, 1989.

ISBN: 0-9694-1150-2   81 p.
** tailored treats for persons with food allergies

F35   McNicol, Jane. *The Great big food experiment: how to identify and control your child's food intolerances.* Toronto, ON: Stoddart, 1990.
ISBN: 0-7737-5344-3   160 p.

F36   Meizel, Janet E. *Your food-allergic child: a parent's guide.* Bedford, MA: Mills and Sanderson, 1988.
ISBN: 0-9381-7916-0   278 p.

F37   Moore, Pauline. *New milk-free, egg-free recipes for children: nutritional therapy for allergenic symptoms including eczema, asthma, diarrhea, colic, coeliac disease and ulcerative colitis.* London: Foulsham, 1986.
160 p. illustrated

F38   Thomas, Linda L. *Caring and cooking for the allergic child.* rev. New York: Sterling, 1980.
ISBN: 0-8069-5552-X   141 p. illustrated
** gluten-free, milk-free, egg-free recipes for diarrhea, babies and toddlers, the allergic child, and the whole family; with allergy-detection suggestions

F39   Williams, Margaret L. *Cooking without: recipes for the allergic child (and family).* Ambler, PA: Gimbal Corp., 1989.
ISBN: 0-9607-0460-4   73 p. illustrated
** recipes are for children with food allergies

FOR HYPERACTIVE CHILDREN

F40   Ash, Janet and Roberts, Dulcie. *Hyperactive child: happiness is junk-free food.* rev. ed. New York: Thorsons, 1990.
ISBN: 0-7225-2379-3   221 p.
** recipes using natural food

F41   Feingold, Ben F. and Feingold, Helene S. *The Feingold Cookbook for hyperactive children, and others with problems associated with food additives and salicylates.* New York: Random House, 1979.
ISBN: 0-3944-1232-X   327 p. illustrated
** recipes do not contain artificial coloring, flavors, two preservatives (butylated hydroxytoluene [BHT] and butylated hydroxyanisole [BHA]), or fruits and vegetables containing natural salicylates

F42   Finsand, Mary Jane. *Caring and cooking for the hyperactive child.* New York: Sterling, 1981.
ISBN: 0-8069-8980-7   192 p.
** based on Dr. Ben F. Feingold's dietary guidelines for hyperactive-child syndrome patients

F43   Hollands, Elizabeth A. *How a mother copes with hyperactivity.* Altona, MB: Friesen, 1983.
ISBN: 0-8892-5557-1   119 p. illustrated
** cookery for the hyperactive child

F44   Robb, Phyllis. *Cooking for hyperactive and allergic children.* Fort Wayne, IN: Cedar Creek Publishers, 1980.

ISBN: 0-9353-1600-0   235 p. illustrated
** based on Dr. Feingold's diet guidelines: without
artificial coloring/flavoring, BHA, BHT, and salicylates;
many recipes are refined-sugar-free and/or milk-free

F45   Roth, June. *Cooking for your hyperactive child: more
than 200 artificial-additive-free recipes.* Chicago:
Contemporary Books, 1977.
ISBN: 0-8092-7832-4   271 p. illustrated
** recipes contain no food additives and clearly indicate
whether a dish is free of natural salicylate, dairy
products, egg, wheat, corn, or sugar; also includes a guide
for identifying foods that contain "hidden" allergens, a
four-day natural salicylate-free diet, and a four-day
diversified rotation diet

F46   Stevens, Laura J. and Stoner, Rosemary B. *How to
improve your child's behavior through diet.* Garden City,
NY: Doubleday, 1979.
ISBN: 0-3851-4820-8   346 p.
** designed for children with food allergies and
emotional problems; recipes contain no refined foods and
sugar; limited amount of milk; no artificial colors or
flavors, and no BHA or BHT

F47   Stevens, Laura J.; Stevens, George E.; and Stoner,
Rosemary B. *How to feed your hyperactive child.*
Garden City, NY: Doubleday, 1977.
ISBN: 0-3851-2465-1   240 p. illustrated
** recipes based on Dr. Feingold's guidelines (without
artificial colorings and flavorings, BHT, BHA, and

salicylates) and appeal to children and teenagers

F48   Tydeman, Ann. *Cooking with pure ingredients: family recipes for the hyperactive.* Norwalk, CT: Australian National University Press, 1979.
ISBN: 0-7081-0746-X   200 p. illustrated
** features natural ingredients for hyperactive-child syndrome patients

GLUTEN-FREE DIET

F49   Canadian Celiac Association. *A Guide for the diabetic celiac.* Mississauga, ON: Canadian Celiac Association, 1990.
ISBN: 0-9210-2602-1   42 p. illustrated
** contains gluten-free recipes

F50   Canadian Celiac Association. *Celiac disease needs a die. for life: the handbook for celiacs and their families.* Mississauga, ON: Canadian Celiac Association, 1988.
ISBN: 0-9210-2600-5   80 p. illustrated
** includes gluten-free recipes

F51   Coffey, Lynette. *Wheatless cooking: including gluten-free and sugar-free recipes.* Berkeley, CA: Ten Speed Press, 1985.
ISBN: 0-8981-5156-2   88 p. illustrated, some color

F52   Degenerative Disease Control Group. *Overcome disease*

nutritionally: non-gluten baking and other recipes from the Ogilvie research kitchen. New Mexico: Degenerative Disease Control Group, 1981.
40 p.   illustrated

F53   Friesen, Joyce. *Gluten free anytime.* Edmonton, AB: D. Wall, 1989.   176 p.

F54   Greer, Rita. *Gluten-free cooking.* 3rd ed. New York: Thorsons, 1989.
ISBN: 0-7225-2201-0   128 p.

F55   Hagman, Bette. *The Gluten-free gourmet: living well without wheat.* New York: Holt, 1990.
ISBN: 0-8050-1210-9   235 p.
** over 200 gluten-free recipes (with milk substitutes) for breads, desserts, breakfast, appetizers, snacks, brunches, pizza, main dishes, and holiday dishes

F56   Kisslinger, Juanita. *The Rice flour cookbook.* rev. ed. Sidney, BC: Kisslinger Publications, 1987.
ISBN: 0-9210-1902-5   117 p. illustrated
** rice-flour recipes that are gluten-free for celiac disease sufferers also published under the title *The joy of gluten-free cooking*

F57   Leicht, Libby. *A Cookbook for celiac (sprue) /diabetics and singles who need one to two portion servings only.* 2nd rev. ed. Pender Island, BC: 1982.
65 p.   illustrated
** contains gluten-free, low-fat, and low-sugar recipes

F58   Powers, Margaret. *Gluten free and good!*   Old Town
       Press, 1983.
       ISBN: 0-9610-1400-8   113 p.
       ** prepared for patients with celiac disease

F59   Rawcliffe, Peter. *Gluten-free diet.* St. Clarita, CA:
       Optima, 1990.
       ISBN: 0-3561-9675-5   128 p.
       ** prepared for celiac disease patients

F60   Redjou, Pat Cassady. *The No-gluten solution: the
       cooking guide for people who are sick and tired of being
       sick and tired.* Vancouver, WA: Print and Publish, Inc.,
       1990.
       ISBN: 0-9626-0520-4   158 p. illustrated
       ** designed for patients with celiac disease

F61   Reid, Chris. *Gluten-free and easy: recipes for a gluten
       allergy diet.* Victoria, BC: C. Reid, 1983.
       ISBN: 0-9691-4840-2   138 p.

F62   Ridgway, Judy. *Wheat and gluten free cookery: over 100
       recipes for allergy sufferers.* London: Century Arrow,
       1986.
       ISBN: 0-0994-6650-3   135 p. illustrated

F63   Wood, Marion N. *Coping with the gluten-free diet.*
       Springfield, IL: Thomas, 1982.
       ISBN: 0-3980-4718-9   150 p.
       ** for patients with celiac disease

GLUTEN-FREE
MILK-FREE DIET

F64 Hills, Hilda Cherry. *Good food, milk free, grain free: the
easy-to-follow, money-saving nutrition plan that has
helped thousands regain mental and physical health.*
New Canaan, CT: Keats, 1980.
ISBN: 0-8798-3201-0   154 p.
** designed for schizophrenics and patients with celiac
disease

F65 Martin, Jeanne Marie. *All natural allergy recipes:
breads, desserts and main dishes: gluten and dairy-free.*
Vancouver, BC: J.M.M. Publications, 1986.
108 p. illustrated

GLUTEN-FREE MILK-FREE
EGG-FREE DIET

F66 American Dietetic Association. *Gluten intolerance: a
resource including recipes.* Chicago: American Dietetic
Association, 1985.
ISBN: 0-8809-1013-5   99 p.
** a part of the *Food sensitivity series*, designed for
persons with celiac disease; includes discussion and
treatment for gluten intolerance; recipes indicate the non-
containing allergens: wheat, egg, or milk; with tips for
substitutions for making completely gluten-free dishes

F67   Autry, Gloria Diener and Allen, T. Diener. *The Color-coded allergy cookbook: the key to good eating for the food-sensitive.* Indianapolis, IN: Bobbs-Merrill, 1983.
ISBN: 0-6725-2746-4   392 p.
** contains more than 900 recipes, all free of cow's milk, wheat, and eggs; includes appetizers, main dishes, and desserts; recipes non-color-coded are the Basic Building-Block plan (for initial testing periods); color coded for the types of grains to test and add

F68   Cole, Candia Lea. *Not milk--nut milks!: 40 of the most original dairy-free milk recipes ever!* Santa Barbara, CA: Woodbridge Press, 1990.
ISBN: 0-8800-7184-2
** recipes do not use eggs, milk, or wheat

F69   Gibson, Sheila; Templeton, Louise; and Gibson, Robin. *Cook yourself a favour: 350 recipes to help you help yourself to better health.* new ed. New York: Thorsons, 1986.
ISBN: 0-7225-1320-8   144 p. illustrated
** recipes omit eggs, milk, or wheat

F70   Greer, Rita. *Wheat, milk and egg-free cooking.* 2nd ed. New York: Thorsons, 1989.
ISBN: 0-7225-2202-9   144 p.
** from *A special diet cookbook* series

F71   Hamrick, Beck and Wiesenfeld, Stephen L. *The Egg-free, milk-free, wheat-free cookbook.* New York: Harper and Row, 1982.

ISBN: 0-0601-4978-7   274 p. illustrated
** recipes indicate the non-containing allergens

F72   Hunter, John; Jones, Virginia Alun; and Workman,
       Elizabeth. *Food intolerance: are the foods you eat
       making you sick? Test yourself using the "exclusion
       diet".* Tucson, AZ: The Body Press, 1986.
       ISBN: 0-8958-6474-6   127 p.
       ** recipes are marked for exclusion (for initial testing),
       wheat-free, milk-free, egg-free, or for arthritis sufferers

F73   Roth, June. *The Allergy gourmet.* Chicago, IL:
       Contemporary Books, 1983.
       ISBN: 0-8092-5612-6   294 p. illustrated
       ** recipes marked dairy-free, egg-free, or gluten-free

F74   Workman, Elizabeth; Hunter, John; and Jones, Virginia
       Alun. *The Allergy diet: how to overcome your food
       intolerance.* New York: Larousse, 1985.
       ISBN: 0-1302-2450-2   119 p. illustrated, color
       ** recipes are marked for exclusion, gluten-free, milk-
       free, or egg-free diets

GLUTEN-FREE MILK-FREE
EGG-FREE CORN-FREE DIET

F75   Allergy Information Association. *The Allergy cookbook:
       diets unlimited for limited diets.* 2nd rev. ed. Toronto,
       ON: Methuen, 1986.
       ISBN: 0-4588-0690-0   148 p.

** provides allergen contents and substitutions for milk, egg, gluten, wheat, corn, salicylate, yeast, and reduced sugar

F76   Jones, Marjorie Hurt. *The Allergy self-help cookbook: over 325 natural foods recipes, free of wheat, milk, eggs, corn, yeast, sugar and other common food allergens.* Emmaus, PA: Rodale Press, 1984.
ISBN: 0-8785-7505-7   385 p.
** recipes and samples of a diversified rotation diet for allergy patients

F77   Lashford, Stephanie. *The Allergy cookbook.* Rev. and enl. ed. Bath, Avon: Ashgrove Press, 1986.
ISBN: 0-9067-9874-4   192 p. illustrated, some color
** four recipe categories: egg-free, white-flour-free, corn-free, and milk-free

F78   Little, Billie. *Recipes for allergics.* New York: Bantam, 1982.
ISBN: 0-5532-2538-3   266 p.
** recipes arranged by corn allergy, egg allergy, and milk allergy; each of the three groups includes wheat-free recipes

F79   Mandell, Fran Gare. *Dr. Mandell's Allergy-free cookbook.* New York: Gulf and Western, 1981.
ISBN: 0-6718-3603-X   252 p.
** includes fasting and menu of rotary diversified diet free of allergens such as sugarcane, soy, egg, corn, wheat,

yeast, and milk; all recipes provide substitution list for allergens

F80   Nonken, Pamela Peckarsk and Hirsch, S. Roger. *The Allergy cookbook and food-buying guide: a practical approach to cooking and buying food for people who are allergic to foods.* New York: Warner Books, 1982.
ISBN: 0-4463-7173-4   302 p.
** contains recipes free of corn, eggs, milk, soy, wheat, and yeast; lists what foods are safe to buy by category and by brand name; lists foods to avoid, and foods to substitute for allergens

F81   Rudoff, Carol. *The Allergy baker: wheat-free, milk-free, egg-free, corn-free, soy-free.* 3rd ed. Menlo Park, CA: Allergy Publications, 1990.
ISBN: 0-9300-4813-X   114 p. illustrated

F82   Shattuck, Ruth R. *The Allergy cookbook: tasty, nutritious cooking without wheat, corn, milk or eggs.* rev. ed. New York, NY: New American Library, 1986.
ISBN: 0-4522-5450-7   304 p.

F83   Traub, Terry. *The Food allergy detection program: complete with over 300 allergen-free recipes.* New York: Frederick Fell Publishers, 1983.
ISBN: 0-8119-0592-6   236 p.
** Part 1 includes detection of allergens and preparation of the elimination diet; Part 2 contains milk-free, egg-free, gluten-free, and corn-free recipes

GLUTEN-FREE MILK-FREE
YEAST-FREE DIET

F84   Greenberg, Ron and Nori, Angela. *Freedom from allergy cookbook: 207 wheat, yeast and milk free recipes.* Vancouver, BC: Blue Poppy Press, 1988.
ISBN: 0-8892-5905-4   118 p.

MILK-FREE DIET

F85   American Dietetic Association. *Lactose intolerance: a resource including recipes.* Chicago: American Dietetic Association, 1985.
ISBN: 0-8809-1012-7   77 p.

F86   Borgwardt, Barbara Newby. *The No milk cookbook: delicious milk-free recipes and ideas for the entire family.* rev. ed. West Allis, WI: Parkway Publications, 1982.
ISBN: 0-9608-3980-1   89 p.   illustrated

F87   Burlant, Arlene. *Lactose-free cooking: over 200 recipes for people sensitive to dairy products.* Wayne, NJ: Lockley Publishers, 1990.
ISBN: 0-9626-9410-X   221 p. illustrated
** includes nutrients and diabetic food exchanges for each recipe

F88   Carper, Steve. *No milk today: how to live with lactose intolerance.* New York: Simon and Schuster, 1986.
ISBN: 0-6716-0301-9   286 p.

F89   Hostage, Jacqueline E. *Living-- without milk: a cookbook and nutritional guide for those who should avoid dairy products.* 3rd ed. White Hall, VA: Betterway Publications, 1981.
ISBN: 0-9326-2005-1   139 p. illustrated

F90   Kidder, Beth. *The Milk-free kitchen: living well without dairy products: 450 family-style recipes.* New York: Henry Holt, 1991.
ISBN: 0-8050-1255-9   458 p.
** recipes from breakfast items, appetizers, and desserts to main dishes; a small portion previously published as *Cooking without milk*, 1988

F91   Martens, Richard A. and Martens, Sherlyn. *The Milk sugar dilemma: living with lactose intolerance.* 2nd ed., rev. and expanded. East Lansing, MI: Medi-Ed Press, 1987.
ISBN: 0-9367-4101-5   260 p. illustrated

F92   Zukin, Jane. *Dairy free cookbook.* Rocklin, CA: Prima Pub. and Communications, 1991.
ISBN: 1-5595-8088-7   322 p.
** includes milk-free recipes for lactose-intolerant patients

F93   Zukin, Jane. *Milk-free holiday cooking.* Iowa City, IA: Commercial Writing Service, 1989.
120 p. illustrated
** recipes for appetizers, beverages, soups, salads, breads, main dishes, side dishes, desserts, and candies,

and further subdivided by major holidays including Jewish holidays

MILK-FREE EGG-FREE DIET

F94   Sainsbury, Isobel S. *The Milk-free and milk/egg-free cookbook: how to prepare easy, delicious foods for people on special diets and their families.* New York: Arco, 1979.
ISBN: 0-6680-4701-1   148 p.

F95   Ratner, Ellen. *Savory soups.* Menlo Park, CA: Allergy Publications, 1988.
ISBN: 0-9616-7087-8   116 p. illustrated
** recipes are milk-free, egg-free, corn-free, and soy-free; side dishes, main entries, chilled desserts, and fruit soups; from the *Allergy kitchen* series

SELECTED ASSOCIATIONS
AND FOUNDATIONS

American Celiac Society
45 Gifford Avenue, Jersey City, New Jersey 07304
201-432-1207

Asthma and Allergy Foundation of America
1717 Massachusetts Avenue, Suite 305, Washington, DC 20036
202-265-0265

Celiac Sprue Association USA
P.O. Box 31700, Omaha, Nebraska 68103-0700

Feingold Association of the US
P.O. Box 6550, Alexandria, Virginia 22306
800-321-FAUS
703-768-FAUS

Gluten Intolerance Group of North America
P.O. Box 23053, Seattle, Washington 98102-0353
206-325-6980

Midwest Gluten Intolerance Group
5660 Rebecca Lane, Minnetonka, Minnesota 55345

National Celiac-Sprue Society
5 Jeffrey Road, Wayland, Massachusetts 01778

GASTROINTESTINAL
DISEASES AND DISORDERS (G)

The GASTROINTESTINAL system is composed of the stomach and the intestines. It extracts nutrient- and energy-yielding molecules from foods and digests them into smaller sub-units that can be absorbed. Much of the treatment of gastrointestinal diseases and disorders depends on supplying the correct diet for each particular type of gastrointestinal disturbance. The area is exposed to all kinds of dietary indiscretions, and it is affected by mental and emotional disturbances to a greater extent than are the rest of the organs involved in the processes of digestion and metabolism.

Data from several national surveys provide evidence that these gastrointestinal conditions are extremely prevalent and cause considerable impairment of health and functional ability in the American population.

CIRRHOSIS and other chronic liver diseases are the only digestive system disorders among the 10 leading causes of death aside from cancer. For this standing, the most powerful dietary culprit is alcohol consumption.

HEARTBURN, an inflammation of the lower esophagus, caused by the backflow of stomach acids, can occur when the lower esophageal sphincter does not contract properly. Alcohol, dietary fat, and both regular and decaffeinated coffee have been demonstrated to reduce sphincter pressure and to increase reflux.

DIVERTICULOSIS occurs when diverticula, abnormal outpocketings of the intestinal wall, form in the colon and cause pain in the left lower abdomen, without fever. A high-fiber diet or fiber supplements are recommended by some in clinical management of uncomplicated diverticular disease.

GASTRIC AND DUODENAL ULCERS are local erosions of the mucosa that result from excessive production of gastric acid and pepsin or from decreased mucosal resistance to these substances. The role of nutritional factors in the etiology of ulcers is uncertain. The bland milk-and-cream-based Sippy diet, used in former years, is no longer recommended as treatment. Today, ulcer patients typically are encouraged to consume a varied and balanced diet, taken slowly in four or five small meals a day, but limited in alcohol, coffee, and other substances that lead to discomfort and pain. However, bland and ulcer diets probably are not detrimental to most persons if they are used for a short time and may be of psychological benefit to some.

Dietary fat, fiber, and alcohol are significant factors associated with gastrointestinal diseases. Evidence that dietary fiber helps treat and prevent constipation and manage chronic diverticular disease suggests the prudence of consuming diets higher in fiber and lower in fat.

For persons suffering from celiac sprue and lactose intolerance, consult the section on Food Intolerance. Following are some selected contemporary diets for various gastrointestinal diseases and disorders. For additional high-fiber, soft foods, and bland dietbooks included in other chapters, see the Diet Plan Locator Guide and the Keyword Index.

DIGESTIVE DISORDERS

G1   Bircher-Benner Klinik. *Bircher-Benner Nutrition plan for digestive problems: a comprehensive guide, with suggestions for diet menus and recipes.* Edited by Ralph Bircher. Translated by Timothy McManus. New York: Jove Publications, 1978.
ISBN: 0-5150-4226-9   142 p.

G2   Matsen, Jonn. *Eating alive: prevention thru good digestion.* North Vancouver, BC: Crompton Books, 1988.
ISBN: 0-9693-5860-1   300 p. illustrated
** a naturopathic cookbook for persons who suffer from digestive diseases

DIVERTICULOSIS

G3   American Digestive Disease Society. *The "Irritable bowel" diet.* New York: The Society, 1980s.
68 p.   illustrated
** designed for patients with irritable bowel syndrome or diverticulosis; this diet plan is targeted to alleviate the following symptoms: constipation/pain, flatus, intermittent diarrhea/constipation, heartburn, nausea, and vomiting;

part of the *ADDS dietary plans* series

LIVER AND
GALLBLADDER DISORDERS

G4   Bircher-Benner Klinik. *Bircher-Benner Nutrition plan for liver and gallbladder problems; a comprehensive guide, with suggestions for diet menus and recipes.* Edited by Ralph Bircher. Translated by Klaus Musmann. New York: Jove Publications, 1978.
ISBN: 0-5150-4229-3   124 p.

ULCER

G5   American Digestive Disease Society. *The "Ulcer" diet: an ADDS dietary plan for ulcers and other acid conditions.* New York: The Society, 1980s.
62 p. illustrated
** for gastric and duodenal ulcers, hiatal hernia, esophagitis, gastritis, duodenitis, heartburn, acid reflux, and other acid conditions; includes list of foods to avoid, base-line diet with foods to try and not to try, step-by-step guide to test for food intolerances and sensitivities; sample menus included without recipes; part of the *ADDS dietary plans* series

G6   Berland, Theodore and Spellberg, Mitchell A. *Living with your ulcer.* New York: St. Martin's Press, 1971.
178 p. illustrated

G7   Bruyere, Toni Marsh and Robey, Sidney Jean. *For gourmets with ulcers: a unique cookbook that tells you how to prepare delectable meals with ulcer-diet foods.* New York: Norton, 1981.
ISBN: 0-3930-0984-X   226 p.

G8   Duncan, Ben. *Soothing food: a new view of cooking for ulcers and difficult stomachs.* New York: Hippocrene Books, 1972.
ISBN: 0-8825-4013-0   180 p.
** includes recipes and suggestions about foods to be avoided, questionable foods, costs, fats, prepacked foods, equipment and seasoning

G9   Liddell, Caroline and Ross, Nickey. *Ulcer superdiet.* London: Pitman, 1977.
ISBN: 0-2730-0110-8   124 p.

G10   Roth, June. *The Troubled tummy cookbook.* Chicago, IL: Henry Regnery Co., 1976.
ISBN: 0-8092-8178-3   254 p. illustrated
** designed for ulcer patients requiring a bland-diet; recipes include liquid, soft, strict bland, regular bland, postgastrectomy, low-residue, high-residue, low-fat, low-sodium, low-purine, and gluten-free diets

G11   Schultz, Cecilia L. *The Bland-diet cookbook: over 200 delicious recipes for individuals who must restrict their diets to soothing mild foods.* New York: Putnam's Sons, 1978.
ISBN: 0-3991-1857-8   91 p.   illustrated

** recipes include bland diet for ulcer patients, bland low-residue diet, and bland low-fat diet

SELECTED ASSOCIATIONS
AND FOUNDATIONS

American Digestive Disease Society
60 E. 42nd Street, Room 411, New York, New York 10165

National Digestive Diseases Advisory Board
1801 Rockville Pike, Suite 500, Rockville, Maryland 20852
301-496-6045

National Digestive Diseases Information Clearinghouse
Box NDDIC, Bethesda, Maryland 20892
301-468-6344

National Ulcer Foundation
675 Main Street, Melrose, Massachusetts
617-665-6210

United Ostomy Association
Suite 12036 Executive Park, Irvine, California 92714
714-660-8624

MUSCULAR-SKELETAL
DISEASES AND DISORDERS (MS)

Major skeletal diseases influenced by nutrition include rickets, osteomalacia, and osteoporosis. Rickets, the "softening" of bones in children, and its adult form, osteomalacia, have been largely eradicated in the industrialized world by milk fortification, enrichment of infant foods with vitamin D, the use of vitamin D supplements by children, and improved environmental conditions that promote adequate exposure to sunlight.

ARTHRITIS occurs in two forms. The most common type is osteoarthritis, a chronic non-inflammatory arthritis also known as osteoarthrosis or degenerative joint disease. Typical characteristics are pain, stiffness, joint enlargement, and limitation of joint motion. Diagnosis is through X-ray. About 90% of adults over the age of 50 suffer from this. Another type of arthritis is rheumatoid arthritis, a chronic inflammatory disease of unknown cause affecting any synovial joint and associated tendon sheath. The progress and duration of arthritis varies. The goal of therapeutic management is to delay progression, preserve joint function, reduce pain, and control inflammation.

MULTIPLE SCLEROSIS is an inflammatory disease of the central nervous system, characterized by chronic progression of neurologic dysfunction. It may be caused by an autoimmune disease linked to a viral infection. The symptoms were once thought to develop gradually, but this is not necessarily true. In about 40% of cases the onset may occur in less than a few hours. The disease is rare in children; and in about two-thirds of cases, it begins between ages 20 and 40. The duration of the disease varies from a few months to an average of 30 years and there is no specific drug therapy.

The relationship of dietary fat consumption and the progression of both arthritis and multiple sclerosis has been examined in recent studies. When multiple sclerosis patients at early and late stages are on a low-saturated fat diet (less than or equal to 20 g fat/day) or are given the addition of Omega-3 and Omega-6 polyunsaturated fatty acids, the severity of deterioration and frequency of relapses are reduced. In other studies, Omega-3 fatty acid decreased the severity of arthritis (in human cell samples). The effect of fish oil, containing Omega-3 fatty acid, has also been linked to reduce cholesterol level and the severity of diabetes, migraines, and psoriasis.

OSTEOPOROSIS, or loss of bone mass, has become the most significant bone disease in Western countries. An estimated 1.3 million fractures of the vertebrae, hips, forearms, and other bones in those 45 years of age and older were complicated by osteoporosis. It can be classified into primary and secondary forms.

Primary osteoporosis, specifically involutional osteoporosis, has two forms. Type I is postmenopausal osteoporosis which is the accelerated decrease in bone mass that occurs when estrogen levels decline after menopause. In postmenopausal women, estrogen-replacement therapy has been the best documented method of preventing osteoporosis. Type II is age-related osteoporosis, the inevitable loss of bone mass with age that occurs in both men and women.

Secondary osteoporosis may develop at any age as a consequence of endocrinologic and gastrointestinal conditions or metabolic disorders, as well as prolonged bedrest and states of weightlessness, that result in bone demineralization.

Although much is yet to be learned about how diet can affect the development of this disease, sufficient scientific evidence now exists to make nutrition a focus of programs to prevent or to treat osteoporosis. Dietary factors of particular concern are calcium, phosphate, vitamin D (and calcitriol, its hormonally active form), protein, sodium, calories, and alcohol. Increased exercise and decreased cigarette smoking also may decrease the risk for osteoporosis. During the first three to four decades of life, ingesting adequate calcium, maintaining appropriate body weight, exercising, restricting alcohol, and avoiding smoking are evidently appropriate prevention strategies for osteoporosis.

Most interest in the dietary control of osteoporosis focuses on calcium. Although current epidemiologic and clinical evidence is uncertain, chronic low calcium intake may decrease peak bone mass, especially during adolescence. Some of the high-calcium foods are milk, cheese, yogurt, collard greens, turnip greens, tofu, sardines with bones, and salmon with bones.

Following are some selected contemporary orthodox and unorthodox diets for muscular-skeletal diseases and disorders. For additional low-fat and high-calcium dietbooks included in other chapters, see the Diet Plan Locator Guide and the Keyword Index.

ARTHRITIS

MS1   Airola, Paavo O. *There is a cure for arthritis.* West Nyack, NY: Parker, 1988.
ISBN: 0-1391-4671-7   200 p.
** presents biological medicine and naturopathic methods of treatment for arthritis; a part of the *Reward classics series*

MS2   Alexander, Dale. *Arthritis and common sense #2.* West Hartford, CT: Witkower Press, 1984.
ISBN: 0-9116-3817-2   291 p. illustrated

MS3   Bingham, Beverly. *Cooking with fragile hands: kitchen help for arthritics.* Naples, FL: Creative Cuisine, Inc., 1985.
ISBN: 0-9614-1220-8   384 p. illustrated
** recipes from appetizers and desserts to main dishes; containing many kitchen photographs, hints and tips on food preparation

MS4   Bircher-Benner Klinik. *Bircher-Benner Arthritis and rheumatism nutrition plan; a comprehensive guide with*

suggestions for diet menus and recipes. Edited by Ralph Bircher. Translated by Lotte Erlich. Los Angeles: Nash Pub., 1972.
ISBN: 0-8402-8029-7   124 p.

MS5   Dong, Collin H. and Banks, Jane. *The Arthritic's cookbook: appetizing recipes to fit the diet prescribed by a medical doctor who has treated thousands of cases of rheumatic diseases with remarkable success.* New York: Thomas Y. Crowell, 1973.
ISBN: 0-6900-0086-3   184 p.
** recipes do not use meats, fruits, tomatoes, dairy products, egg yolks, yogurt, any acid (vinegar), pepper, chocolate, dry roasted nuts, soft drinks, alcoholic beverages, additives, preservatives, or chemicals

MS6   Fredericks, Carlton. *Arthritis, don't learn to live with it.* New York: Perigee Books, 1985.
ISBN: 0-3995-1133-4   221 p.

MS7   Hills, Margaret. *Curing arthritis cookbook.* London: Sheldon, 1986.
ISBN: 0-8596-9524-7   112 p.
** a part of the *Overcoming common problems* series

MS8   Kushi, Aveline. *Arthritis: cooking for health.* Tokyo: Japan Publications, 1988.
ISBN: 0-8704-0677-9   181 p. illustrated
** includes macrobiotic diet recipes for arthritis and is a part of the *Macrobiotic food and cooking series*

MS9 Laver, Mary and Smith, Margaret. *Arthritic cookbook.*
London: Hamlyn, 1983.
ISBN: 0-6003-2338-2   128 p. illustrated, some
color

MS10 Macfarlane, Ann. *Are you cooking comfortably?* British
Gas, 1986.
ISBN: 0-9035-4538-1   100 p.
** for patients suffering from arthritis

MS11 MacFarlane, Helen Beverley. *Diets to help arthritis.* 1st.
rev. format ed. New York: Thorsons, distributed by
Sterling Pub. Co., 1988.
ISBN: 0-7225-1730-0   48 p.

MS12 McIlwraith, Michael. *The Arthritis diet cookbook.*
London: Gollancz, 1988.
ISBN: 0-5750-4265-6   168 p.

MS13 Wade, Carlson. *Carlson Wade's Factbook on arthritis,
nutrition, and natural therapy.* New Canaan, CT: Keats
Pub., 1976.   124 p.
** includes naturopathic recipes for arthritis; part of the
A Pivot original health book series

MS14 Warmbrand, Max. *Overcoming arthritis and other
rheumatic diseases.* Old Greenwich, CT: Devin-Adair
Co., 1976.
ISBN: 0-8159-6311-4   220 p.
** a naturopathic cookbook for arthritis

BACK PAIN

MS15 Green, Lawrence E.; O'Rorke, Maureen; and Ceresa,
Carol. *The Bad back diet book: a commonsense program*
of diet and exercise. San Francisco, CA: Chronicle
Books, 1987.
ISBN: 0-8770-1416-7   123 p. illustrated, some
color
** low-calorie cookery and exercise for backaches

MULTIPLE SCLEROSIS

MS16 Fitzgerald, Geraldine and Briscoe, Fenella. *Multiple*
sclerosis: healthy menus to help in the management of
multiple sclerosis. New York: Thorsons, distributed in
USA by Sterling, 1989.
ISBN: 0-7225-1810-2   127 p. illustrated
** published in collaboration with Action for Research
into Multiple Sclerosis

MS17 Forsythe, Elizabeth. *The Low-fat gourmet: a doctor's*
cookbook for heart disease and MS [multiple sclerosis].
London: Pelham Books, 1980.
ISBN: 0-7207-1226-2   154 p. illustrated

MS18 Swank, Roy L. and Dugan, Barbara Brewer. *The*
Multiple sclerosis diet book: a low-fat diet for the
treatment of M.S. rev. and expanded ed. Garden City,
NY: Doubleday, 1987.
ISBN: 0-3852-3279-9   391 p.

** recipes for all types of dishes including oriental cuisines with fat and oil content listings; sample menus for one-week low-fat and three-day eating out

OSTEOPOROSIS

MS19 Appleton, Nancy. *Healthy bones.* Garden City Park, NY: Avery Pub. Group, 1990.
ISBN: 0-8952-9462-1
** recipes to prevent osteoporosis

MS20 Ettinger, Victor G. and Fredal, Judy. *Recipes for better bones: cooking for today's most popular tastes to prevent tomorrow's most unwanted ailment--osteoporosis.* New York: Putnam, 1988.
ISBN: 0-3995-1401-5   175 p. illustrated
** contains high-calcium, low-fat, high-fiber, high-complex-carbohydrate, and low-sugar recipes to prevent osteoporosis; each recipe indicates calcium and caloric content

MS21 Goulder, Lois and Lutwak, Leo. *The Strong bones diet: the high calcium, low calorie way to prevent osteoporosis.* Gainesville, FL: Triad Pub. Co., 1988.
ISBN: 0-9374-0420-9   222 p.

MS22 Marks, Betty. *The High-calcium, low-calorie cookbook: more than 250 delicious recipes.* Chicago: Contemporary Books, 1987.
ISBN: 0-8092-4579-5   271 p.

** high-calcium, low-calorie, low-cholesterol, low-fat, low-sodium, and no-sugar recipes; each details calorie contents and nutritional values

MS23 Ness, Joanne and Subak-Sharpe, Genell. *The Calcium-requirement cookbook: 200 recipes that supply necessary calcium-rich foods to prevent the bone loss that often begins in a woman's thirties.* New York: M. Evans, 1985.
ISBN: 0-8713-1453-3   191 p.
** high-calcium, low-cholesterol, low-calorie recipes with calcium and caloric content listed

SELECTED ASSOCIATIONS
AND FOUNDATIONS

American Juvenile Arthritis Organization
1314 Spring Street, N.W., Atlanta, Georgia 30309
404-872-7100

Arthritis Advisory Committee
Center for Drug Evaluation and Research
Food and Drug Administration (HFD-9), Room 8B-45, 5600 Fishers Lane, Rockville, Maryland 20857
301-443-4695

Arthritis Care
5 Grosvenor Crescent, London S1X 7ER, England
1-235-0902

Arthritis Foundation
1314 Spring Street, N.W., Atlanta, Georgia 30309
404-872-7100

British Society for Rheumatology
3 St. Andrew's Place, Regent's Park, London NW1 4LE,
England
1-224-3739

International Federation of Multiple Sclerosis Society
3/9 Heddon Street, London W1R 7LE, England
1-734-9120

National Arthritis Advisory Board
Building 31/4C-32, Bethesda, Maryland 20892
301-496-0801

National Arthritis and Musculoskeletal and Skin Diseases
Advisory Council
National Institutes of Health, Bethesda, Maryland 20892
301-496-7277

National Institute of Arthritis and Musculoskeletal and Skin
Diseases
National Institutes of Health, Bethesda, Maryland 20892
301-496-7277

National Multiple Sclerosis Society
205 East 42nd Street, New York, New York 10017
212-986-3240

National Osteoporosis Foundation
2100 M Street, N.W., Suite 602, Washington, DC 20037
202-223-2226

ORAL AND DENTAL
DISEASES AND DISORDERS (OR)

DENTAL CARIES AND PERIODONTAL DISEASE are significant and widespread public health problems in the United States. They are rarely life threatening but can cause substantial expense, pain, restriction of activity, and work loss.

DENTAL CARIES, or tooth decay, is caused by a progressive dissolution of mineral from tooth surfaces by acid produced by oral bacteria. Advanced disease can result in tooth loss. The number of decayed, missing, and filled permanent teeth increases steadily with age.

Despite the complex etiology of dental caries, the causative role of dietary sugar, especially sucrose, is well established. Caries-producing bacteria have such a high need for simple sugars--glucose, fructose, lactose, maltose, and sucrose-- that they readily metabolize into acids that demineralize teeth. Sugars in solution are more readily cleared from the mouth than sugars in solid foods and, therefore, are more likely to have only a transient influence on plaque acidity. Foods that adhere to the teeth are more cariogenic than those that wash off quickly.

The efficacy of fluoride in the prevention of tooth decay is well documented. It is generally assumed to prevent caries by decreasing the solubility of tooth enamel, promoting

155

remineralization of the enamel surface, modifying the chemical interactions in plaque, or inhibiting lactic acid production by cariogenic bacteria.

PERIODONTAL DISEASE includes a spectrum of pathologic conditions ranging from gingivitis, or minor gum inflammation, to periodontitis, or severe loss of the bone structure supporting the teeth. Advanced disease results in loosening and eventual loss of teeth.

Like dental caries, the etiology of this disease includes specific microbiologic, environmental, and systemic components. The gingival sulcus, the space between the gums and the teeth, harbors bacteria that directly and indirectly affect the formation of periodontal lesions and the later destruction of periodontal tissues and their cellular components. Environmental influences on the gums include dietary sugars and other factors that promote the formation of plaque on tooth surfaces, entrapment of food in periodontal lesions, and poor dental hygiene. Persons who are diabetic, immunosuppressed, or genetically susceptible are especially prone to periodontal disease.

Dietary factors of principal interest in dental diseases are sugars and fluoride. Frequent consumption of sugars, especially sucrose, promotes formation of dental plaque, the key predisposing cause of both caries and periodontal disease.

A SOFT DIET OR PUREED DIET may be appropriate for persons without teeth or with poorly fitting dentures; post-oral or maxillary surgery patients; those having oral radiation treatment; and individuals with strictures of the intestinal tract.

For more low-sugar and soft-food dietbooks included in other chapters, consult the Diet Plan Locator Guide and the Keyword Index.

FOR DENTAL HEALTH

OR1 *California Dental Association Low-sugar cookbook.*
Sacramento, CA: the Association, 1988.
28 p.   illustrated
** for better teeth by using less sugar

OR2 Holler, John L. *An Inside look, or, the tooth about your teeth.* Stockton, CA: Carrie Company, 1980.
47 p.   illustrated
** preventive dentistry in the kitchen

OR3 *Look Ma, no cavities cookbook: a cookbook of low-sugar and sugar-free recipes.* rev. ed.   Concord, NH: Auxiliary to the New Hampshire Dental Society, 1979.
55 p.   illustrated
** designed for dental health maintenance

OR4 *Super smart snacks: recipes for healthy teeth.* Olympia, WA: Division of Health, 1989.
28 p.   illustrated
** prepared for children by the Nutrition and Dental Health Consortium

SOFT AND
LIQUID DIET

OR5   Anderson, Beth. *The Healing kitchen: a guide to liquid diet.* Graton, CA: Healing Kitchen, 1989.
48 p. illustrated
** designed for patients with a broken jaw; high-protein and high-calorie liquid diet recipes prepared with a blender, a food processor, and/or a strainer; includes a special section on Mori-Nu Tofu for soups, drinks, and desserts

OR6   Chamberlain, Anne S. *The Soft foods cookbook.* Garden City, NY: Doubleday, 1973.
ISBN: 0-3850-3284-6   130 p.
** for persons with deglutition disorders; recipes for semi-soft, blended, dessert, and extra nutritious dishes

OR7   Daly, Katherine M. and Boyne, Philip J. *Nutrition and eating problems of oral and head-neck surgeries: a guide to soft and liquid meals.* Springfield, IL: Thomas, 1985.
ISBN: 0-3980-4914-9   402 p. illustrated
** designed for patients after mouth surgery, head surgery, neck surgery, or mandible surgery

OR8   Goldberg, Phyllis Z. *So what if you can't chew, eat hearty!: recipes and a guide for the healthy and happy eating of soft and pureed foods.* Springfield, IL: Thomas, 1980.
ISBN: 0-3980-4065-6   137 p. illustrated
** for mastication disorders or patients recovering from

mouth surgery; recipes include protein and caloric contents

OR9   Niven, Penelope. *The I hate to chew cookbook: a gourmet guide for adults who wear orthodontic braces.* New Castle, IN: Straight Status, 1984.
** a soft-food cookbook

OR10   Niven, Penelope and McJunkin, Jack. *Teen cuisine: a cookbook for young people who wear orthodontic braces.* New Castle, IN: Straight Status Press, 1987.
66 p.   illustrated

OR11   Norris, Rosalie N. and Powell, Janet C. *Easy-to-chew and easy-on-salt: easy-to-chew and pureed foods for a sodium-controlled diet.* East Brunswick, NJ: Cornwall Books, 1982.
ISBN: 0-8453-4718-7   177 p.
** recipes in Part 1 include easy-to-chew foods, and in Part II, pureed foods; caloric and sodium content included for each recipe

OR12   Rosenthal, Gail. *Smooth food for all with dental problems-- and everyone else.* Washington, DC: Library of Congress, 1985.
123 p.   illustrated
** a soft-food cookbook

OR13   Wilson, J. Randy. *Non-chew cookbook.* Ottawa, ON: Canadian Hospital Association, 1986.
ISBN: 0-9616-2990-8   200 p.

** includes soft-food recipes for mastication disorder patients

SELECTED ASSOCIATIONS AND FOUNDATIONS

American Dental Association
211 East Chicago Avenue, Chicago, Illinois 60611
312-440-2500

National Advisory Dental Research Council
National Institutes of Health, Bethesda, Maryland 20892
301-496-9469

National Institute of Dental Research
National Institutes of Health, Bethesda, Maryland 20892
301-496-9469

National Foundation for the Prevention of Oral Disease
7125 East Lincoln Drive, Scottsdale, Arizona 85253
602-948-7000

RENAL AND KIDNEY
DISEASES AND DISORDERS (R)

The KIDNEYS are responsible for maintaining normal composition of the blood. Most of the waste products in the blood, except carbon dioxide, that result from metabolism in the body are eliminated through the kidney. Glomeruli, contained in the kidney nephrons, filter the blood, reabsorb selected minerals in the kidney tubules, then excrete the final waste products through the ureters into the bladder.

When the overall glomerular filtration rate is reduced below a certain level, the kidney can no longer perform adequate filtration, reabsorption, and excretion routines, thus some ingested waste substances become excessive in the body. Chronic renal failure is the consequence of longstanding and progressive renal damage and is usually irreversible. Some of the most common causes of chronic renal failure are chronic glomerular disease, chronic infections, hypertension, and diabetes mellitus.

Chronic renal failure causes pervasive disorders in appetite as well as in the body's absorption, excretion, and metabolism of many nutrients. Consequently, nutritional therapy is essential in managing this condition.

The goal of dietary management in renal failure is to

adjust the intake of nutrients to meet the profoundly altered needs and capacities of the patient's renal system. In the patient on chronic dialysis, a different spectrum of problems may emerge. Protein restriction is a therapeutic measure prescribed for patients with advanced renal disease and dialysis patients must follow a protein-, potassium-, and phosphate-restricted maintenance diet.

The following books include contemporary diets for renal/kidney diseases and disorders. For additional low-salt and low-protein dietbooks listed in other chapters, consult the Diet Plan Locator Guide and the Keyword Index.

IN GENERAL

R1   Bateman, E. C.; Livesey, R.; and Judd, P.; editors. *Good food and the artificial kidney; the Royal Free Hospital Renal Unit cookery book.* 2nd rev. ed. London: the Hospital, 1972.
106 p. illustrated

R2   Cleveland Clinic Foundation. *The Cleveland Clinic Foundation Creative cooking for renal diabetic diets.* Chesterland, OH: Senay Pub., 1987.
ISBN: 0-9415-1101-4   154 p.

R3   Cleveland Clinic Foundation. *The Cleveland Clinic Foundation Creative cooking for renal diets.* Chesterland, OH: Senay Pub., 1987.
ISBN: 0-9415-1100-6   248 p.

R4   Cost, Jacquelyn S. *Dietary management of renal disease.*
       Thorofare, NJ: Charles B. Slack, 1975.
       ISBN: 0-9135-9027-4   161 p. illustrated

R5   Harbour, Linda and Wood, Susan. *Diet manual for
       patients with renal disease.* Birmingham, AL: University
       of Alabama Hospital, 1979.
       76 p.   illustrated

R6   Harum, Peggy. *Renal lifestyles manual and diet guide,
       1989.* Marina Del Rey, CA: R & D Laboratories, 1989.
       168 p. illustrated

R7   Hill, Novella S. and Dept. of the Air Force, U.S.A. *Diet
       for patients with renal disease.* Washington, DC: Dept.
       of the Air Force, Headquarters,U.S. Air Force, 1985.
       41 p.   illustrated

R8   Kane, Tyra C. *Diet manual for patients with kidney
       disease.* Houston: Baylor College of Medicine, 1978.
       219 p. illustrated
       ** prepared with support from the Renal Program for
       Texas, the Regional Medical Program of Texas

R9   Kidney Foundation of Iowa. *Understanding your renal
       diabetic diet.* Iowa City, IA: Kidney Foundation of Iowa,
       1980.
       60 p.   illustrated

R10   Kidney Foundation of Iowa. *Understanding your renal
       diet.* Iowa City, IA: Kidney Foundation of Iowa, 1979.

57 p. illustrated

R11   Robinson, Sharon Gannaway. *The Hillcrest Happy kidney kookbook.* Tulsa, OK: Hillcrest Medical Center, 1987. 160 p.

FOR CHRONIC RENAL AND KIDNEY FAILURE PATIENTS

R12   Curtis, Judith A. *The Renal patient's guide to good eating: a cookbook for patients by a patient.* Springfield, IL: Thomas, 1989.
ISBN: 0-3980-5611-0   199 p. illustrated
** low-salt, low-potassium, low-phosphorus, and low-protein recipes prepared for patients with chronic kidney failure

R13   Keenan, Emma W. *Kidney patients' wellness diet--tasty recipes: low protein, low potassium, low sodium, and low fat diet: combined renal and triglyceride diet.* Virginia Beach, VA: Grunwald and Radcliff, 1986.
ISBN: 0-9151-3311-3   84 p.
** endorsed by the National Kidney Foundation of Georgia, Inc. for patients with chronic kidney failure or elevated serum triglyceride

R14   National Kidney Foundation of Massachusetts. *The Eclectic gourmet: more than just a cookbook.* Brookline, MA: National Kidney Foundation of Massachusetts, 1986.

129 p. illustrated
** meals minding chronic renal failure or chronic kidney diseases prepared by the Council on Renal Nutrition of New England; contains glossary of cooking terms and helpful hints for serving, planning, and preparing foods; includes table of food equivalents and nutritional analysis table

R15   Vennegoor, Marianne. *Enjoying food on a renal diet.* London: King's Fund, 1982.
ISBN: 0-1972-4618-4   156 p.
** includes recipes for acute renal insufficiency and chronic renal failure sufferers

FOR DIALYSIS PATIENTS

R16   Council on Renal Nutrition of Northern California and Northern Nevada. *Carbohydrate and sodium controlled recipes: especially for diabetic and CAPD [continuous ambulatory peritoneal dialysis] renal patients.* Lexena, KS: Cookbook Publishers, 1983.
** features recipes that are low in salt and low in carbohydrates

R17   Greene, Meredith C.; editor. *The Gourmet renal nutrition cookbook: with 74 recipes contributed by the dialysis patients of Lenox Hill Hospital.* New York: Lenox Hill Hospital, 1980.
89 p.   illustrated

R18 Illinois Council on Renal Nutrition. *Everyday eating: a cookbook for the dialysis patient and family.* Chicago: National Kidney Foundation of Illinois, 1984.
126 p. illustrated
** salt-free recipes accommodating kidney diseases or chronic renal failure, and patients receiving dialysis or hemodialysis

LOW-PROTEIN DIET

R19 Bounds, Sarah. *Low-protein cooking.* New York: Thorsons, 1983.
ISBN: 0-7225-0828-X   128 p. illustrated
** from the *Cooking for special diets* series

R20 Downey, R. M. *Protein restricted recipes.* Washington, DC: Dept. of the Air Force, Headquarters, U.S. Air Force, 1982.
41 p. illustrated
** contains low-protein recipes

R21 Krawitt, Laura P. and Weinberger, Emily K. *Practical low protein cookery.* Springfield, IL: Thomas, 1971.
110 p. illustrated
** designed for kidney-disease patients

LOW-PROTEIN LOW-SALT
LOW-POTASSIUM DIET

R22   Illinois Council on Renal Nutrition. *Fun food recipes for renal diets: a guide to good and healthful eating for persons who must control their intake of protein, sodium and potassium.* Chicago: The Council, 1977.   61 p.

R23   Margie, Joyce Daly; Anderson, Carl F.; Nelson, Ralph A.; and Hunt, James C. *The Mayo Clinic Renal diet cookbook.* New York: Golden Press, 1974.
ISBN: 0-3074-9262-1   307 p. illustrated, some color
** low-protein, low-sodium, and low-potassium recipes distributed by the National Kidney Foundation

LOW-SALT DIET

R24   Council on Renal Nutrition of Northern California and Northern Nevada. *Sodium controlled recipes: especially for renal patients.* Lexena, KS: Cookbook Publishers, 1983.
56 p.   illustrated

R25   Law, Marian; editor. *The Renal family cookbook.* Downsview, ON: Renal Family Inc., 1983.
ISBN: 0-9691-3490-8   64 p.   illustrated
** salt-free recipes for kidney-disease patients in co-operation with the Association of Nephrology Dietitians of Canada

SELECTED ASSOCIATIONS
AND FOUNDATIONS

American Association of Kidney Patients
1 Davis Blvd., Suite LL1, Tampa, Florida 33606
813-251-0725

American Kidney Fund
6110 Executive Blvd., Suite 1010, Rockville, Maryland 20852
800-638-8299
301-881-3052

EDTA - European Renal Association
Department of Nephrology
Hospital Puerta Hierro, E-28035 Madrid, Spain
1-216-2240

National Kidney and Urologic Diseases Information
Clearinghouse
P.O. Box NKUDIC, Bethesda, Maryland 20892
301-468-6345

National Kidney Foundation
30 E. 33rd Street, New York, New York 10016
800-622-9010
212-889-2210

WEIGHT DISORDERS - OBESITY (W)

OBESITY is the condition of having excess body fat classified by some as a major complex medical disease caused by a mixture of genetic, psychological, and environmental factors. It has undoubtedly contributed to many of the leading causes of death in the United States. Obesity has been directly linked to cancer, heart attack, high blood pressure, stroke, diabetes, gout, arthritis, reproduction problems, gallbladder disease, and many other ailments. To maintain proper weight is no longer simply for attractive physical appearance but is a survivor's must.

Although obesity has been recognized as a health problem, the effective treatment is difficult due to the not-yet-understood causes of obesity. Some of the known factors are genetic determination, overeating, altered metabolism of adipose tissue, altered thermogenesis (the process by which calories are converted into heat), lack of exercise, and possible side effects of certain prescriptions.

Weight gain can be grouped into two categories: upper- and lower- body obesity. Upper-body obesity results from accumulation of large fat cells in the abdominal region, is more common in men, and is associated with increased cardiovascular risk. Lower-body obesity, with accumulation of fat in the hips, gluteal regions, and extremities, is more common in women and has not been linked to increased cardiovascular risk factors. Furthermore, adipose cells are insulin-resistant in the abdominal region but usually are insulin-sensitive in the gluteal region. Thus, upper body obesity also predicts an increased risk for diabetes.

Although the importance of maintaining proper weight has long been recognized, the means of achieving it and the definition of obesity have remained in the center of heated debates. Most researchers agree on the importance of physical exercise in weight control but a commonly agreed upon dietary plan has not been created. From very low-calorie to high-calorie diets, low-carbohydrate to high-carbohydrate diets, vegetarian to high-protein meat-based diets, following is a wide and interesting array of choices from which to select a diet that will work in losing or controlling weight. For additional low-fat, high-complex-carbohydrate, and high-fiber dietbooks included in other chapters, consult the Diet Plan Locator Guide and the Keyword Index.

IN GENERAL

W1   Abravanel, Elliot D. and King, Elizabeth A. *Dr. Abravanel's Anti-craving weight loss diet: based on the 8-week Skinny School program.* New York: Bantam Books, 1990.
ISBN: 0-5530-5771-5   268 p. illustrated

W2   Abravanel, Elliot D. and King, Elizabeth A. *Dr.*

Abravanel's Body type diet and lifetime nutrition plan.
New York, NY: Bantam Books, 1983.
ISBN: 0-5530-5036-2   248 p. illustrated
** includes weight-reducing recipes and exercises

W3   Annechild, Annette. *Wok your way skinny!* New York:
      Simon and Schuster, 1982.
      ISBN: 0-6714-2691-5   160 p.
      ** features weight-reducing stir-fry recipes

W4   Berger, Stuart and Cohen, Marcia. *The Southampton diet.*
      New York: Simon and Schuster, 1982.
      ISBN: 0-6714-4525-1   366 p.
      ** includes weight-reducing recipes

W5   Better Homes and Gardens. *Better Homes and Gardens
      Good food and fitness.* Des Moines, IA: Meredith Corp.,
      1981.
      ISBN: 0-6960-0635-9   95 p.   illustrated
      ** presents recipes for weight reduction

W6   Brody, Jane E. *Jane Brody's Good food gourmet:
      recipes and menus for delicious and healthful
      entertaining.* New York: W.W. Norton, 1990.
      ISBN: 0-3930-2878-X

W7   Crenshaw, Mary Ann. *The Super foods diet.* New York:
      Macmillan, 1983.
      ISBN: 0-0252-8820-2   241 p.
      ** a weight-reduction diet book

W8   Eades, Michael R. *Thin so fast*. New York: Warner
Books, 1989.
ISBN: 0-4465-1497-7   336 p.

W9   Gates, Ronda. *Nutrition nuggets recipes*. Lake Oswego,
OR: Lifestyles Four-Heart Press, 1990.   96 p.
** cooking for weight reduction

W10   George, Phyllis and Adler, Bill. *The I love America diet*.
New York: W. Morrow, 1983.
ISBN: 0-6880-1621-9   248 p. illustrated
** includes weight-reducing recipes based on the federal
dietary guidelines for Americans and official U.S.
weight-control recommendations

W11   Goldberg, Larry. *Controlled cheating: the Fats Goldberg
take it off, keep it off diet program*. Garden City, NY:
Doubleday, 1981.
ISBN: 0-3851-7379-2   289 p.
** weight-reduction cooking

W12   Hackett, Arlyn. *The Slim chef: a cookbook for the
healthy gourmet*. Secaucus, NJ: Lyle Stuart, 1987.
ISBN: 0-8184-0449-3   190 p. illustrated, some
color

W13   Lemieux, Joanne. *Diet signs*. Washington, DC:
Acropolis Books, 1982.
ISBN: 0-8749-1495-7   253 p. illustrated
** details relationship between astrological signs and diet
and includes recipes and exercises for weight loss

W14   Leonard, Jon N. *The Live longer now quick weight-loss program.* New York: Grosset and Dunlap, 1980.
ISBN: 0-4481-4337-2   243 p. illustrated

W15   Levene, Peter. *Healthy slimming.* Poole, Dorset: Javelin Books, distributed by Sterling, 1985.
ISBN: 0-7137-1572-3   128 p. illustrated

W16   Liederman, David and Schwartz, Joan. *David's Delicious weight-loss program: conquering compulsive eating and lowering cholesterol.* New York: St. Martin's Press, 1990.
ISBN: 0-3120-4293-0   270 p.

W17   McNaught, Chris. *The Beef lover's guide to weight control and lower cholesterol.* The Woodlands, TX: Portfolio Pub., 1989.
ISBN: 0-9432-5527-9   236 p. illustrated, some color

W18   Moses, Antoinette. *The Inglewood way to health.* New York: David and Charles, distributed by Sterling Pub. Co., 1990.
ISBN: 0-7153-9388-X   128 p.
** weight-loss cuisine

W19   Nidetch, Jean. *Weight Watchers Food plan diet cookbook: nearly 600 savory recipes: the complete up-to-date food plan used by the world's most successful weight-control organization.* New York: New American Library, 1982.

ISBN: 0-4530-1007-5   440 p. illustrated
** features all four food groups; includes full-choice plan menu, limited-choice plan menu, and no-choice plan menu; each recipe indicates the type of plans, calories, exchanges, and nutritive values (protein, fat, carbohydrate, and sodium)

W20   Nidetch, Jean. *Weight Watchers Quick Success Program cookbook.* New York: New American Library, 1989.
ISBN: 0-4530-1016-4   440 p. illustrated, some color
** recipes based on six exchanges for fruits, vegetables, fat, protein, bread, and milk; also includes eight-week menu planner including reduced-sodium menu and vegetarian menu; each recipe provides calories, exchanges, and nutritive values (protein, fat, cholesterol, fiber, carbohydrate, calcium, and sodium)

W21   Nidetch, Jean. *Weight Watchers Quick Start Plus Program cookbook: including personal choice food selections.* New York: New American Library, 1986.
ISBN: 0-4522-5831-6   486 p. illustrated, some color

W22   Rechtschaffen, Joseph S. and Carola, Robert. *Dr. Rechtschaffen's Diet for lifetime weight control and better health.* New York: Ballantine Books, 1982.
ISBN: 0-3453-0252-4   163 p.

W23   Robertson, Donald S. and Robertson, Carol P. *The Snowbird diet: 12 days to a slender lifetime.* New York:

Warner Books, 1986.
ISBN: 0-4463-8283-3   290 p. illustrated
** highlights weight-reducing recipes, exercises, and
psychological aspects of weight loss

W24   Schiffman, Susan S. and Scobey, Joan. *The Nutri/System
Flavor Set-Point weight loss cookbook.* Boston: Little,
Brown, 1990.
ISBN: 0-3167-7311-5   340 p.

W25   Simmons, Richard. *Richard Simmons' Better body book.*
New York: Warner Books, 1983.
ISBN: 0-4465-1263-X   354 p. illustrated
** recipes and exercises for weight loss

W26   Simmons, Richard. *Richard Simmons' Never-say-diet
cookbook: over 100 new dishes you can enjoy and still
stay slim.* New York: Warner, 1982.
ISBN: 0-4463-7078-9   216 p. illustrated
**   recipes based on author's Live-it dietary principles;
also includes exercise routines

W27   Simonson, Maria and Heilman, Joan Rattner. *The
Complete university medical diet.* New York: Rawson
Associates, 1983.
ISBN: 0-8925-6225-0   242 p. illustrated
** includes weight-reducing recipes, discussions of
psychological aspects of obesity and weight loss, and
group therapy for weight reduction; Maria Simonson is
associated with the Health, Weight, and Stress Program at
Johns Hopkins

W28   Tiffany, Carol. *Everywoman's diet handbook*. Garden City, NY: Doubleday, 1980. 138 p.
** provides weight-reducing recipes and food-composition tables

W29   Weale, Margaret. *The Slimmer's microwave cookbook*. North Pomfret, VT: David and Charles, 1983.
ISBN: 0-7153-8392-2   120 p. illustrated, some color

W30   Weight Watchers International. *Meals in minutes cookbook: over 300 quick new recipes based on the Fast and Flexible Program*. New York: New American Library, 1990.
ISBN: 0-4530-1020-2   406 p. illustrated, color
** features microwave and low-budget recipes; also has eight-week menu with two-week vegetarian, two-week sodium-reduced, and two-week cholesterol-reduced planners

FOR CHILDREN AND TEENAGERS

W31   Dachman, Ken. *The Dachman Diet for kids: a complete guide to healthy weight loss*. New York, NY: World Almanac Publications, distributed in USA by Ballantine Books, 1986.
ISBN: 0-3453-3313-6   223 p.
** recipes are low in calorie content

W32   Eden, Alvin N. and Boyar, Andrea P. *Dr. Eden's Healthy kids: the essential diet, exercise, and nutrition program.* New York: New American Library, 1987.
ISBN: 0-4522-5948-7   285 p.
** designed for children and includes high-fiber, low-fat, and low-salt recipes as well as exercise routines

W33   Lansky, Vicki. *Fat-proofing your children -- so that they never become diet-addicted adults.* New York: Bantam, 1988.
ISBN: 0-5530-5134-2   256 p. illustrated
** on the prevention of obesity in children

W34   Matthews, Dee; Zullo, Allan; and Nash, Bruce. *The You can do it! kids diet.* New York: Holt, Rinehart and Winston, 1985.
ISBN: 0-0306-9653-4   256 p. illustrated
** a weight-reduction cookbook compiled for the prevention of childhood obesity

W35   McKinnon, Manon. *Creative calorie-counting for kids: a guide for Mom and Dad.* Boston: Quinlan Press, 1987.
90 p. illustrated
** low-calorie weight-loss recipes designed for infants and children; includes *A kid's guide,* a separate 10-p. section

W36   Paul, Aileen. *The Kid's diet cookbook.* Garden City, NY: Doubleday, 1980.
ISBN: 0-3851-3659-5   179 p. illustrated
** low-calorie recipes for dieting youngsters to make by

themselves, with suggestions for a weight-reduction program using record keeping and rewards; also extensive calorie charts

W37   Perkins, Eric. *Staying thin for kids: the family guide to health and fitness.* New York: Nautilus Books, 1988. ISBN: 0-9350-5539-8   189 p.
** includes weight-loss recipes and physical fitness for children

W38   Woolfolk, Dorothy A. *The Teenage surefire diet cookbook.* New York: Watts, 1979.
ISBN: 0-5310-2268-4   118 p. illustrated
** presents a weight-loss program developed especially for teenagers; has a basic meal plan emphasizing nutrition and taste; more than 90 recipes

FOR MIDDLE-AGED PERSONS

W39   Miller, Peter M. *The Hilton Head Over-35 diet: change your metabolism: look and feel years younger.* New York: Warner Books, 1989.
ISBN: 0-4465-1430-6   212 p. illustrated
** contains weight-reducing diet and exercise routines prepared for the middle-aged by the Hilton Head Health Institute

W40   Spodnik, Jean Perry and Gibbons, Barbara. *The 35-plus diet for women: the breakthrough metabolism diet developed at Kaiser Permanente for women over 35.*

New York: Harper and Row, 1987.
ISBN: 0-0601-5718-6   231 p.
** a weight-loss diet prepared for middle-aged women by the Kaiser Permanente Medical Center, Cleveland, Ohio

HIGH-CARBOHYDRATE DIET

W41   Cohen-Rose, Sandra and Rose, Colin Penfield. *The New Canadian high energy diet: the high carbohydrate, high nutrient way to stay slim, healthy, and energetic: the diet proven successfull in thousands of private consultations.* Montreal, PQ: Corona Publishers, 1981.
ISBN: 0-9196-3100-2   372 p. illustrated
** includes weight-reducing recipes that are high in carbohydrates

W42   Gross, Joy. *The 30-day way to the born-again body: a total regimen plus the new natural carbohydrate diet that can make you stay thinner, look younger, live longer.* New York: Berkley Pub. Group, 1981.
ISBN: 0-4250-4733-4   287 p.

HIGH-CARBOHYDRATE
LOW-CALORIE DIET

W43   Wurtman, Judith J. and Leibenstein, Margaret. *The Carbohydrate craver's diet cookbook.*   Boston: Houghton Mifflin, 1984.
ISBN: 0-3953-5424-2   308 p.

** contains high-carbohydrate and low-calorie recipes

HIGH-CARBOHYDRATE
LOW-FAT DIET

W44   Connor, Sonja L. and Connor, William E. *The New American diet system.* New York: Simon and Schuster, 1991.
ISBN: 0-6716-8705-0   574 p. illustrated
** features low-fat and high-carbohydrate recipes

HIGH-CARBOHYDRATE
LOW-FAT LOW-SALT DIET

W45   Brody, Jane E. *Jane Brody's Good food book: living the high-carbohydrate way: with over 350 recipes.* New York: Bantam Books, 1987.
ISBN: 0-5533-4346-7   700 p. illustrated
** recipes are high-carbohydrate, low-fat, low-sugar, low-salt, low-protein, and low-calorie

W46   Time-Life Books; editors of. *Eating right: recipes for health.* Alexandria, VA: Time-Life Books, 1987.
ISBN: 0-8094-6163-3   144 p. illustrated, color
** provides high-carbohydrate, low-fat, low-salt recipes; part of the *Fitness, health and nutrition* series; calories, carbohydrate, protein, fat, calcium, sodium, and iron content is indicated for each recipe plus the percentages of carbohydrate, protein, and fat

HIGH-COMPLEX-
CARBOHYDRATE DIET

W47   Better Homes and Gardens. *Better Homes and Gardens Dieter's cook book.* Des Moines, IA: Meredith Corp., 1982.
ISBN: 0-6960-0745-2   384 p. illustrated, some color
** includes complex-carbohydrate diet recipes for weight loss

W48   Celli, Elisa. *The Pasta diet: lose 10 pounds in 14 days then stay slim forever!* New York: Warner Books, 1984.
ISBN: 0-4465-1300-8   256 p.
** a weight-reducing diet plan high in complex carbohydrates; recipes include caloric content; also includes exercise routines, 10-pound 14-day menu plan, and 10-pound 30-day maintenance plan

W49   Pritikin, Nathan. *The Pritikin Permanent weight-loss manual.* Toronto, ON: Bantam Books, 1982.
ISBN: 0-5532-0494-7   396 p. illustrated
** a weight-loss diet plan including recipes that are high in complex carbohydrates and low in calories

HIGH-COMPLEX-CARBOHYDRATE
LOW-CALORIE LOW-SALT DIET

W50   Roth, June. *The Pasta-lover's diet book.* New York:

Macmillan, 1986.
ISBN: 0-0201-0240-2
** features high-complex-carbohydrate, low-calorie and low-salt pasta recipes

HIGH-COMPLEX-CARBOHYDRATE
LOW-FAT DIET

W51   Ross, Shirley. *The Complex carbohydrate handbook.*
New York: Morrow, 1981.
ISBN: 0-6880-0593-4   241 p.
** includes low-fat and complex-carbohydrate recipes

HIGH-COMPLEX-CARBOHYDRATE
LOW-SALT VEGETARIAN DIET

W52   McDougall, Mary A. *The McDougall Health-supporting cookbook.* Piscataway, NJ: New Century Publishers, 1985-1986.
ISBN: 0-8329-0393-0   2 vols.
** a vegetarian approach stressing complex carbohydrates and low salt

HIGH-COMPLEX-CARBOHYDRATE
VEGETARIAN DIET

W53   McDougall, John A. *The McDougall program: Twelve days to dynamic health.* New York: New American

Library Books, 1990.
ISBN: 0-4530-0659-0   436 p.   illustrated
** vegetarian cooking with complex-carbohydrate
recipes

W54   McDougall, John A. and McDougall, Mary A. *The McDougall Plan for super health and life-long weight loss.* Piscataway, NJ: New Century Publishers, 1983.
ISBN: 0-8329-0289-6   340 p. illustrated
** includes weight-reducing vegetarian recipes that are high in complex carbohydrates

HIGH-FIBER DIET

W55   Brassel, Helen. *The Natural foods recipe book: 800 low-calorie dishes to help you lose weight.* New York: Arco, 1984.
ISBN: 0-6680-5631-2   305 p.
** high-fiber and low-calorie recipes from appetizers, salads, and desserts to soups and main entries; special section on meatless protein and tofu recipes; recipes include caloric content

W56   Brumback, Roger A. and Brumback, Mary H. *The Dietary fiber weight-control handbook: the high-fiber path to eating right, being healthy, and never being hungry.* Chicago: Year Book Medical Publishers, 1989.
ISBN: 0-8151-0749-8   176 p.

W57   Deprey, Irene. *The New Canadian fiber diet.* New York:

Vantage Press, 1987.
ISBN: 0-5330-6880-0   123 p. illustrated
** high-fiber recipes for weight reduction

W58   Homola, Samuel. *Dr. Homola's Macro-nutrient diet for quick permanent weight loss*. West Nyack, NY: Parker Pub. Co., 1981.
ISBN: 0-1321-6952-5   240 p.
** a weight-reducing diet with high-fiber recipes using natural ingredients

HIGH-FIBER
LOW-CALORIE DIET

W59   Baker, Yvonne G. *Guilt-free cooking: an introduction to naturally good cooking for those who love to eat and want to do it right*. Denver, CO: Accent Books, 1985.
ISBN: 0-8963-6179-9   174 p. illustrated
** recipes are high-fiber, high-protein, low-calorie, and low-cholesterol

W60   Chester, Helen. *The High fibre calorie-controlled cookbook*. London: Ward Lock, 1986.
ISBN: 0-7063-6477-5   96 p.   illustrated, color

W61   Eyton, Audrey. *Audrey Eyton's Even easier F-Plan*. London: Allen Lane, 1984.
ISBN: 0-7139-1714-8   288 p.
** includes high-fiber and low-calorie recipes

W62 Eyton, Audrey. *The F Plus diet.* Toronto, ON: Bantam Books, 1986.
ISBN: 0-5530-5099-0
** high-fiber and low-calorie weight-reducing recipes

HIGH-FIBER
LOW-FAT DIET

W63 Corlin, Judith and Miller, Mary Susan. *The Scarsdale nutritionist's weight loss cookbook.* New York: Simon and Schuster, 1982.
ISBN: 0-6714-5794-2   191 p.
** recipes are low-fat, low-salt, low-sugar, low-starch, high-fiber, and have high water content

W64 Ferguson, Sybil. *The Diet Center cookbook: from the five-phase program that has worked for over 4 million dieters - nutritious, low-cost, easy-to-prepare, seasonal menus and recipes to help you lose weight quickly and permanently.* New York: Simon and Schuster, 1986.
ISBN: 0-6716-0445-7   121 p. illustrated
** high-fiber, low-fat, and high-complex-carbohydrate recipes arranged by seasons providing calories, exchanges, and nutritive values (protein, carbohydrate, fat, cholesterol, fiber, and sodium)

W65 Katahn, Martin. *T-factor diet: lose weight safely and quickly without cutting calories - or even counting them.* New York: Bantam, 1989.
ISBN: 0-3930-2693-0   301 p. illustrated

** the "Thin-Factor" via a low-fat and high-fiber diet; includes exercise and psychological aspects of weight reduction, T-factor program for children and adolescents, plus food, fat, and fiber content tables

W66   Lowry, Eve and Ennis, Carla Mulligan. *Living lean and loving it.* St. Louis, MO: Mosby/Forman, 1988.
ISBN: 0-8016-3215-3   280 p. illustrated, some color
** low-fat and high-fiber recipes included

W67   Westland, Pamela. *High-fiber cookbook: recipes for good health.* New York: Arco Pub., 1982.
ISBN: 0-1338-7555-5   156 p. illustrated, color
** each high-fiber and low-fat recipe indicates caloric, fat, and fiber content

HIGH-FIBER LOW-FAT
LOW-CALORIE LOW-SUGAR DIET

W68   *Slim and fit cooking.* New York: Cornerstone Library, 1983.
ISBN: 0-3461-2590-1   192 p.
** contains recipes that are high-fiber, low-calorie, low-sugar, and low-fat

HIGH-PROTEIN
LOW-CALORIE DIET

W69 Hayden, Naura. *The Hip, high-prote, low-cal, easy-does-it cookbook.* New York: Bibli O'Phile, distributed by Dutton, 1984.
ISBN: 0-9421-0405-6   254 p. illustrated
** presents high-protein and low-calorie recipes with protein and caloric contents

HIGH-PROTEIN
LOW-CARBOHYDRATE DIET

W70 Ezrin, Calvin and Kowalski, Robert E. *The Endocrine control diet: how to beat the metabolic trap and lose weight permanently.* New York: Harper and Row, 1990.
ISBN: 0-0601-5919-7   256 p. illustrated
** includes insulin metabolism and other endocrine aspects of obesity

LOW-CALORIE DIET

W71 American Dietetic Association. *Getting down to basics: a dieter's guide plus 42 great recipes.* Chicago, IL: American Dietetic Association in cooperation with the U.S. Dept. of Agriculture, 1982.
48 p. illustrated, some color
** low-calorie recipes for weight reduction

W72 Better Homes and Gardens. *Better Homes and Gardens Eat and stay slim.* 3rd ed. Des Moines, IA: Meredith Corp., 1990.

ISBN: 0-6960-1917-5   128 p. illustrated
** contains low-calorie recipes for weight loss

W73   Burke, Jeanette Silveira. *Beautiful food for your beautiful body.* rev. and expanded ed.   Reedley, CA: The Author, 1981.   271 p.
** features weight-reducing low-calorie recipes

W74   Carroll, Mary Harrison. *Elegant low-calorie cooking.* San Ramon, CA: Ortho Information Services, 1988.
ISBN: 0-8972-1154-5   128 p. illustrated, color
** California Culinary Academy Series; caloric content included for each recipe

W75   Coco, James and Paone, Marion. *The James Coco diet.* Toronto, ON: Bantam, 1984.
ISBN: 0-5532-4514-7   257 p.
** includes low-calorie recipes and caloric content tables for foods

W76   Cooking Light Magazine. *Cooking light breads, grains and pastas: 80 hearty and flavorful recipes for breads, biscuits, waffles, rice, macaroni--and much more.* New York: Warner Books, 1991.
ISBN: 0-4463-9182-4   84 p.   illustrated, color

W77   Darden, Ellington. *32 days to a 32 inch waist.* Dallas, TX: Taylor, 1990.
ISBN: 0-8783-3710-5   149 p. illustrated
** a low-calorie weight-reducing cookbook, plus exercises

W78   Deeming, Sue. *Eat light: the healthy, satisfying way to lose and keep off weight, complete with recipes and menus.* Tucson, AZ: HP Books, 1985.
ISBN: 0-8958-6351-0   176 p. illustrated, color
** contains low-calorie recipes

W79   Devine, Mary; editor. *Low-calorie cooking.* London: Marshall Cavendish Books Ltd., 1985.
ISBN: 0-8630-7379-4   60 p.   illustrated

W80   Fobel, Jim. *Jim Fobel's Diet feasts: an inspired new cuisine, healthy, hearty, delicious.* New York: Doubleday, 1990.
ISBN: 0-3852-6001-6   196 p. illustrated, color
** low-calorie recipes produced by Jane Ross Associates, Inc., and Bellwether Books

W81   Franey, Pierre and Flaste, Richard. *Pierre Franey's Low-calorie gourmet: the New York Times 60-minute gourmet's lighter approach to classic cuisine.* New York: Random House, 1989.
ISBN: 0-8129-1836-3   276p.

W82   Harvey, Lee and Chambers, Helen. *Family favorites on a diet.* Ottawa, ON: A.D. Harvey Nutrition Consultants, 1986.
ISBN: 0-9692-3690-5   162 p.
** includes low-calorie recipes for weight reduction

W83   Herskowitz, Joel. *The Popcorn plus diet.* New York: Pharos Books, distributed in USA by Ballantine Books,

1987.
ISBN: 0-3453-4400-6   160 p. illustrated
** a popcorn cookbook which contains weight-reducing, low-calorie recipes

W84   Hewitt, Donald W. *Diet without danger: a physician's guide to shedding unwanted weight with safety and sanity.* Mountain View, CA: Pacific Press Pub. Association, 1980.
** includes low-calorie recipes

W85   Jones, Jeanne. *Fitness first: a 14-day diet and exercise program.* San Francisco: 101 Productions, distributed by Scribner, 1980.
ISBN: 0-8928-6162-2   154 p. illustrated
** provides low-calorie recipes and exercises for weight loss

W86   Katahn, Martin and Katahn, Terri. *The Rotation diet cookbook.* New York: Norton, 1987.
445 p. illustrated
** recipes based on rotation diet: calorie intake level rotates; recipes use fruits, vegetables, whole grains, lean meat, fish, and poultry; each recipe provides nutritive values and caloric content

W87   Kronschnabel, Darlene. *Ideals low calorie cookbook.* Milwaukee, WI: Ideals Pub. Corp., 1981.
ISBN: 0-8249-3003-7   63 p.   illustrated, color

W88   Leveille, Gilbert A. *The Setpoint diet: the food and*

exercise connection for lasting weight control. New
York: Ballantine Book, 1985.
ISBN: 0-3453-2196-0   307 p.
** Setpoint Diet includes exercise and five eating plans
reflecting five different calorie intakes: 1200, 1500, 1800,
2100, and 2400; includes exercise tips and menus for
adults, adolescents, and older adults with varied calorie
intakes; each recipe indicates calories

W89   Lindauer, Lois Lyons. *The Diet Workshop wild weekend
      diet.* New York: Dell Pub. Co., 1985.
      ISBN: 0-4401-2034-9   301 p. illustrated
      ** presents weight-reducing low-calorie recipes

W90   Maplesden, Dr. *The Universal diet.* Winnipeg, MB: R.P.
      Frye, 1986.
      ISBN: 0-9197-4144-4   140 p.
      ** contains low-calorie recipes for weight loss

W91   Myerson, Bess and Adler, Bill. *The I love New York
      diet.* New York: Warner, 1983.
      251 p.
      ** weight-reducing cuisine containing low-calorie recipes

W92   Niedermayer, Flo. *300 and under: low-calorie entrees
      the whole family will enjoy.* Regina, SK: J.B. Pub., 1986.
      ISBN: 0-9198-4548-7   142 p. illustrated, color
      ** includes low-calorie recipes and exercises to reduce
      weight

W93   Perkins, Eric. *The Staying thin cookbook.* New York:

Nautilus Books, 1988.
ISBN: 0-9350-5538-X   197 p.
** features low-calorie recipes for weight loss

W94   Principal, Victoria. *The Diet Principal.* New York:
Simon and Schuster, 1987.
ISBN: 0-6715-3082-8   256 p. illustrated, some
color
** includes three complete easy-to-follow diet plans:
bikini diet (quick weight-loss plan), 30-day diet for loss
(more sustained weight-loss plan), and diet for life
(weight maintenance plan); recipes included for each diet
plan

W95   Pritikin, Nathan. *The Pritikin promise: 28 days to a
longer healthier life.* New York: Simon and Schuster,
1985.
ISBN: 0-6715-4634-1   516 p. illustrated
** contains low-calorie recipes

W96   Sachet, Paul; Morgan, Brian L. G.; and Morgan, Roberta.
*The Paris diet: the European revolution in weight
control.* New York: Villard Books,1990.
ISBN: 0-3945-8216-0   316 p.
** a weight-reducing low-calorie cookbook

W97   Schlemme, Carolyn. *Low-calorie meals.* Oakland, CA:
Third Party Pub., 1987.
ISBN: 0-8991-4023-8   96 p.   illustrated
** a part of *The great American cookbook series*;
includes a list of 700 food items in 100-calorie servings

W98　Stein, Laura. *The Bloomingdale's Eat healthy diet.* New York: St. Martin's Press, 1986.
ISBN: 0-3120-8516-8　　223 p. illustrated
** low-calorie recipes included

W99　Theriot, Jude W. *New American light cuisine.* Gretna, LA: Pelican Publishing Co., 1988.
ISBN: 0-8828-9690-3　　207 p. illustrated
** more than 150 recipes for gourmet and ethnic dishes each 300 calories or less per serving; every recipe indicates calories and nutritive contents (carbohydrate, fat, protein, cholesterol, and fiber)

W100　Torine, Len. *Light Cuisine.* Gaithersburg, MD: American Cooking Guild, 1988.
ISBN: 0-9423-2032-8　　64 p.
** a low-calorie cookbook for weight reduction

W101　Underwood, Greer. *Gourmet light: simple and sophisticated recipes for the calorie-conscious cook.* Chester, CT: Globe Pequot Press, 1985.
ISBN: 0-8710-6872-9　　326 p. illustrated
** includes low-calorie recipes from stocks and sauces to desserts; calories and nutritive values (protein, carbohydrate, fat, and sodium) detailed

W102　Weight Watchers International. *Weight Watchers New international cookbook: based on the 1986 Quick Start Plus Program.* New York: New American Library, 1985.
ISBN: 0-4530-0011-3　　384 p. illustrated, color
** recipes arranged by country of origin; each low-

calorie recipe indicates exchange, nutritive, and caloric values

W103 Woolf, Hilda. *Leanline cookery for every occasion.* London: Robson Books, 1983.
ISBN: 0-8605-1209-6   145 p. illustrated
** includes low-calorie recipes for weight reduction

W104 Wright, Jennifer M. *Count your calories cookbook.* rev. and expanded ed.   Christchurch, NZ: Whitcoulls Publishers, distributed by ISBS, Portland, OR, 1985.
ISBN: 0-7233-0742-3   135 p. illustrated, color

LOW-CALORIE
FAST AND SIMPLE CUISINE

W105 Better Homes and Gardens. *Better Homes and Gardens Fast-fixin' diet recipes.* Des Moines, IA: Meredith, 1988.
ISBN: 0-6960-1756-3   80 p. illustrated, color
** low-calorie quick and simple recipes with caloric content included

W106 Weight Watchers International. *Weight Watchers Quick and easy menu cookbook: over 250 seasonal recipes and menus based on the Quick Success Program.* New York: New American Library, 1987.
ISBN: 0-4530-1015-6   339 p. illustrated, some color
** low-calorie recipes arranged by 12 months; based on best-buy seasonal fruits and vegetables; also includes a

six-week menu and each recipe has exchange, nutritive, and caloric values

LOW-CALORIE ORIENTAL CUISINE

W107 Dyer, Ceil. *Slim wok cookery.* Tucson, AZ: HP Books, 1986.
ISBN: 0-8958-6412-6   160 p. illustrated, color
** Chinese wok recipes that are low-calorie for weight reduction

W108 Leong, James. *The Low calorie Chinese gourmet cookbook.* New York: Pinnacle, 1982.
ISBN: 0-5234-1850-7   136 p. illustrated

LOW-CALORIE SPA CUISINE

W109 Cluff, Sheila and Brown, Eleanor. *The Ultimate recipe for fitness: spa cuisine from The Oaks at Ojai and The Palms at Palm Springs.* Ojai, CA: Fitness Publications, 1990.
ISBN: 0-9618-8053-8   190 p. illustrated
** recipes are high-carbohydrate, low-fat, no-salt, low-cholesterol, and low-sugar; apple juice concentrate as sweetener; 28-day dinner menu and fitness tips; each recipe provides carbohydrate, protein, fat, and sodium content

W110 Kulick, Florence and Matthews, Florence. *The Hamptons health spa diet cookbook.* Sag Harbor, NY: Permanent Press, 1983.
ISBN: 0-9329-6628-4   216 p. illustrated
** contains low-calorie recipes based on cuisine developed by the authors for the International Health and Beauty Spa at Gurney's Inn, Montauk, New York

W111 Safdie, Edward J. *New spa food: hearty, healthy recipes from the Norwich Inn and Spa.* New York: C.N. Potter, 1990.
ISBN: 0-5175-7534-5   154 p. illustrated, color
** a low-calorie recipe book

LOW-CALORIE
MICROWAVE CUISINE

W112 Cone, Marcia and Snyder, Thelma. *Microwave diet cookery: low calorie menus for all seasons.* New York: Simon and Schuster, 1988.
ISBN: 0-6716-2388-5   319 p. illustrated, color
** low-calorie recipes arranged by four seasons with caloric content listings

W113 Crocker, Betty. *Best recipes for low-calorie microwaving.* New York: Prentice Hall, 1990.
ISBN: 0-1306-8123-7   112 p. illustrated, color
** part of the Betty Crocker red spoon collection; caloric content provided for each recipe

W114 Dwyer, Karen Kangas. *Easy livin' low-calorie microwave cooking.* New York: St. Martin's Press, 1990.
ISBN: 0-3120-3821-6   355 p. illustrated

W115 Microwave Times; editors of. *Microwave lite one-dish meals: under 350 calories.* Chicago: Contemporary, 1987.
ISBN: 0-8902-4531-0   166 p.
** quick and easy recipes with a section for special occasions; calories listed for each recipe

LOW-CALORIE
LOW-SALT DIET

W116 Gibbons, Barbara. *Light and spicy: over 350 low-calorie, full-flavor recipes.* New York: Harper and Row, 1989.
ISBN: 0-0609-6361-1   160 p. illustrated, some color
** low-calorie and low-salt recipes providing caloric content

W117 Weight Watchers International. *Weight Watchers Healthy life-style cookbook: over 250 recipes based on the personal choice program.* New York: Dutton, 1991.
ISBN: 0-4530-1023-7   358 p. illustrated, some color
** includes recipes that are low-salt, low-cholesterol, and low-calorie

LOW-CALORIE LOW-SALT
LOW-SUGAR DIET

W118 Beck, Judy and Matthews, William Andrew. *Judy Beck's Gourmet cookbook for a slimmer you.* New York: Simon and Schuster, 1983.
ISBN: 0-6714-7462-6   206 p.
** contains low-calorie, low-salt, and sugar-free recipes

LOW-CARBOHYDRATE DIET

W119 Atkins, Robert C. *Dr. Atkins' Health revolution: how complementary medicine can extend your life.* New York: Bantam Books, 1990.
ISBN: 0-5532-8360-X   437 p.
** a low-carbohydrate diet book including case studies on diet therapy

W120 Heller, Rachael F. and Heller, Richard F. *The Carbohydrate addict's diet: the lifelong solution to yo-yo dieting.* New York: Dutton, 1991.
ISBN: 0-5252-4953-2   283 p.

W121 Kaufman, William I. *The New low carbohydrate diet.* New York: Berkley Publishing Group, 1981.
ISBN: 0-5150-8264-3   64 p.

LOW-CARBOHYDRATE
LOW-CALORIE DIET

W122 Patten, Marguerite. *Diet cookbook*. New York: Exeter
Books, distributed by Bookthrift, 1983.
ISBN: 0-6710-5965-3   224 p. illustrated, color
** low-carbohydrate and low-calorie recipes for crash
and short-term diets, low-cholesterol diets, and diets for
children and the elderly; each recipe includes caloric and
carbohydrate content

LOW-CARBOHYDRATE
LOW-CALORIE LOW-FAT DIET

W123 Hinman, Bobbie and Snyder, Millie. *More lean and
luscious*. Rocklin, CA: Prima Pub. and Communications,
distributed by St. Martin's Press, 1988.
ISBN: 0-9146-2942-9   461 p. illustrated
** provides low-calorie, low-fat, and low-carbohydrate
recipes; each recipe includes caloric values, exchanges,
and nutritive values (protein, carbohydrate, sodium, and
cholesterol)

LOW-CARBOHYDRATE
LOW-CALORIE LOW-SALT DIET

W124 Pinion Press; editors of. *The Weight wokker: a cookbook*.
Calgary, AB: Pinion Press, 1983.
ISBN: 0-9201-2500-X
** low-calorie, low-carbohydrate, and low-salt recipes
cooked with a wok oriental style

LOW-FAT DIET

W125 Bailey, Covert and Bishop, Lea. *Target recipes.* Boston: Houghton Mifflin, 1985.
ISBN: 0-3953-7699-8   168 p.
** includes low-fat recipes for weight reduction

W126 Bounds, Sarah. *Fat-free cooking.* New York: Thorsons, 1985.
ISBN: 0-7225-1173-6   128 p.

W127 Burt, Lizzie and Mercer, Nelda. *High fit -- low fat.* Nashville, TN: Favorite Recipes Press, 1989.
ISBN: 0-8719-7260-3   160 p. illustrated, some color

W128 Carper, Jean and Eyton, Audrey. *The Revolutionary 7-unit low fat diet: the diet that lets you enjoy pasta, bread, potatoes, and even a drink, while losing up to 7 pounds in 7 days.* New York: Rawson, Wade, 1981.
ISBN: 0-8925-6156-4   216 p. illustrated

W129 Cockburn-Smith, Beth. *Low-fat cookbook.* London: Hamlyn, 1984.
ISBN: 0-6003-2406-0   128 p. illustrated, some color

W130 Conley, Rosemary and Bourne, Patricia. *Rosemary Conley's Hip and thigh diet cookbook.* London: Arrow, 1990.
ISBN: 0-0996-6250-7   238 p. illustrated

** recipes are low in fat content

W131 Ewing, Scott. *Scott Ewing's Low-fat luxury cookbook.*
New York: Thorsons, 1988.
ISBN: 0-7225-1650-9   176 p.

W132 Gaunt, LaRene. *Recipes to lower your fat thermostat.*
Provo, UT: Vitality House International, 1984.
ISBN: 0-9125-4702-2   398 p. illustrated, some
color

W133 Guenther, Joan P. *Simply elegant: low fat choices.*
Palatine, IL: J. P. Guenther, 1991.
300 p.
**   recipes with an international flair

W134 Herman, Barry and Lawren, Bill. *The Long life gourmet
cookbook: the revolutionary gourmet cookbook, based on
America's safest and most effective diets, that enables
you to eat hearty portions of truly delicious foods without
fear of gaining weight while adding high-quality, vital
and productive years to your life.* New York: Simon and
Schuster, 1984.
ISBN: 0-6714-7000-0   352 p.
** contains recipes that are low in fat content

W135 Hinman, Bobbie and Snyder, Millie. *Lean and luscious:
over 400 easy-to-prepare, delicious recipes for today's
low-fat lifestyle.* Rocklin, CA: Prima Publishing and
Communications, distributed by St. Martin's Press, 1987.
ISBN: 0-9146-2920-4   450 p. illustrated

W136 Jacob, Yvonne. *Creative cooking the lowfat way: a lifetime approach to healthy eating.* Phoenix, AZ: Yvonne Jacob, 1989.
ISBN: 0-9622-9710-0   284 p. illustrated
** a weight-reduction cookbook

W137 Kreitzman, Sue. *Complete slim cuisine.* New York: Bantam, 1990.
ISBN: 0-5930-1874-5   353 p.
** contains low-fat recipes

W138 Lampen, Nevada. *More fat-free recipes.* London: Faber and Faber, 1984.
ISBN: 0-5711-3178-6   102 p.

W139 Methven, Barbara. *Low-fat microwave meals.* Minnetonka, MN: Cy DeCosse, 1989.
ISBN: 0-8657-3567-0   159 p. illustrated, color
** includes step-by-step pictorial instructions for most recipes; exchanges and nutritive values included for each recipe

W140 Moquette-Magee, Elaine. *Fight fat and win: how to eat a low-fat diet without changing your lifestyle.* Minneapolis, MN: DCI Pub., 1990.
ISBN: 0-9377-2165-4   244 p.

W141 Noh, Chin-Hwa. *Low-fat Korean cooking: fish, shellfish and vegetable.* Elizabeth, NJ: Hollym International Corp., 1985.
ISBN: 0-9308-7847-7   76 p. illustrated, color

** low-fat recipes with step-by step color picture instructions for boiled, steamed, stir-fried, broiled, deep-fried, pan-fried dishes, and vegetables and salads

W142 Parker, Valerie. *A Lowfat lifeline for the '90s: how to survive in a fat-filled world: delicious new recipes and all you need to know to help you shop, cook, and eat when you're not on a diet.* Lake Oswego, OR: Lowfat Publications, 1990.
ISBN: 0-9626-3980-X   278 p. illustrated
** calories and fat content included with each recipe

W143 Pritikin, Robert. *The New Pritikin program: the easy and delicious way to shed fat, lower your cholesterol, and stay fit.* New York: Simon and Schuster, 1990.
ISBN: 0-6716-6163-9   368 p.
** a low-fat diet book

W144 Remington, Dennis W.; Fisher, A. Garth; and Parent, Edward A. *How to lower your fat thermostat: the no-diet reprogramming plan for lifelong weight control.* Provo, UT: Vitality House International, 1983.
ISBN: 0-9125-4701-4   236 p. illustrated

W145 Rubey, Jane. *Lowfat international cuisine.* San Leandro, CA: Bristol Pub. Enterprises, 1989.
ISBN: 0-9119-5492-9   172 p. illustrated, some color

W146 Saynor, Reg and Ryan, Frank. *The Eskimo diet cookbook.* Ebury, distributed by Random Century, North

Pomfret, VT, 1990.
ISBN: 0-8522-3937-8   192 p.
** includes low-fat recipes

W147   Smith, Margaret Jane. *All-American low-fat meals in minutes: recipes and menus for special occasions or everyday.* Minnetonka, MN: DCI Pub., 1990.
ISBN: 0-9377-2173-5

W148   Spear, Ruth A. *Low fat and loving it: how to lower your fat intake and still eat the foods you love: 200 delicious recipes.* New York: Warner Books, 1991.
ISBN: 0-4465-1535-3   318 p.
** weight-reducing recipes also aimed at cancer prevention and coronary heart disease prevention

W149   Wang, Lydia. *The New Chinese cooking for health and fitness.* Tokyo, Japan: Gakken Co., distributed in USA through Harper and Row, 1986.
ISBN: 0-8704-0730-9   120 p. illustrated, some color
** contains low-fat Chinese recipes

W150   Westland, Pamela. *Low-fat cookery.* London: Grafton, 1986.
ISBN: 0-5860-6697-7   248 p.

LOW-FAT
LOW-CALORIE DIET

W151 Bluestein, Barry and Morrissey, Kevin. *Light sauces: delicious low-calorie, low-fat, low-cholesterol recipes.* Chicago: Contemporary Books, 1991.
ISBN: 0-8092-4063-7

W152 Claessens, Sharon and the Rodale Food Center. *The Lose weight naturally cookbook.* Emmaus, PA: Rodale Press, 1985.
ISBN: 0-8785-7539-1   391 p. illustrated, color

W153 Cooking Light Magazine. *Cooking light microwave: 80 nutritious and tempting recipes for soups, salads, main courses, desserts, and beverages.* New York, NY: Warner Books, 1991.
ISBN: 0-4463-9181-6   78 p.   illustrated, color
** low-calorie and low-fat recipes included

W154 Grad, Laurie Burrows. *Make it easy, make it light: more than 200 quick recipes for tasty, healthful dishes.* New York: Simon and Schuster, 1987.
ISBN: 0-6716-2538-1   364 p.
** contains low-calorie and low-fat recipes from appetizers to desserts; calories, cooking notes, accompaniments for dishes, and suggestions for variations

W155 Hughes, Nancy S. *The Four-course, 400-calorie meal cookbook: quick and easy recipes for delicious low-calorie, low-fat dinners.* Chicago: Contemporary Books, 1991.
ISBN: 0-8092-4058-0   182 p.

W156 Kreitzman, Sue and the editors of Consumer Reports Books. *Slim cuisine: innovative techniques for healthful cooking.* Mount Vernon, NY: Consumer Reports Books, 1991.
ISBN: 0-8904-3187-6
** includes weight-reducing recipes that are low in fat and calories

W157 Shulman, Martha Rose. *Mediterranean light: delicious recipes from the world's healthiest cuisine.* New York: Bantam Books, 1989.
ISBN: 0-5530-5352-3   424 p. illustrated
** a low-calorie and low-fat Mediterranean cookbook arranged by types of foods; each recipe includes caloric content and nutritive values of fat, protein, carbohydrate, cholesterol, and sodium

LOW-FAT LOW-CALORIE
LOW-SALT DIET

W158 Crocker, Betty. *Betty Crocker's Eat and lose weight: the complete five-point program for weight control and health.* New York: Prentice Hall, 1990.
ISBN: 0-1307-4303-8   271 p. illustrated, color
** low-calorie low-fat low-sodium recipes with microwave adaptations included; the five points are eat smart, exercise, set goals, keep good records, and design your lifestyle

W159 Grace, Louise P. *The 30-minute light gourmet.* Dallas,

TX: Taylor Pub. Co., 1990.
ISBN: 0-8783-3617-6
** low-fat, low-salt, and low-calorie cuisine

W160 Jones, Jeanne. *Cook it light: healthy light cuisine to please your palate and keep you fit.* New York: Macmillan, 1987.
ISBN: 0-0202-1781-1   297 p. illustrated, some color
** weight-reducing low-cholesterol, low-fat, low-calorie, and low-salt recipes

W161 Kidushim-Allen, Deborah. *Light desserts: the low calorie, low salt, low fat way.* New York: Harper and Row, 1981.
ISBN: 0-0625-0486-X   182 p. illustrated

W162 Renggli, Seppi and Grodnick, Susan. *The Four Seasons Spa cuisine.* New York: Simon and Schuster, 1986.
ISBN: 0-6715-4440-3   348 p. illustrated
** low-salt, low-fat, low-calorie, and low-cholesterol recipes with Japanese and Indonesian spices or condiments

LOW-FAT LOW-CALORIE
LOW-SALT LOW-SUGAR DIET

W163 Consumer Guide. *Low calorie, low sodium, low cholesterol, low sugar, low fat cookbook: stay slender and healthy with these easy-to-make great tasting recipes.*

Skokie, IL: Consumer Guide, 1985.
192 p.   illustrated

W164 Cooking Light Magazine. *Cooking light cookbook 1991.*
Birmingham, AL: Oxmoor House, 1990.
ISBN: 0-8487-1029-0   272 p. illustrated
** includes exercise routines for fitness

W165 Crocker, Betty. *Betty Crocker's Light and easy cooking:
recipes for today's interest in wholesome cooking and
moderate use of salt, sugar and fat.* New York: Prentice
Hall, 1983.
ISBN: 0-1308-3288-X   256 p. illustrated, color

W166 Darling, Renny. *Renny Darling's Cooking great! looking
great! feeling great!: the moderation diet: the only
sensible way to stay slim and healthy: 350 deliciously
light recipes: low-calorie, low-cholesterol, low-fat, low-
sugar, low-sodium.* Beverly Hills, CA: Royal House
Publishing Co., 1990.
ISBN: 0-9304-4030-7   253 p. illustrated
** recipes provide caloric content

W167 Health Travel International. *Spa dining: luscious low-
calorie recipes from America's great spas.* New York:
St. Martin's Press, 1985.
ISBN: 0-3127-4927-9   243 p.
** international low-red meat, low-cholesterol, low-
calorie, low-fat, low-sugar, and low-salt preparations;
arranged by 16 spas (addresses included); each recipe
provides caloric values

W168 Patton, Tim and Manno, Karen. *Spa recipes from the Spa at Palm-Aire.* Wilmington, DE: Middle Atlantic Press, distributed by Lanham Book Network, 1989.
ISBN: 0-9126-0872-2   166 p.
** a weight-loss diet providing low-calorie, low-fat, sugar-free, and low-salt recipes

W169 Prince, Francine. *Francine Prince's Vitamin diet for quick and easy weight loss.* New York: Simon and Schuster, 1982.
ISBN: 0-3461-2521-9   206 p.
** vitamins A, C, D, E, and B-50 complex are targeted for this diet; recipes are low-calorie, low-fat, low-cholesterol, high-fiber, no-salt, and no-sugar; also provides a one-week crash diet menu

LOW-FAT LOW-CALORIE LOW-SUGAR DIET

W170 Gallagher, Kathy. *The I'm sick of carrot sticks cookbook: enjoy the food you eat while losing weight: over 50 complete gourmet menus, each containing fewer than 600 calories.* New York: Macmillan, 1984.
ISBN: 0-0254-2070-4   194 p.
** low-calorie, low-fat, and low-sugar recipes included; also provides 51 complete dinner menus with less than 600 calories each

W171 Gibbons, Barbara. *The Light and easy cookbook.* New York: Macmillan, 1980.

ISBN: 0-0254-3120-X   260 p.
** low-fat, low-calorie, low-sugar recipes

LOW-FAT LOW-SALT DIET

W172 Arsaga, Cindy and Masullo, Ginny. *Eating healthy in the fast lane.* 2nd ed. Fayetteville, AR: Yarrow House, 1990.
ISBN: 0-9625-1881-6   82 p. illustrated
** quick and easy recipes, low-fat and low-salt

W173 McMahan, Jacqueline Higuera. *The Healthy fiesta.* Lake Hughes, CA: Olive Press, 1990.
ISBN: 0-9612-1509-7   187 p. illustrated
** includes recipes of Mexican dishes that are low in fat and salt

LOW-FAT LOW-SALT
LOW-SUGAR DIET

W174 Jencks, Tina. *In good taste: a creative collection of delicious easy to prepare, low-fat recipes, free of sugar and salt.* Berkeley, CA: Lancaster-Miller, 1980.
ISBN: 0-8958-1020-4   142 p. illustrated

W175 McCormick, Kathy. *Lean and healthy: a food lover's guide.* Olympia, WA: Capitol Neighborhood Press, 1984. 90 p. illustrated
** includes low-fat, low-salt, and sugar-free recipes

W176 Miller, Jeannette L. and Van Waardhuizen, Carol. *The Healthy holiday cookbook.* 2nd ed. West Des Moines, IA: American Heart Association, Iowa Affiliate, 1988. 127 p. illustrated
** features low-salt, low-fat, and sugar-free recipes

W177 Paine, Harriett and Dillard, Maureen. *Cook for the health of it!: it's easy to cook with less fat, sugar and salt.* Downey, CA: CHEC Publications, 1983. 132 p.

LOW-FAT LOW-SUGAR DIET

W178 Applebee, Jackie. *Low-fat and no-fat cooking: wholesome recipes for those who have to cut down on fat.* 2nd ed. New York: Thorsons, 1989. ISBN: 0-7225-2207-X 96 p.

W179 Cirillo, Lee Mangione. *Lite sweet delites: delicious treats without guilt.* Rochester, NY: Specialty Cookbooks Publishers, 1989. ISBN: 0-9623-2250-4 226 p. illustrated
** recipes are low-fat and sweetened with fructose sugar substitutes

W180 Goddard, Liza and Baldwin, Ann. *Not naughty but nice.* Ward Lock, distributed by Sterling Pub. Co., New York, 1987. ISBN: 0-7063-6586-0 128 p.
** includes low-fat and sugar-free recipes

W181 Rohrer, Virginia. *Total health cookbook: low-fat, low-sugar recipes to help you cook right and feel great.* Wheaton, IL: Tyndale House Publishers, 1980.
ISBN: 0-8423-7288-1   156 p. illustrated

W182 Takahashi, Yoko I. and Cassiday, Bruce. *The Tokyo diet: lose weight the Japanese way.* New York: William Morrow, 1985.
ISBN: 0-6880-2865-9   204 p.
** low-fat, low-cholesterol, low-sugar recipes without bread, dairy products, or baked goods; also includes a 15-day menu

VEGETARIAN DIET

W183 Elliot, Rose. *Vegetarian slimming.* Chapmans, distributed by Barnes & Noble Bks.-Imports, Savage, MD, 1991.
ISBN: 1-8559-2517-6   320 p.

W184 Leneman, Leah. *Slimming the vegetarian way.* rev. and reset ed. New York: Thorsons, 1989.
ISBN: 0-7225-1587-1   144 p.
** includes vegetarian weight loss recipes

W185 Shulman, Martha Rose. *The Almost meatless diet book.* Papermac, distributed by St. Martin's Press, New York, 1990.
ISBN: 0-3335-2500-0   280 p.
** provides recipes for weight reduction

SELECTED ASSOCIATIONS
AND FOUNDATIONS

Abundantly Yours
P.O. Box 151134, San Diego, California 92115
619-697-9862

Association for the Study of Obesity
Department of Nutrition and Dietetics
St. George's Hospital
Blackshaw Road, London SW17 0QT, England
1-672-1225

Lean Line
151 New World Way, South Plainfield, New Jersey 07080
800-624-3108 (in New Jersey)
800-526-0965 (in New York)
201-757-7677

National Association to Advance Fat Acceptance
P.O. Box 188620, Sacramento, California 95818
916-443-0303

Obesity Foundation
5600 S. Quebec, Suite 160-D, Englewood, Colorado 80111
303-779-4833

Overeaters Anonymous
National Office
P.O. Box 92870, Los Angeles, California 90009
213-542-8363

TOPS Club
(Take Off Pounds Sensibly)
P.O. Box 07360, 4575 S. Fifth Street, Milwaukee, Wisconsin
53207
414-482-4620

HEALING IN GENERAL
AND
OTHER DISORDERS (H)

OTHER DISORDERS

ASTHMA, ECZEMA, AND HAY FEVER

H1   Bennett, Carol. *Asthma and eczema.* New York: Thorsons, 1989.
ISBN: 0-7225-1821-8   160 p.
** contains recipes that are milk-free; from *A special diet cookbook* series

H2   Turner, Roger Newman. *Diets to help asthma and hay fever.* rev. ed. New York: Thorsons, 1989.
ISBN: 0-7225-1933-8   47 p.

CANDIDIASIS

H3   Burton, Gail. *The Candida control cookbook: good food for yeast-sensitive people.* New York: New American Library, 1989.

ISBN: 0-4530-0661-2   224 p.
** for candidiasis patients; no-sugar, no-fruits, gluten-free, milk-free, non-alcoholic, no dried herbs, no red meat, no mushrooms, and others; daily carbohydrate consumption is restricted to 60-100 grams; all recipes include carbohydrate content

H4   Connolly, Pat and Associates of the Price-Pottenger Nutrition Foundation. *Candida albicans yeast-free cookbook: how to use good nutrition to fight the exploding epidemic of yeast- and fungal-related diseases!* New Canaan, CT: Keats Pub., 1985.
ISBN: 0-8798-3409-9   149 p. illustrated
** includes how to live with candida albicans and features sugar-free, yeast-free recipes from breakfast and appetizers to desserts and beverages; each recipe indicates carbohydrate content

H5   Crook, William G. *The Yeast connection: a medical breakthrough.* 2nd ed. Jackson, TN: Professional Books, 1984.
ISBN: 0-9334-7806-2   336 p. illustrated
** a low-carbohydrate cookbook for candidiasis and mycotoxicoses

H6   Crook, William G. and Jones, Marjorie Hurt. *The Yeast connection cookbook: a guide to good nutrition and better health.* Jackson, TN: Professional Books, 1989.
ISBN: 0-9334-7816-X   379 p. illustrated
** for persons who suffer from candidiasis

DEPRESSION

H7　　Roth, June. *The Food/depression connection: how to detect neuro-allergies: more than 200 artificial-additive-free recipes: food-sensitivity checklist with each recipe: related allergy foods and menu planning: guide to high vitamin and mineral foods: four-day diversified rotary diet.* Chicago: Contemporary Books, 1978
ISBN: 0-8092-7897-9　　　258 p.
** milk-free, egg-free, sugar-free, wheat-free, barley-free, oat-free, corn-free, rye-free, rice-free recipes for patients with chronic depression

HEADACHES

H8　　Annechild, Annette and Johnson, Laura. *Yeast-free living: if you suffer from headaches, tiredness, recurring infections, allergies and upset stomach, this book could change your life.* New York: Perigee, 1986.

H9　　Bircher-Benner Klinik. *Bircher-Benner Nutrition plan for headache and migraine patients; a comprehensive guide, with suggestions for diet menus and recipes.* Edited by Ralph Bircher. Translated by Timothy McManus. New York: Pyramid Books, 1977.　　　158 p.

H10　　Grasso, Patricia Holter and Stump, Jan Schaller. *The Headache cookbook: a tool for migraine self help.* Bowie, MD: R. J. Brady Co., 1984.
ISBN: 0-8930-3512-2　　　376 p. illustrated

H11   Wentworth, Josie A. *The Migraine prevention cookbook:
      menus and recipes for controlling dietary causes of
      headaches.* Garden City Park, NY: Avery, 1983.
      ISBN: 0-3851-8052-7   202 p.
      ** Part I: description of the migraine and suspected
      offenders such as hypoglycemia, chocolate, cheese, citrus
      fruit, and alcohol; Part II: recipes from breakfast, lunches,
      and dinners to snacks without using the suspected
      offenders

IMMUNITY

H12   Berger, Stuart M. *Dr. Berger's Immune power cookbook.*
      New York: New American Library, 1989.
      ISBN: 0-4511-6048-7   301 p. illustrated
      ** recipes to improve one's immunity prepared by
      Rosemary E. McCoy; a companion volume and practical
      application of the principles underlying the *Immune
      power diet*

H13   Berger, Stuart M. *Dr. Berger's Immune power diet.*
      New York: New American Library, 1985.
      ISBN: 0-4530-0483-0   278 p.
      ** weight-reducing diet recipes aimed also at improving
      immunity

H14   Brighthope, Ian; Maier, Ruth; and Fitzgerald, Peter. *A
      Recipe for health: building a strong immune system.*
      Charlton, Victoria: McCulloch, 1989.
      ISBN: 0-9496-4626-1   176 p. illustrated

H15   Galland, Leo and Buchman, Dian Dincin. *Superimmunity for kids*. New York: Dell Pub., 1989.
ISBN: 0-3852-9827-7   315 p.

MENTALLY AND
PHYSICALLY HANDICAPPED

H16   Marshall, Rosamund M. *My cook book*. Kidderminster, Hereford and Worcester: BIMH Publications, 1983.
ISBN: 0-9060-5434-6   136 p. illustrated
** step-by-step easy-to-follow instructions accompanying pictures throughout this book published by the British Institute of Mental Handicap; part 1 explains kitchen equipment, safety tips, hygiene, storing food, and nutrition of foods; part 2 includes simple recipes; part 3 presents advanced recipes; and part 4 is menu planning

H17   Smolen, Maxine. *Wheelchair recipes from the collection of Momma Wheels*. Port Washington, NY: Ashley Books, 1987.
ISBN: 0-8794-9171-X
** cookery for the physically handicapped

PKU
[PHENYLKETONURIA]

H18   Lorimer, Cathy. *Low-protein cuisine*. Glendale Heights, IL: C.L. Lorimer, 1990.   45 p.
** low-phenylalanine and low-protein recipes prepared

for those with phenylketonuria

H19   Schuett, Virginia E. *Low protein cookery for PKU
      (phenylketonuria).* 2nd ed. rev. and expanded. Madison,
      WI: University of Wisconsin Press, 1988.
      ISBN: 0-2991-1140-7   569 p. illustrated
      ** contains low-phenylalanine and low-protein recipes for
      those with phenylketonuria; phenylalanine, protein, and
      caloric contents listed; includes helpful hints for holiday,
      special occasions, picnics, babysitters, travel, and
      everyday tips

PROSTATE DISORDERS

H20   Bircher-Benner Klinik. *Bircher-Benner Nutrition plan for
      prostate problems; a comprehensive guide with
      suggestions for diet menus and recipes.* Translated by
      Kenneth C. Taylor. Edited by Ralph Bircher. Los
      Angeles: Nash Pub., 1973.
      ISBN: 0-8402-8046-7   105 p.

SKIN
DISEASES AND DISORDERS

H21   Bircher-Benner Klinik. *Bircher-Benner Nutrition plan for
      skin problems; a comprehensive guide with suggestions
      for diet menus and recipes.* Edited by Ralph Bircher.
      Translated by Dora Laurence. Los Angeles: Nash Pub.,
      1973.

ISBN: 0-8402-8047-5   110 p.

H22   Kirsta, Alix. *Good Housekeeping eating for healthy skin.*
New York: Good Housekeeping, 1989.
ISBN: 0-8522-3717-0   160 p.
** recipes for healthy dishes using natural foods

HEALING
IN GENERAL

H23   Bricklin, Mark and Claessens, Sharon. *The Natural
healing cookbook: over 450 delicious ways to get better
and stay healthy.* Emmaus, PA: Rodale, 1981.
ISBN: 0-8785-7338-0   460 p. illustrated
** recipes designed for healing circulatory, digestive,
skeletal, and psychological problems, and many other
diseases

H24   Christopher, John R. *Regenerative diet.*   Springville,
UT: Christopher Publications, 1987.   275 p.
** a vegetarian cookbook

H25   Cunningham, Marci. *Natural remedies, recipes and
realities.* Gibbon Glade, PA: Backwoods Books, 1986.
ISBN: 0-9388-3300-6   184 p. illustrated
** features folk medicine

H26   Evergreen Foundation Staff. *Healing with whole foods:
includes the art of cooking and grains and vegetables:
food as medicine for the body and mind.* Berkeley, CA:

North Atlantic Books, 1990.
ISBN: 0-9381-9064-4   450 p. illustrated

H27   Goodman, Harriet Wilinsky and Morse, Barbara. *Just what the doctor ordered: gourmet recipes developed with Boston's Beth Israel Hospital for low-calorie, diabetic, low-fat, low-cholesterol, low-sodium, bland, high-fiber, and renal diets*. New York: Holt, Rinehart, and Winston, 1983.
ISBN: 0-8514-0621-1   674 p. illustrated
** recipes developed by Boston's Beth Israel Hospital

H28   Hagiwara, Yoshihide. *Green barley essence: health benefits of nature's ideal "fast food"*. Adapted and edited by Doug Smith and Dan McTague. New Canaan, CT: Keats, 1985.
ISBN: 0-8798-3418-8   147 p. illustrated
** a cookbook on the therapeutic use of dried green barley juice; translated from (in Japanese) *ky oi no kenk ogen bakuyrokuso*

H29   Harbhajan Singh Khalsa, Yogiji. *Foods for health and healing: remedies and recipes: based on the teachings of Yogi Bhajan*. Berkeley, CA: Spiritual Community, 1988.
ISBN: 0-9138-5215-5   140 p. illustrated

H30   Hausman, Patricia and Hurley, Judith Benn. *The Healing foods: the ultimate authority on the curative power of nutrition*. Emmaus, PA: Rodale, 1989.
ISBN: 0-8785-7812-9   461 p.
** an encyclopedic book arranged alphabetically by

types of foods and disorders; within each section, nutritional values, healing power, and recipes provided or disorder introduced, dietary treatment suggested, and recipes given

H31 Nilson, Bee. *Cooking for special diets*. 3rd ed. Harmondsworth, London: Penguin Books, 1981. ISBN: 0-1404-6095-0   479 p. illustrated

H32 Prevention Magazine; editors of. *The Healing foods cookbook: 400 delicious recipes with curative power*. Emmaus, PA: Rodale Press, distributed by St. Martins, 1991. ISBN: 0-8785-7956-7

H33 Rector-Page, Linda. *Cooking for healthy healing: a reference for healing diets and recipes*. California, 1990. 704 p.

H34 Shurtleff, William and Aoyagi, Akiko. *The Book of kudzu: a culinary and healing guide: 13 medical preparations*. Garden City Park, NY: Avery, 1985. ISBN: 0-8952-9287-4   102 p. illustrated ** includes 53 recipes and medical treatment with kudzu for common colds, diarrhea, colitis, kidney disorders, gonorrhea, and other ailments

H35 Wigmore, Ann. *The Wheatgrass book*. Garden City Park, NY: Avery, 1985. ISBN: 0-8952-9234-3   126 p. illustrated ** a cookbook on the therapeutic use of wheatgrass, vegetable juices, and raw foods

HEALING WITH
AYURVEDA

H36 Johari, Harish. *The Healing cuisine: India's art of Ayurvedic cooking.* Rochester, VT: Healing Arts Press, 1990.
ISBN: 0-8928-1382-2
** a vegetarian cookbook

H37 Morningstar, Amadea and Desai, Urmila. *The Ayurvedic cookbook: a personalized guide to good nutrition and health.* Santa Fe, NM: Lotus Press, 1990.
ISBN: 0-9149-5506-3   351 p. illustrated
** Indic macrobiotic recipes based on Ayurveda in which foods affect doshas: Kapha, Vata, and Pitta; each recipe presents effects of the dish on doshas and most healing season to prepare the dish; a balanced meal is believed to include 40-60% whole grains, 10-20% high quality protein, and 30-50% fresh fruits and vegetables

HEALING WITH
FRUITS AND VEGETABLES

H38 Abramowski, O. L. M. *Abramowski's Fruitarian system of healing.* Westville, Natal, South Africa: Essence of Health Pub. Co., 1976.   187 p.

H39   Albright, Nancy. *The Crunchy, juicy cookbook.*
Emmaus, PA: Rodale Press, 1977. 86 p. illustrated
** cuisine using fruits, nuts, and cereals

H40   Blauer, Stephen. *The Juicing book.* Garden City Park,
NY: Avery, 1989.
ISBN: 0-8952-9253-X
** a cookbook on the therapeutic use of fruit and
vegetable juices

H41   Salaman, Maureen Kennedy and Scheer, James F. *Foods
that heal.* Menlo Park, CA: Statford Pub., 1989.
ISBN: 0-9130-8702-5   524 p.
** vegetable and fruit cookery

H42   Thorsons Editorial Board. *The Complete raw juice
therapy.* New York: Thorsons, 1989.
ISBN: 0-7225-1877-3   128 p.
** a cookbook on the therapeutic use of fruit and
vegetable juices

HEALING WITH
HERBS

H43   Heinerman, John. *The Complete book of spices: their
medical nutritional, and culinary uses.* New Canaan, CT:
Keats Pub., 1983.
ISBN: 0-8798-3281-9   183 p. illustrated

H44   Houdret, Jessica. *Herbs in healthy home cooking.* Bath,

Avon: Ashgrove Press, 1987.
ISBN: 0-9067-9882-5   159 p. illustrated

H45   Kent, Amnon. *It's in your kitchen cabinet: using herbs
and spices for a healthier body.* Forest Hills, NY: Kent,
1987.
ISBN: 0-9433-1300-7   69 p.
** a cookbook on the therapeutic use of herbs

H46   Klein, Erica Levy. *Skinny spices: 50 nifty homemade
spice blends that can make any diet delicious.* Chicago,
IL: Surrey Books, 1991.
ISBN: 0-9406-2524-5

H47   Messegue, Maurice. *A Kitchen herbal: making the most
of herbs for cookery and health.* London: Collins, 1984.
ISBN: 0-3302-8090-1   255 p. illustrated

H48   Rose, Jeanne. *Jeanne Rose's Herbal guide to food:
eating healthy the herbal way.* Berkeley, CA: North
Atlantic Books, 1989.
ISBN: 1-5564-3063-9   252 p. illustrated

HEALING WITH
MACROBIOTICS

H49   Kushi, Michio. *Natural healing through macrobiotics.*
Tokyo: Japan Publications, 1979.
ISBN: 0-8704-0457-1   304 p. illustrated
** a macrobiotic cookbook applying naturopathy,

previously published as *The macrobiotic way of natural healing*

H50 Turner, Kristina. *The Self-healing cookbook: a macrobiotic primer for healing body, mind and moods with whole, natural foods.* 2nd ed. rev. Grass Valley, CA: Earthtones Press, 1987.
ISBN: 0-9456-6810-4   209 p. illustrated

H51 Wittels, Beatrice. *I choose to be well diet cookbook.* Elkins Park, PA: CSC Press, 1983.
ISBN: 0-9610-7800-6   336 p. illustrated
** a macrobiotic diet book for the ill person

SELECTED ASSOCIATIONS AND FOUNDATIONS

Foundation for Depression and Manic Depression
7 E. 67th Street, New York, New York 10021
212-772-3400

Information Exchange on Young Adult Chronic Patients (Mental Health)
151 S. Main Street, Suite 212, New City, New York 10956
914-634-0050

National Headache Foundation
5252 N. Western Avenue, Chicago, Illinois 60625
800-523-8858 (in Illinois)
800-843-2256 (outside Illinois)
312-878-5558

National Migraine Foundation
5252 N. Western Avenue, Chicago, IL 60625
312-878-7715

SECTION II

DIETS

FOR

GENERAL HEALTH

LIFE STAGES (L)

PREGNANCY studies have shown that nutrition affects the pregnancy's course and outcome. Nutritional status before pregnancy is also a major factor that affects the health of a pregnant woman and her infant. The best diet for any pregnancy is one that begins before conception.

Extra energy and nutrients are needed to support the growth of maternal tissues, such as the uterus and breast, and the increased metabolic demands of pregnancy as well as the growth of the fetus and placenta. During lactation, the energy and nutrients provided in milk, and those required for its production, must be replaced.

Intake of sufficient energy and nutrients to attain optimal nutritional status, including appropriate weight before pregnancy and adequate weight gain during pregnancy, improves infant birth weight and reduces infant mortality and morbidity. Evidence relating maternal diet to child health indicates that well-nourished mothers produce healthier children.

CHILDREN'S nutrient requirements, in relation to body size, are greater than adults. A child needs protein for the maintenance of body tissues, changes in body composition, and synthesis of new muscles. Inadequate intakes of vitamins and minerals are reflected in slow growth rates, inadequate mineralization of bones, and very low body reserves of micronutrients. Snacks become an important source of calories and nutrients and may contribute as much as one-third of the calories and fat, one-fifth of the protein, and nearly one-half of the carbohydrates 10-year-old children consume. These patterns emphasize the need for parents and schools to provide appropriate levels of daily physical activity, appropriate meals, and nutritious snacks without promoting tooth decay.

ADOLESCENCE demands significant increases in calories and nutrient intake to support rapid growth rate and increased body size. Irregular eating patterns are common, reflecting a growing independence from the family and the teenager's increasingly busy social life including athletic, academic, and vocational activities. Consuming the appropriate amount and form of energy and nutrients for a developmental age is important for good health. Avoiding excessive intake of fat, sodium, and sugar for children and adolescents is of critical importance, offering specific advantages in wellness.

Nutrients most often consumed in insufficient amounts are iron, calcium, riboflavin, and vitamin A. The adolescent need for iron increases as the result of expanding blood volume and increased tissue mass. In addition to augmented needs, females must replace iron lost through menstruation. Nutrient needs can best be met when diets contain a wide variety of foods.

ATHLETES, in accelerated physical training, need more energy. Food intake must be adjusted and consideration given to an appropriate dietary balance of 30 percent fats, 50 to 55 percent carbohydrates, and 15 percent proteins.

ELDERLY persons approach one side of the life-long aging process continuum which is marked by steady deterioration of bodily functions in matured adults and the accumulation of chronic disabilities and diseases. The rate of the aging process is influenced by genetic and environmental forces and differs among individuals from varied physiologic, psychological, and social vantage points. Thus, chronological age by itself becomes less reliable as an index of the physiologic or psychological condition when nutritional needs of the geriatric population are dealt with.

Older persons have a high prevalence of chronic disease, use medications heavily, and are relatively sedentary. Senior citizens should consume sufficient nutrients, adequate calcium, and calories, and sustain levels of physical activity that maintain desirable body weight. Then the onset of chronic disease may be prevented or delayed, and may be less severe.

Following is a selection of contemporary cookbooks designed for pregnant women, infants and toddlers, children and teenagers, athletes, and senior citizens.

PREGNANCY
IN GENERAL

L1   Brewer, Gail Sforza and Brewer, Thomas H. *The Brewer Medical diet for normal and high-risk pregnancy: a leading obstetrician's guide to every stage of pregnancy.* New York: Simon and Schuster, 1983.
ISBN: 0-6714-2635-4   244 p.

L2   Cronin, Isaac and Brewer, Gail Sforza. *Eating for two: the complete pregnancy nutrition cookbook, insure a healthy future for you and your unborn baby!* New York: Bantam, 1983.
ISBN: 0-5532-3372-6   322 p.
** features detailed nutritional needs and recipes for during pregnancy and after giving birth using natural foods; also covers vegetarian main courses; each recipe includes protein and caloric content

L3   Duff, Susan. *The Post-pregnancy diet: how to regain your figure after your baby is born.* New York: New American Library, 1989.
ISBN: 0-4530-0595-0   168 p.
** includes weight-reducing recipes and exercise for women

L4   Eisenberg, Arlene; Murkoff, Heidi Eisenberg; and Hathaway, Sandee Eisenberg. *What to eat when you're expecting.* New York: Workman, 1986.
ISBN: 0-8948-0015-9   349 p.

L5   Erick, Miriam. *D.I.E.T.* during pregnancy: the complete guide and calendar*. Newly rev. Brookline, MA: Grinnen-Barrett Pub. Co., distributed by Talman, 1987.
ISBN: 0-9613-0634-3   244 p. illustrated
** D.I.E.T. stands for Developing Intelligent Eating Techniques; designed for expectant mothers and infants; revised edition of *Pregnancy and nutrition*

L6   Gazella, Jacqueline Gibson. *Nutrition for the childbearing year*. Wayzata, MN: Woodland Pub. Co., 1979.
ISBN: 0-9341-0401-8   173 p. illustrated
** a cookbook designed for nutritional needs during pregnancy

L7   *Good Housekeeping Eating for a healthy baby*. New York: Good Housekeeping, 1990.
ISBN: 0-8522-3772-3   160 p.
** features recipes for pregnant women

L8   Kamen, Betty and Kamen Si. *The Kamen Plan for total nutrition during pregnancy*. New York: Appleton-Century-Crofts, 1981.
ISBN: 0-8385-5079-7   234 p. illustrated
** provides menu planning and recipes using vegetables, meat, fish, grains, tofu and other soybean products, legumes, home-made yogurt, sprouting, and pickling; also has sections on nutritional needs, negative intake, ills and ailments, and next time around

L9   Klein, Diane. *Eating right for two: the complete nutrition guide and cookbook for a healthy pregnancy.* New York: Ballantine Books, 1983.
ISBN: 0-3453-0915-4   331 p. illustrated

L10   Lashford, Stephanie. *The 12 month pregnancy: your diet, from pre-conception, to motherhood.* Bath, Avon: Ashgrove Press, 1985.
ISBN: 0-9067-9842-6   141 p. illustrated

L11   Lewis, Catherine. *Good food before birth.* London: Unwin, 1984.
ISBN: 0-0464-1045-7   240 p.
** recipes prepared for pregnant women and nursing mothers

L12   Liddell, Caroline and Ross, Nickey. *Mother's superdiet: healthy eating for you and your baby.* London: Pitman, 1977.
ISBN: 0-2730-0109-4   122 p. illustrated

L13   Mayle, Peter. *How to be a pregnant father: an illustrated survival guide for the first-time father.* Secaucus, NJ: Lyle Stuart, 1986.
ISBN: 0-8184-0399-3   56 p.   illustrated
** including the pregnant father's cookbook by Len Deighton

L14   McCreary, Jacqueline Michele. *Food for "life" (and for thought): information and recipes for "the pregnant family".* Windsor, ON: J. McCreary, 1982.

ISBN: 0-9691-1890-2   127 p. illustrated

L15 Paananen, Donna. *New mother's cookbook: over 300*
nutritious, delicious recipes for expectant and new
mothers. New York: Exeter Books, 1981.
ISBN: 0-8967-3111-1   80 p. illustrated, color
** all types of dishes for expecting mothers, infants, and
toddlers

L16 Peavy, Linda S. *Have a healthy baby: doctor*
recommended nutritional guide and menus for before,
during and after your baby is born. New York: Drake
Publishers, 1977.
ISBN: 0-8473-1486-3   175 p.

L17 Shannon, Ellen C. *The Expectant mother's guide to*
happy eating. San Diego, CA: A. S. Barnes, 1975.
ISBN: 0-4980-1639-0   152 p.

L18 Smalheiser, Shirley. *The Healthy pregnancy menu*
cookbook. New York: Cornerstone Library, 1983.
ISBN: 0-3461-2590-1   192 p.

L19 Williams, Phyllis S. *Nourishing your unborn child:*
nutrition and natural foods in pregnancy. Rev. ed. New
York: Avon Books, 1982.
ISBN: 0-3806-0657-7   288 p.
** a natural-food cookbook

PREGNANCY
VEGETARIAN DIET

L20   Elliot, Rose. *The Vegetarian mother and baby book.*
New York: Pantheon Books, 1986.
ISBN: 0-3947-4620-1   261 p. illustrated

L21   Gross, Joy and Freifeld, Karen. *The Vegetarian child.*
Secaucus, NJ: Lyle Stuart Inc., 1983.
ISBN: 0-8184-0342-X   224 p.
** vegetarian cookery for pregnancy

L22   Klaper, Michael. *Pregnancy, children and the vegan diet.*
Umatilla, FL: Gentle World, 1987.
ISBN: 0-9614-2482-6   108 p. illustrated

INFANTS and TODDLERS

L23   Castle, Sue. *The Complete guide to preparing baby
foods.* rev. ed. Garden City Park, NY: Doubleday, 1981.
ISBN: 0-3851-5884-X   336 p.
** provides infant nutrition requirements and recipes;
how to store and prepare for all types of baby foods; a
revised edition of *The complete guide to preparing baby
foods at home,* 1973

L24   Coyle, Rena and Messing, Patricia. *Baby let's eat!: how
to feed your baby like the rest of the family. One hundred
easy recipes for wholesome meals and snacks you can all
enjoy together, with complete nutritional guidelines for*

children aged 6 months to 3 years. New York: Workman Publishing Inc., 1987.
ISBN: 0-8948-0300-X   128 p. illustrated
** baby's nutritional needs with recipes for each of the following age groups: 6-12 months, 12-18 months, 18-24 months, and 24-36 months

L25   Flynn-Esquivel, Sheila and Orleans, Valerie. *The Culinary kid: a nutrition guide and cookbook for parents and kid.* Orange, CA: St. Joseph Hospital, 1986.
ISBN: 0-9616-8570-0   157 p.
** medical nutritional tips for toddlers, preteens, and teenagers during healthy and sick times; recipes of breakfasts, salads, soups, sandwiches, main entrees, drinks, snacks, and desserts

L26   Helmer, Barbara Sloan. *The Better baby food cookbook.* Minneapolis, MN: Bethany Fellowship, Inc., 1980.
ISBN: 0-8712-3018-6   127 p.

L27   Karmel, Annabel. *The Complete baby meal planner.* Toronto, ON: Doubleday Canada, 1991.
ISBN: 0-3852-5336-2
** includes infant nutrition, recipes, and menus

L28   Kimmel, Martha; Kimmel, David; and Goldenson, Suzanne. *Mommy made--and daddy too: home cooking for a healthy baby and toddler.* New York: Bantam, 1990.
ISBN: 0-5533-4866-3   308 p.
** includes sections on nutritional needs of infants and

toddlers

L29   Knight, Karin and Lumley, Jeannie. *The Baby cookbook: a complete guide to nutrition, feeding, and cooking for babies six months to two years of age.* New York: Quill, 1985.
ISBN: 0-6880-4950-8   302 p.
** with section on infant nutrition

L30   Lansky, Vicki. *Vicki Lansky's Feed me! I'm yours: baby food made easy, delicious, nutritious and fun things you can cook up for your kids!* rev. ed. Deephaven, MN: Meadowbrook, Inc., distributed by New York: Simon and Schuster, 1986.
ISBN: 0-8816-6072-8   121 p. illustrated
** baby-food cookery from scratch; finger foods, toddler food, snacks, breakfast, seasonal recipes; kitchen crafts, potpourris, and birthday party menu for 1-5 year olds

L31   Madden, Chris Casson. *Baby's first helpings: super-healthy meals for super-healthy kids.* Garden City Park, NY: Doubleday, 1983.
ISBN: 0-3851-9143-X   159 p. illustrated

L32   Paris-Turner, Becky. *Canada cooks!: baby's choice.* North Vancouver, BC: Whitecap Books, 1989.
ISBN: 0-9210-6169-2   160 p. illustrated, color
** includes a section on infant nutrition

L33   Payne, Alma. *The Baby food book.* Boston, MA: Little, Brown and Co., 1977.

ISBN: 0-3166-9543-2   178 p.
** part 1, general discussion of infant nutritional needs
including a special section for vegetarian parents; part 2,
baby-food recipes for cereals, fruits, main dishes,
desserts, vegetarian main dishes, baby sandwiches, and
finger foods

L34   Turner, Mary and Turner, James. *Making your own baby
food: give your child the very best! a healthier and safer
way to feed your growing infant - and save money too!
with family-tested recipes.* revised, updated, and
expanded ed. New York: Bantam, 1976.
ISBN: 0-5531-1066-7   146 p.
** basic infant and prenatal nutritional listings; discusses
the baby-food industry; recipes for all types of baby food

INFANTS and TODDLERS
VEGETARIAN DIET

L35   Kenyon, Judy. *Diet for a healthy baby: vegetarian food
alternatives for your baby and young child.* Van Nuys,
CA: Kenyon, 1979.
ISBN: 0-9604-4920-5   40 p.   illustrated
** presents infant nutrition and vegetable recipes

INFANTS and TODDLERS
MICROWAVE CUISINE

L36   Behan, Eileen. *Microwave cooking for your baby and*

child: the ABCs of creating quick, nutritious meals for little ones. New York: Villard Books, 1991.
ISBN: 0-3945-8419-8   233 p. illustrated
** includes infant nutrition and recipes

INFANTS and TODDLERS
WITH NATURAL INGREDIENTS

L37   Firkaly, Susan Tate. *Into the mouths of babes: a natural foods cookbook for infants and toddlers.* White Hall, VA: Betterway Publications, 1984.
ISBN: 0-9326-2035-3   168 p. illustrated
** includes shopper's guide to whole foods, nutritional needs for pregnancy and infancy, coping with food allergies, and recipes for 4-6 months, 7-9 months, 10-12 months, 1-3 years; whole family recipes and recipes for allergic children

L38   Hunter, Carol. *The Best healthy baby cookbook.* rev. and expanded ed. New York: Thorsons, 1990.
ISBN: 0-7225-2281-9   128 p.
** recipes using natural food

L39   Kenda, Margaret Elizabeth and Williams, Phyllis S. *The Natural baby food cookbook.* updated and rev. New York: Avon, 1982.
ISBN: 0-3806-0640-2   217 p.
** natural-food cuisine

L40   Toms, Laraine. *Cooking for your baby the natural way.*

New York: Sterling, 1984.
ISBN: 0-8069-7826-0   128 p. illustrated
** baby-food recipes including homemade yogurt,
casseroles, snacks, and ice cream

CHILDREN and TEENAGERS

L41   Berman, Christine and Fromer, Jacki. *Meals without
squeals: child care food guide and cookbook.* Palo Alto,
CA: Bull Pub. Co., 1991.
ISBN: 0-9235-2110-0
** children's nutritional needs included

L42   Bunker, Caroline. *Feed your child safely.* Ebury, 1990.
ISBN: 0-8522-3823-1   160 p.
** provides child nutrition health aspects

L43   Cooper, Phyllis. *More please: nutritious meals, recipes
and parties for children.* West Vancouver, BC: P.M.
Cooper Pub., 1989.
ISBN: 1-5505-6020-4   138 p. illustrated, color

L44   Ellison, Sheila and Gray, Judith. *365 foods kids love to
eat.* Foster City, CA: Forward March, distributed in USA
by Publishers Group West, 1989.
ISBN: 0-9620-4675-2   365 p. illustrated

L45   Gow, Emma-Lee and Smith, Janet. *The Lunchbox book.*
Ebury, 1988.
ISBN: 0-8522-3765-0   63 p.

** recipes for packed lunches

L46   Hess, Mary Abbott; Hunt, Anne Elise; and Stone, Barbara
      Motenko. *A Healthy head start: a worry free guide to*
      feeding young children. New York: Holt, 1990.
      ISBN: 0-8050-1329-6   324 p. illustrated

L47   Lang, Jenifer Harvey. *Jenifer Lang Cooks for kids: 153*
      recipes and ideas for good food that kids love to eat.
      New York: Harmony Books, 1991.
      ISBN: 0-5175-8417-4

L48   Moore, Carolyn E.; Kerr, Mimi H.; and Shulman, Robert
      J. *Young chef's nutrition guide and cookbook.* New
      York: Barron's, 1990.
      ISBN: 0-8120-5789-9   281 p. illustrated

L49   Pay, Joanna. *Cooking for kids the healthy way:*
      wholesome recipes with child-appeal. London: Dunitz,
      1986.
      ISBN: 0-9482-6910-4   124 p. illustrated, some
      color

L50   Prince, Francine and Prince, Harold. *Feed your kids*
      bright. New York: Simon and Schuster, 1987.
      ISBN: 0-6716-0522-4   284 p.
      ** includes discussions of nutritional effects on children's
      intelligence and moods

L51   Tracy, Lisa. *Kidfood: how to get your kids to eat right*
      right from the start - and like it. New York: Dell, 1989.

ISBN: 0-4405-0245-4   324 p.

L52   Wishik, Cindy S. *Kids dish it up--sugar-free: a versatile teaching tool for beginning cooks.* Port Angeles, WA: Peninsula Publ., 1982.
ISBN: 0-9181-4622-4   1 vol. (unpaged)
illustrated

CHILDREN and TEENAGERS
DESSERTS and SNACKS

L53   Lansky, Vicki. *The Taming of the C.A.N.D.Y.* monster: *Continuously Advertised Nutritionally Deficient Yummies!* Deephaven, MN: Book Peddlers, 1988.
ISBN: 0-9167-7307-8   136 p. illustrated
** advise for shopping in supermarkets, nutritional guidelines and tips for kids; recipes for brownbag lunches, alternatives to junk foods and desserts, milk-free dishes, and microwave dishes

L54   Warner, Penny. *Healthy snacks for kids: a wide variety of creative treats, drinks and meals you can prepare in a jiffy.* San Leandro, CA: Bristol Publishing Enterprises, 1989.
ISBN: 0-9119-5498-8   176 p. illustrated, some color
** contains sugar-free and salt-free snack recipes with fresh easy-to-find ingredients; part of the *Nitty Gritty cookbook*

L55   Warren, Jean. *Super snacks: seasonal sugarless snacks for young children: no sugar, no honey, no artificial sweeteners.* Alderwood Manor, WA: Warren Pub. House, distributed by Gryphon House, Mt. Rainier, MD, 1983. 63 p. illustrated

CHILDREN and TEENAGERS
WITH NATURAL INGREDIENTS

L56   Better Homes and Gardens. *Better Homes and Gardens Healthy foods for hungry kids.* Des Moines, IA: Meredith Corp., 1987.
ISBN: 0-6960-1690-7   80 p.   illustrated, color
** recipes using natural foods

L57   Lashford, Stephanie. *The Kitchen crew: a children's wholefood cookery book.* Bath, Avon: Ashgrove, 1986.
ISBN: 0-9067-9863-9   96 p.   illustrated, color
** recipes using natural food

L58   Schauss, Alexander G.; Meyer, Barbara Friedlander; and Meyer, Arnold. *Eating for A's: a delicious 12-week nutrition plan to improving your child's academic and athletic performance.* New York: Pocket Books, 1991.
ISBN: 0-6717-2814-8
** recipes with natural foods; children's nutritional needs, health, and hygiene detailed

ATHLETES

L59 Berkoff, Frances G.; Lauer, Barbara J.; and Talbot, Yves. *Power eating: how to play hard and eat smart for the time of your life.* Montreal, PQ: Communiplex, 1989. ISBN: 2-9801-4810-5   240 p. illustrated, some color
** presents nutritional needs for athletes

L60 Clark, Nancy. *The Athlete's kitchen: the essential nutrition guide for active men and women: from quick-energy snacks to fortifying feasts, over 200 recipes for a wholesome and delicious diet.* New York: Bantam, 1983. ISBN: 0-5532-3211-8   322 p.
** with supermarket shopping guides; low-fat, low-cholesterol, high-complex-carbohydrate, and low-salt recipes for breakfast, lunch, dinner; lacto-ovo-vegetarian recipes included

L61 Goulart, Frances Sheridan. *The Official eating to win cookbook: super foods for super athletic performance.* New York: Stein and Day, 1983. ISBN: 0-8128-8142-7   287 p.
** recipes of all types of dishes with variation suggestions based on "winning combination" guidelines: more exercise, more raw foods, less meat, less sugar, less protein, more carbohydrates, less fat, more fiber, and less refined foods

L62 Michael, Jane Wilkens. *Breakfast, lunch, and dinner of champions: star athletes' diet programs for maximum energy and performance.* New York: Quill, 1984. ISBN: 0-6880-3195-1   263 p. illustrated

L63   Peterson, Marilyn Shope and Martinsen, Charlene S. *The Athlete's cookbook: easy recipes and nutritional guidelines for active people* Seattle: Smuggler's Cove Publishing, 1980.
ISBN: 0-9184-8405-7   191 p. illustrated
** recipes arranged by sport categories; caloric content with each recipe

L64   Pritikin, Nathan. *Diet for runners.* New York: Simon and Schuster, 1985.
ISBN: 0-6715-5623-1   256 p.
** includes low-cholesterol recipes and discusses physiological and nutritional aspects of runners

L65   Tanny, Mandy. *Muscular gourmet: a natural foods cookbook with over 300 high-powered, low-calorie recipes plus hard-hitting tips on diet and exercise to build the body you want.* New York: Harper and Row, 1988.
ISBN: 0-0609-6096-5   237 p. illustrated
** high-protein and low-calorie recipes using natural ingredients for bodybuilding

L66   Wollin, Roberta and Gan, Sheila; compilers. *Eating and competing: favorite recipes, diet and training tips from international olympic and world class athletes, 1920-1984.* Atlanta, GA: Philmay Enterprises, 1984.
ISBN: 0-9428-9406-5   260 p.
** provides recipes with international flair and athlete's nutritional needs

ELDERLY

L67   Casale, Anne. *The Long life cookbook: delectable recipes for two: low sodium, low cholesterol, low sugar.* New York: Ballantine Books, 1987.
ISBN: 0-3453-3377-2   387 p. illustrated
** includes low-cholesterol, low-salt, sugar-free, and low-fat recipes for the aged

L68   Friedlander, Barbara and Petersen, Marilyn. *Dr. Frank's No-aging diet cookbook.* New York: Dial Press, 1977.
ISBN: 0-8037-1958-2   148 p.
** based on *Dr. Frank's no-aging diet*; preserve youthfulness with nucleic-acid-rich foods, repair bodies, remove and retard wrinkles; specific weekly regimen of fish and daily liquids

L69   Gray Panthers of San Francisco. *Cheap and nutritious (and delicious) cookbook: a project of the Gray Panthers of San Francisco.* San Francisco, CA: Gray Panthers of San Francisco, 1984.
130 p.
** includes recipes and nutritional needs for middle-aged and aged persons

L70   Gustafson, Helen. *The Reluctant cook.* Berkeley, CA: Celestial Arts, 1990.
ISBN: 0-8908-7594-4   93 p.
** features quick and easy recipes for senior citizens and references to catalogues and companies of special interest to older, disabled, or handicapped people

L71   Harlow, Jan; Liggett, Irene; and Mandel, Evelyn. *The Good age cookbook: recipes from the Institute for creative aging.* Boston: Houghton Mifflin, 1979.
ISBN: 0-3952-7781-7   221 p. illustrated
** designed for people over 65 years of age; includes low-calorie, low-fat, low-cholesterol, and low-salt cuisine for singles or couples

L72   Jester, Pat. *Age buster cookbook.* West Des Moines, IA: Creative Foods Ltd., 1985.
ISBN: 0-9615-7080-6   96 p. illustrated
** reduced-salt recipes prepared for persons 65 and older

L73   Klinger, Judith Lannefeld; compiler. *Mealtime manual for people with disabilities and the aging.* 2nd ed. Camden, NJ: Campbell Soup Co., 1978.
269 p. illustrated
** recipes for physically handicapped and aged; includes self-help devices for the disabled; in cooperation with the Institute of Rehabilitation Medicine, New York University Medical Center, and Campbell Soup Company

L74   LaLanne, Elaine and Benyo, Richard. *Fitness after 50 workout.* Lexington, MA: S. Greene, distributed by NY: Viking Penguin, 1989.
ISBN: 0-8289-0669-6   165 p. illustrated
** targeted for middle-aged and aged persons; includes natural-food cooking and exercise for persons older than 50

L75   Lees, Dan and Lees, Molly. *Cooking in retirement.*

London: Christopher Helm, 1987.
ISBN: 0-7470-2001-9   182 p. illustrated, some color
** recipes and nutritional needs for the older person

L76   McFarlane, Marilyn. *The Older Americans cookbook: easy-to-fix, low-cost, delicious dishes designed to meet the nutritional needs of older people.* Greensboro, NC: Tudor, 1988.
ISBN: 0-9363-8950-2   201 p.
** designed for senior citizens; includes a six-week suggested menu plan with meal preparation, shopping and nutrition tips, and recipes for a low-sodium and low-cholesterol diet

L77   Oliver, Margo. *Margo Oliver's Cookbook for seniors: nutritious recipes for one, two, or more.* North Vancouver, BC: Bellingham, 1989.
ISBN: 0-8890-8695-8   261 p. illustrated

L78   Wilson, Jane Weston. *Eating well when you just can't eat the way you used to: over 250 recipes that please the palate and lift the spirits.* New York: Workman, 1987.
ISBN: 0-8948-0943-1   390 p. illustrated
** low-salt, low-fat, low-sugar, and high-fiber recipes designed for persons over 50 years of age

SELECTED ASSOCIATIONS
AND FOUNDATIONS

American Board of Nutrition
9650 Rockville Pike, Bethesda, Maryland 20814
301-530-7110

American Dietetic Association
216 W. Jackson Blvd., Suite 800, Chicago, Illinois 60606
312-899-0040

American Institute of Nutrition
9650 Rockville Pike, Bethesda, Maryland 20814
301-530-7050

American Red Cross
431 18th Street, N.W., Washington, DC 20006
202-737-8300

Concerned Relatives of Nursing Home Patients
P.O. Box 18820, Cleveland Heights, Ohio 44118
216-321-0403

Dietary Guidelines Advisory Committee
Human Nutrition Information Service
Department of Agriculture
Federal Building, 6505 Belcrest Rd., Hyattsville, Maryland
20782
301-436-5090

International Academy of Nutrition and Preventive Medicine
P.O. Box 5832, Lincoln, Nebraska 68505
402-467-2716

International Baby Food Action Network
3255 Hennepin Avenue, S., Suite 220, Minneapolis, Minnesota
55408
612-823-1571

National Advisory Council on Maternal, Infant and Fetal
Nutrition
Supplemental Foods Program Division
Food and Nutrition Service
Department of Agriculture
3103 Park Center Drive, Alexandria, Virginia 22302
703-756-3746

National Association of Childbearing Center
3123 Gottschall Road, Perkiomenville, Pennsylvania 18074
215-234-8068

National Center for Education in Maternal and Child Health
38th and R Streets, N.W., Washington, DC 20057
202-625-8400

National Child Nutrition Project
1501 Cherry Street, 3rd floor, Philadelphia, Pennsylvania
215-247-7439

National Council on Patient Information and Education
666 11th Street, N.W., Suite 810, Washington, DC 20001
202-347-6711

National Maternal and Child Health Clearinghouse
38th and R Streets, N.W., Washington, DC 20057
202-625-8410

Pregnancy and Infant Loss Center
1421 East Wayzata Blvd., #40, Wayzata, Minnesota 55391
612-473-9372

MACROBIOTIC DIET (M)

Translated from the Greek, "macro" means "large" or "great", and "bios" signifies "life". Together they are used to describe a lifestyle including a simple, balanced diet that aims to promote health and longevity. Today's macrobiotics was revived and reestablished by a Japanese named George Ohsawa. He and his followers suggest that sickness and unhappiness are nature's way of urging us to adopt a proper diet and way of life. Macrobiotics is not just a diet but a religious as well as a philosophical practice of Zen.

A MACROBIOTIC DIET is based on whole grain and traditional foods in harmony with the seasons. It advocates the use of whole grains, beans, and locally grown vegetables as primary sources of food energy and nutrition. In addition, the diet includes nutritious soyfoods, mineral-rich sea vegetables, and white-meat fish and shellfish to substitute for red meat and poultry. Instead of refined salt and sugar, macrobiotic seasonings are sea salt and natural-grain sweeteners such as rice syrup and barley malt.

A proper macrobiotic diet consists of 50-60% whole grains, 20-25% cooked vegetables, 5% raw vegetables, 5% sea vegetables, 5-10% beans, 5% soup, 5% condiments, and others. This type of dietary practice has generated alarming long-term effects according to medical research. Vitamin B-12, vitamin D, riboflavin, calcium, and iron deficiencies are some of the negative aspects of this diet. Consequently, there is a high prevalence of rickets in infants on macrobiotic diets. Compared to their peer groups, infants and children on a macrobiotic diet are smaller in weight and height. Gross motor and language development are also slower in the macrobiotic infants. To overcome the above side effects, an adapted macrobiotic diet is recommended to include a source of dietary fat, fatty fish, and dairy products. Following is a selection of contemporary macrobiotic dietbooks.

M1   Aihara, Cornellia. *The Calendar cookbook.* Oroville, CA: George Ohsawa Macrobiotic Foundation, 1979. ISBN: 0-9188-6032-6   250 p. illustrated ** contains macrobiotic diet recipes and daily breakfast/dinner menus from January 1 to December 31

M2   Aihara, Cornellia. *The D-o of cooking: complete macrobiotic cooking for the seasons.* Oroville, CA: George Ohsawa Macrobiotic Foundation, 1982. ISBN: 0-9188-6039-3   230 p. illustrated

M3   Aihara, Cornellia. *Macrobiotic kitchen: key to good health.* Tokyo: Japan Publications, distributed in USA by Harper and Row, 1982. ISBN: 0-8704-0514-4   140 p. illustrated ** a Japanese cookbook using whole grains and vegetables and originally published as *The Chico-san cookbook: a unique guidebook to natural foods cooking,* 1972

M4   Albert, Rachel. *Cooking with Rachel: creative vegetarian and macrobiotic cuisine.* Oroville, CA: George Ohsawa Macrobiotic Foundation, 1989.
ISBN: 0-9188-6049-0   328 p. illustrated

M5   Cowmeadow, Oliver. *An Introduction to macrobiotics: the natural way to health and happiness.* New York: Thorsons, 1987.
ISBN: 0-7225-1414-X   160 p. illustrated

M6   Diamond, Harvey and Diamond, Marilyn. *Fit for life.* New York, NY: Warner Books, 1985.
ISBN: 0-4465-1322-9   241 p.
** a macrobiotic diet book

M7   Diamond, Marilyn. *A New way of eating: the proper foods, combinations, and recipes to start you on the road to health.* New York: Warner Books, 1987.
ISBN: 0-4463-8404-6   156 p. illustrated
** contains macrobiotic diet recipes

M8   East West Journal; editors of. *Whole world cookbook: international macrobiotic cuisine.* Garden City Park, NY: Avery Pub. Group, 1984.
ISBN: 0-8952-9231-9   124 p. illustrated
** macrobiotic recipes of French, Italian, Japanese, Chinese, American, Latin American, and Middle Eastern cuisines; also includes transitional recipes for making the change from a standard Western-style diet to a more natural diet

M9   Esko, Edward and Esko, Wendy. *Macrobiotic cooking for everyone.* Tokyo: Japan Publications, distributed in USA through Harper and Row, 1980.
ISBN: 0-8704-0469-5   272 p. illustrated

M10 Esko, Wendy. *Aveline Kushi's Introducing macrobiotic cooking.* Tokyo: Japan Publications, 1987.
ISBN: 0-8704-0690-6   221 p. illustrated

M11 Ferre, Julia. *Basic macrobiotic cooking: procedures of grain and vegetable cookery.* Oroville, CA: George Ohsawa Macrobiotic Foundation, 1987.
ISBN: 0-9188-6047-4   275 p. illustrated
** recipes of grains, vegetables, noodles, sea vegetables, legumes, fish, and eggs

M12 George Ohsawa Macrobiotic Foundation. *The First macrobiotic cookbook.* rev. ed. Oroville, CA: George Ohsawa Macrobiotic Foundation, 1984.
ISBN: 0-9188-6042-3   121 p. illustrated
** a Zen cookbook

M13 Henkel, Pamela and Koch, Lee. *As easy as 1,2,3: a mostly macrobiotic cookbook.* Oroville, CA: George Ohsawa Macrobiotic Foundation, 1990.
ISBN: 0-9188-6051-2   126 p.
** quick and easy recipes using vegetables, whole grains, tofu and other soybean products from main dishes to desserts

M14 Kagemori, Teruha. *Healthful eating for healthy living: a*

macrobiotic approach. Ville St. Laurent, PQ: T. Kagemori, 1984.
ISBN: 0-9691-9450-1   180 p. illustrated

M15   Koblin, Seymour A. *Food for life: the macrobiotic approach to discovering personal balance.* San Diego, CA: Soulstar Creations, 1990.
ISBN: 0-9625-0001-1   100 p. illustrated

M16   Kushi, Aveline and Esko, Wendy. *The Changing seasons macrobiotic cookbook.* Garden City Park, NY: Avery Pub. Group, 1985.
ISBN: 0-8952-9232-7   265 p. illustrated

M17   Kushi, Aveline and Esko, Wendy. *Macrobiotic family favorites.* Tokyo, Japan: Japan Publications, 1987.
ISBN: 0-8704-0620-5   207 p. illustrated

M18   Kushi, Aveline and Esko, Wendy. *The Quick and natural macrobiotic cookbook.* Chicago: Contemporary Books, 1989.
ISBN: 0-8092-4436-5   306 p. illustrated
** recipes for six days including breakfast, lunch, and dinners

M19   Kushi, Aveline and Jack, Alex. *Aveline Kushi's Complete guide to macrobiotic cooking for health, harmony, and peace.* New York: Warner Books, 1985.
ISBN: 0-4463-7982-4   414 p. illustrated
** includes how to prepare brown rice, miso soup, tofu, and other natural foods the macrobiotic way in today's

kitchen; how to harmonize with seasons and make use of the medicinal energies of different foods; festive menus for holidays and special occasions

M20 Lerman, Andrea Bliss. *The Macrobiotic community cookbook: favorite recipes from America's macrobiotic leaders.* Garden City Park, NY: Avery Pub. Group, 1989.
ISBN: 0-8952-9396-X   199 p. illustrated

M21 Marquardt, Suzanne. *Suzanne's Natural food cookbook.* Hantsport, NS: Lancelot Press, 1986.
ISBN: 0-8899-9328-9   127 p. illustrated
** contains macrobiotic diet recipes

M22 McCarty, Meredith. *American macrobiotic cuisine.* Eureka, CA: Turning Point Publications, 1986.
ISBN: 0-9349-4702-3   110 p. illustrated
** recipes with whole grains, vegetables (both land and sea), beans, soyfoods, fruits, and some fish

M23 Michell, Keith. *Practically macrobiotic: ingredients, preparation, and cooking of more than 200 delicious macrobiotic recipes.* Rochester, Vt: Healing Arts Press, distributed in USA by Harper and Row, 1988.
ISBN: 0-8928-1278-8   240 p. illustrated

M24 Ohsawa, Lima. *Macrobiotic cuisine.* Tokyo: Japan Publications, 1984.
ISBN: 0-8704-0600-0   175 p. illustrated
** originally published as *The art of just cooking*, 1974

M25 Tauraso, Nicola M. et al. *The GOTACH Center for Health's good health cookbook: a nutritional approach to wellness.* Frederick, MD: Hidden Valley Press, 1984. ISBN: 0-9357-1006-X
** a vegetarian macrobiotic diet book

M26 Weber, Marcea and Weber, Daniel. *Macrobiotics and beyond: a guide to total living.* Garden City Park, NY: Avery Publishing, 1988.
ISBN: 0-8952-9445-1   205 p.
** seasonal macrobiotic recipes; desserts, breakfast, and beverages; special sections: 1. Chinese system of diagnosis, treatment, food, 2. food action in seasonal recipes, 3. food relationship with organs, 4. energies, flavors, 5. recipe suitability for various diets: milk-free, gluten-free, vegan, candida, Pritikin, and raw; a part of the *Natural and healthy books* series

M27 Wollner, Anneliese. *Macrobiotic dessert book.* Translated by Kushi, Gabriele. Tokyo, Japan: Japan Publications, distributed in USA through Harper and Row, 1988.
ISBN: 0-8704-0700-7   107 p. illustrated, some color
** a dessert cookbook using natural foods; translation of *Makrobiotik-Dessertbuch*

M28 Wu, Sylvia. *Cooking with Madame Wu: yin and yang recipes for health and longevity.* New York: McGraw-Hill, 1984.
ISBN: 0-0707-2110-6   256 p.

** a Chinese macrobiotic cookbook

SELECTED ASSOCIATIONS
AND FOUNDATIONS

George Ohsawa Macrobiotic Foundation
1511 Robinson Street, Oroville, California 95965
916-533-7702

NATURAL INGREDIENTS (N)

NATURAL INGREDIENTS are foods that are fresh, whole, unrefined, unpolished, and grown in soils that have not been chemically treated, are free of additives, preservatives, and pesticide sprays. Canning, freezing, dehydrating, using food additives, and milling are normally regarded as processing, while smoking, drying, salting, roasting, pasteurizing, and fermenting are commonly considered natural. However, each author of a natural-food cookbook may offer varied personal definitions.

Fresh organically grown fruits and vegetables, molasses, whole grains, brown sugar, and fresh herbs are examples of natural foods. Advocates of this type of diet believe that fresh, natural, and whole foods are healthier than ordinary processed foods. They also feel that natural foods are the best safeguard against empty calories which provide little redeeming nutritional values: low vitamins, minerals, and proteins.

Contrary to any above claims, there has been no definitive statement about the nutritional superiority of natural foods over processed foods. The added vitamins and minerals in processed foods may surpass the unprocessed ones which also may not be lower in fat, sugar, cholesterol, sodium, and calories. Following is a selection of contemporary natural-ingredient cookbooks.

IN GENERAL

N1   Atlas, Nava. *The Wholefood catalog: a complete guide
      to natural foods.* New York: Fawcett/Columbine, 1988.
      ISBN: 0-4499-0197-1   212 p. illustrated

N2   Bampfylde, Heather and Bampfylde, Zune. *Gourmet food
      naturally.* New York: Larousse, 1983.
      ISBN: 0-8833-2331-1   176 p. illustrated, some
      color
      ** a cookbook with international cuisine

N3   Bass, Lorena Laforest. *Honey and spice: a nutritional
      guide to natural dessert cookery.* Ashland, OR:
      Coriander Press, 1983. 339 p.
      ISBN: 0-9128-3700-4   339 p. illustrated

N4   Blackman, Jackson F. *Working chef's cookbook for
      natural whole foods: a guide for professional and
      amateur chefs with information, philosophy, techniques,
      recipes to develop their fullest intuition, judgment, and
      potential in the preparation of natural whole foods, as
      recommended by nutritional experts and leading
      professionals of past and present.* Morrisville, VT:
      Central Vermont Publishers, 1989.
      ISBN: 0-9621-7476-9   344 p. illustrated

N5   Blate, Michael. *A Way of eating for pleasure and health.*
      Davie, FL: Falkynor Books, 1983.
      ISBN: 0-9168-7815-5   136 p. illustrated
      ** part of the *G-Jo Institute fabulous foods series* and a

natural-food cookbook

N6   Bounds, Sarah. *Food for health and vitality: wholefoods cookbook.* London: Ward Lock, 1985.
ISBN: 0-7063-6404-X   128 p. illustrated, some color
** recipes for dishes using natural food

N7   Bounds, Sarah. *Thorsons' Green cookbook.* New York: Thorsons, 1990.
ISBN: 0-7225-2423-4   159 p.
** includes health-food recipes using natural ingredients

N8   Bounds, Sarah. *Wholefood baking.* Nevato, CA: Hamlyn, 1984.
ISBN: 0-6003-2412-5   124 p. illustrated, some color
** a baking cookbook with natural ingredients

N9   Bragg, Paul C. and Bragg, Patricia. *Bragg Gourmet health recipes: for life extension and vital, healthy living to 120!* rev. new ed. Santa Barbara, CA: Health Science, 1985.
ISBN: 0-8779-0031-0   402 p. illustrated
** natural-ingredient cuisine; previously published as *Bragg health food cookbook*

N10   Brown, Jo Giese. *The Good food compendium: an indispensable guide to sensible nutrition and eating pleasures for those who care about fine care and wholesome living.* Garden City Park, NY: Dolphin

Books, 1981.
ISBN: 0-3851-3523-8   399 p. illustrated
** preparing natural foods

N11   Burros, Marian Fox. *Pure and simple: delicious recipes
       for additive-free cooking: an elegant and easy cookbook
       with up-to-date advice on avoiding ingredients that
       contain chemicals and preservatives.* New York: Berkley
       Pub. Group, 1982.
       ISBN: 0-4250-5643-0   237 p.
       ** low-salt, high-complex-carbohydrate ethnic recipes
       using natural foods from all four food groups

N12   Carroll, David. *The Complete book of natural foods.*
       New York: Summit Books, 1985.
       ISBN: 0-6714-7517-7   269 p. illustrated

N13   Carroll, Mary Harrison. *The Healthy gourmet cookbook.*
       San Ramon, CA: Chevron Chemical Co., 1989.
       ISBN: 0-8972-1194-4   127 p. illustrated, color
       ** a cookbook from the *California Culinary Academy
       series*, calls for natural ingredients

N14   Cavalier, Victoria P. *America's favorites, naturally.*
       Aberdeen, SD: Melius and Peterson Publishing Corp.,
       1987.
       ISBN: 0-9610-1305-2   163 p. illustrated, some
       color
       ** recipes require natural ingredients from all four food
       groups; includes dried foods and vegetarian dishes

N15   Claessens, Sharon. *Healthy cooking: the best, the healthiest recipes selected from cuisines around the world.* Emmaus, PA.: Rodale Press, 1985.
ISBN: 0-8785-7559-6   168 p. illustrated, color
** contains international recipes with natural foods; part of *Prevention total health system*

N16   East West Journal; editors of. *Shopper's guide to natural foods: a consumer's guide to buying and preparing foods for good health.* Garden City Park, NY: Avery Pub. Group, 1987.
ISBN: 0-8952-9233-5   204 p. illustrated

N17   Findlater, Evelyn. *Evelyn Findlater's Natural foods primer: a beginner's guide to choosing and using wholefoods.* New York: Thorsons, 1985.
ISBN: 0-7225-1162-0   112 p. illustrated

N18   Findlater, Evelyn. *Making your own home proteins: tofu, tempeh, soft cheese, yogurt and sprouted seeds.* London: Century, 1985.
ISBN: 0-7126-0817-6   151 p. illustrated

N19   Findlater, Evelyn. *The Natural entertainer: the healthy way to delicious food.* London: Century, 1987.
ISBN: 0-7126-1619-5   192 p. illustrated

N20   Findlater, Evelyn. *Off the shelf: the healthfood shopper's brandname cookbook.* London: Century, 1986.
ISBN: 0-7126-1496-6   252 p. illustrated, some color

** provides recipes using natural foods

N21   Friday, Sandra K. and Hurwitz, Heidi S. *The Food sleuth handbook.* New York: Atheneum, 1982.
ISBN: 0-6891-1246-7   294 p.
** a natural-food cookbook

N22   Gerras, Charles; editor and the staff of Rodale Press. *Rodale's Basic natural foods cookbook: over 1500 easy-to-follow recipes, from the most basic to the most elaborate, using easy-to-find natural ingredients, plus hundreds of practical cooking tips and techniques.* Emmaus, PA: Rodale, 1984.
ISBN: 0-8785-7469-7   899 p. illustrated
** recipes for all types of dishes listed under types of natural foods; basic information for each food is detailed before the recipes

N23   Hewitt, Jean. *The New York Times New natural foods cookbook.* rev. ed. New York: Avon Books, 1983.
ISBN: 0-3806-2687-X   438 p. illustrated
** recipes require ingredients that are basic, fresh, unrefined, non-highly processed and without additives, synthetic or artificial ingredients; includes foods from all four food groups in all types of dishes; revised edition of *The New York Times natural food cookbook*, 1972

N24   Hunt, Janet. *The Holistic cook.* New York: Thorsons, 1986.
ISBN: 0-7225-1243-0   222 p. illustrated
** all recipes call for natural foods

N25 Kilham, Christopher S. *The Bread and Circus Whole food bible: how to select and prepare safe healthful foods without pesticides or chemical additives.* New York: Addison-Wesley, 1991.
ISBN: 0-2015-1762-0   319 p. illustrated
** in Part 1. Whole Food Bible, encyclopedic information on various types of foods; eco reports; Part 2 contains recipes: appetizers, soup, salad, main entrees, desserts; all recipes prepared without artificial coloring, flavors, or preservatives

N26 Kuntz, Bernie. *Whole foods kitchen journal.* Redmond, WA: Elfin Cove Press, 1989.
ISBN: 0-9449-5836-2   389 p. illustrated
** recipes use natural foods including vegetables, seafoods, grains, beans, fruits, poultry, and meat

N27 Middlestead, Maria. *Cooking naturally: wholefood cuisine with flair and finesse.* London: Hodder and Stoughton, 1984.
ISBN: 0-3403-6394-0   263 p. illustrated

N28 Mosimann, Anton. *Cuisine naturelle: the way to better health, longer life and happiness.* London: Papermac, 1987.
ISBN: 0-3333-7972-1   216 p. illustrated, some color
** a natural-food cookbook

N29 Mother Earth News; editors and staff of. *The Fresh foods country cookbook.* Hendersonville, NC: Mother

Earth News, 1984.
ISBN: 0-9384-3211-7   188 p. illustrated, color

N30   Renwick, Ethel Hulbert. *The Real food cookbook.* New
      Canaan, CT: Keats Pub., 1983.
      ISBN: 0-8798-3346-7   272 p. illustrated
      ** cookery with natural foods

N31   Ridgwell, Jenny and Ridgway, Judy. *Healthy eating.*
      New York: Oxford University Press, 1989.
      ISBN: 0-1983-2757-9   112 p.
      ** all dishes feature natural foods

N32   Scribner, Peggy Rhodes. *Adventures in healthful
      cooking.* Stone Mountain, GA: Dogwood Press, 1985.
      ISBN: 0-9614-9780-7   210 p.
      ** natural-food recipes

N33   Williamson, Darcy. *The All natural brown bagger's
      cookbook.* Bend,OR: Maverick Publications, 1986.
      ISBN: 0-8928-8156-9   127 p.

N34   Williamson, Darcy. *The All natural cookie cookbook.*
      Bend, OR: Maverick Publications, 1983.
      ISBN: 0-8928-8086-4   113 p.

N35   Williamson, Darcy. *The All natural salad cookbook.*
      Bend, OR: Maverick Publications, 1982.
      ISBN: 0-8928-8071-6   100 p.

N36   Williamson, Darcy. *The All natural soup cookbook.*

Bend, OR: Maverick Publications, 1985.
ISBN: 0-8928-8070-8   138 p.
** a vegetarian cookbook

WITH TOFU, TEMPEH, AND
OTHER SOYBEAN PRODUCTS

N37   Andersen, Juel. *Juel Andersen's Tofu kitchen: a complete cookbook for the high-protein low-calorie miracle food.* New York: Bantam, 1981.
ISBN: 0-5532-0424-6   210 p. illustrated
** includes tofu- and soymilk-making and recipes using tofu in salad dressing, sandwiches, tofu burgers, for dinner, desserts, and beverages

N38   Bates, Dorothy R. *The Tempeh Cookbook.* Summertown, TN: Book Publishing Company, 1989.
ISBN: 0-9139-9065-5   96 p. illustrated, color
** main dishes of Oriental, Italian, Mexican, American, and International cuisine; appetizers, salads, soups, sandwiches, and desserts; caloric, protein, carbohydrate, and fat content listed for each recipe

N39   Clarke, Christina. *Cook with tofu: the high-protein, low-cost soyfood everyone is discovering: over 150 delicious nutritious recipes you and your family will love.* New York: Avon, 1981.
ISBN: 0-3807-7941-2   223 p.
** lacto-ovo-vegetarian recipes for dips, appetizers, soups, sandwiches, salads, main entrees, sweets, dressing,

and sauces

N40 Clute, Robin; Andersen, Juel; and Andersen, Sigrid. *Juel Andersen's Tempeh primer: a beginner's book of tempeh cookery.* Berkeley, CA: Creative Arts Communications, 1980.
ISBN: 0-9168-7059-6   57 p.   illustrated
** recipes for salads, sandwiches, soups, main entrees, and oven dishes

N41 Cusumano, Camille. *Tofu, tempeh, and other soy delights: enjoying traditional oriental soyfoods in American-style cuisine.* Emmaus, PA: Rodale, 1984.
ISBN: 0-8785-7489-1   261 p. illustrated
** recipes arranged by types of soy products; for breakfast, luncheon, dinner, quick meal, brunch, festive, and vegetarian dishes

N42 Hagler, Louise. *Tofu cookery.* rev. ed. Summertown, TN: Book Pub. Co., 1990.
ISBN: 0-9139-9076-0
** vegan tofu preparations for dips, salads, dressings, soups, main dishes, and desserts

N43 Jones, Dorothea Van Gundy. *The Soybean cookbook: adventures in zestful eating: over 350 imaginative recipes ranging from salads to desserts.* New York: Arco, 1982.
ISBN: 0-6680-1770-8   240 p.

N44 Leneman, Leah. *Soya foods cookery.* New York: Routledge and Kegan Paul, 1988.

ISBN: 0-7102-1028-0   145 p.
** vegan recipes for soya milk, tofu, tempeh, and miso, from main entrees to desserts including tofu ice cream

N45 Liu, Christine Y. C. *Nutritional cooking with tofu: high protein, low cholesterol, low calorie, and sodium controlled recipes.* Ann Arbor, MI: Graphique Publishing, 1984.
ISBN: 0-9610-5667-3
** make soups, main dishes, vegetarian main dishes, desserts, and tofu; each recipe provides calories and nutritive values (protein, carbohydrate, fat, cholesterol, and sodium)

N46 Moriyama, Yukiko. *A Taste of tofu: mastering the art of tofu cookery.* Tokyo: JOIE, Inc., distributed by JP Trading, Inc., Brisbane, CA, 1988.
ISBN: 4-9152-4946-8   104 p. illustrated, color
** includes quick and easy tofu recipes

N47 O'Brien, Jane. *The Magic of tofu and other soybean products: the best of vegetarian cooking: hints and recipes to make the most of an infinitely versatile wholefood.* New York: Thorsons, 1983.
ISBN: 0-7225-0767-4   128 p. illustrated
** includes how to make tofu at home and tofu vegetarian recipes

N48 Paino, John and Messinger, Lisa. *The Tofu book: the new American cuisine.* Garden City Park, NY: Avery,

1990.
ISBN: 0-8952-9409-5

N49   Shurtleff, William and Aoyagi, Akiko. *The Book of tempeh: the delicious, cholesterol-free protein, 130 recipes*. 2nd ed. New York: Harper and Row, 1985.
ISBN: 0-0609-1265-0   173 p. illustrated
** vegetarian recipes for tempeh, dairy products, and eggs

N50   Shurtleff, William and Aoyagi, Akiko. *The Book of tofu: protein source of the future -- now!* Berkeley, CA: Ten Speed Press, 1983.
ISBN: 0-8981-5095-7   1 v.   illustrated

N51   Watanabe, Tokuji and Kishi, Asako. *The Book of soybeans: nature's miracle protein*. Tokyo: Japan Publications, distributed through Harper and Row, 1984.
ISBN: 0-8704-0513-6   191 p. illustrated

N52   Williamson, Kerri Bennett. *The Taming of tofu*. Boise, ID: Pacific Press, 1991.
ISBN: 0-8163-1027-0

SELECTED ASSOCIATIONS
AND FOUNDATIONS

Association of Women in Natural Foods
10159 Brooke Avenue, Chatsworth, California 91311
818-718-6230

Natural Food Associates
P.O. Box 210, Atlanta, Texas 75551
214-796-3612

VEGETARIAN DIET (V)

VEGETARIANISM has attracted an increasing number of people based on a variety of reasons: humantiarian, philosophical, religious, or ecological concerns. A variety of dietary practices are embraced in vegetarianism. First, vegan vegetarians consume only fruits, vegetables, nuts, grains, and legumes, and abstain from all forms of animal foods. Second, lacto-vegetarians have dairy products as well as fruits, vegetables, nuts, grains, and legumes. Third, lacto-ovo-vegetarians eat eggs, dairy products, fruits, vegetables, nuts, grains, and legumes. And last, no-red-meat vegetarians or semivegetarians, the least restricted, consume all foods (such as poultry and fish) except red meats.

In all four types of vegetarian diets, the main and common ingredients are fruits, vegetables, nuts, grains, and legumes. The American Dietetic Association now recognizes that well-planned vegetarian diets can be consistent with good nutritional intake. When plant proteins from a variety of sources are consumed, supplementation occurs and results in a mixture of all essential amino acids in proportions similar to those found in proteins of animal origin. Further, the core of a vegetarian diet consists of high-fiber and high-complex-carbohydrate foods that tend to be low in calories, cholesterol, saturated fat, and sodium, and high in vitamins and some minerals.

Vegetarian diets can fit today's basic dietary guidelines for thwarting cancer, heart attacks, and obesity, and these diets can maintain good general health. This is the key rationale for inclusion of vegetarian cookbooks in this health-related cookbook bibliography. Distinction among four types of vegetarian diets thus becomes less important than the benefits of their collective core. Following is a selection of contemporary vegetarian cookbooks.

IN GENERAL

V1   Baker, Jenny. *Vegetarian student.* London: Faber and Faber, 1986.
ISBN: 0-5711-4525-6   160 p.

V2   Callan, Ginny. *Horn of the Moon cookbook.* New York: Perennial Library, 1987.
ISBN: 0-0609-6038-8   304 p. illustrated
** vegetarian recipes from the Horn of the Moon Cafe, Montpelier, Vermont.

V3   Carper, Jean. *The Food pharmacy guide to good eating: with more than 200 totally healthy recipes.* New York: Bantam, 1991.
ISBN: 0-5530-7285-4   422 p.
** includes the relationship of health and nutrition and vegetarian diet

V4   Chelf, Vicki Rae. *Cooking with the right side of the brain.* Garden City Park, NY: Avery Pub., 1991.

ISBN: 0-8952-9431-1   283 p. illustrated, some color

V5   Cohlmeyer, David. *The Vegetarian chef.* Santa Barbara, CA: Woodbridge Press, 1986.
ISBN: 0-1954-0487-4   179 p.
** seasonal ethnic recipes using vegetables, fruits, eggs, and dairy products

V6   Colbin, Annemarie. *The Book of whole meals: a seasonal guide to assembling balanced vegetarian breakfasts, lunches, and dinners.* New York: Ballantine Books, 1983.
ISBN: 0-3453-0982-0   231 p. illustrated

V7   Conil, Christopher and Conil, Jean. *The All-colour vegetarian recipe book.* London: Foulsham, 1986.
ISBN: 0-5720-1403-1   128 p.

V8   Cox, Michael. *The Subversive vegetarian: tactics, information, and recipes for the conversion of meat eaters.* Santa Barbara, CA: Woodbridge Press Co., 1980.
ISBN: 0-9128-0083-6   128 p. illustrated

V9   Echols, Barbara E. *Barron's Meatless meals: a hearty collection of naturally good recipes.* Woodbury, NY: Barron's, 1983.
ISBN: 0-8120-2163-0   320 p. illustrated, color
** recipes from bread and rice to desserts using bean sprouts and soybean products, eggs, and cheese; revised edition of *Vegetarian delights*, 1981

V10   Elliot, Rose. *The Complete vegetarian cuisine.* New
      York: Pantheon Books, 1988.
      ISBN: 0-3945-7123-1   352 p. illustrated, color
      ** originally published in U.K. as *Rose Elliot's
      vegetarian cookery.*

V11   Gentle World. *The Cookbook for people who love
      animals.* 4th ed. Umatilla, FL: Gentle World, 1987.
      ISBN: 0-9614-2480-X   192 p.
      ** 300 recipes from beginner to gourmet, no meat, no
      eggs, no dairy, no sugar or honey, and no cholesterol

V12   Goldbeck, Nikki and Goldbeck, David. *Nikki and David
      Goldbeck's American Wholefoods cuisine: 1300 delicious
      vegetarian recipes from snacks to gourmet.* New York:
      New American Library, 1987.
      ISBN: 0-7225-1405-0   583 p. illustrated

V13   Hartbarger, Janie Coulter and Hartbarger, Neil J. *Eating
      for the eighties: a complete guide to vegetarian nutrition.*
      New York: Berkley, 1983.
      ISBN: 0-4250-5827-1   331 p.

V14   Hazen, Janet. *Glories of the vegetarian table: a
      collection of contemporary vegetarian recipes and menus.*
      New York: Addison-Wesley, 1988.
      ISBN: 0-2011-2631-1   143 p.
      ** lacto-ovo-vegetarian recipes

V15   Jordan, Julie. *The Cabbagetown Cafe cookbook.*
      Trumansburg, NY: Crossing Press, 1986.

ISBN: 0-8959-4193-7   237 p. illustrated
** vegetarian recipes from Cabbagetown Cafe, Ithaca,
New York

V16   Kendig, Joan and Kendig, Keith. *Modern vegetable
protein cookery.* New York: Arco, 1980.
ISBN: 0-6680-4617-1   339 p. illustrated
** use rice and legumes to obtain complete plant
protein; includes lacto-ovo-vegetarian recipes

V17   Lappe, Frances Moore. *Diet for a small planet.* rev. and
updated. New York: Ballantine Books, 1983.
ISBN: 0-3452-9524-2   496 p. illustrated
** a vegetarian cookbook including ethnic cuisines using
dairy products and eggs

V18   Lemlin, Jeanne. *Vegetarian pleasures: a menu cookbook.*
New York: Alfred A. Knopf, distributed by Random
House, 1986.
ISBN: 0-3947-4302-4   301 p. illustrated
** recipes including the use of eggs and cheese
arranged as quick, informal, elegant, summer, and
breakfast and brunch menus

V19   Madison, Deborah. *The Greens cook book: extraordinary
vegetarian cuisine from the celebrated restaurant.*
Toronto, ON: Bantam Books, 1987.
ISBN: 0-5530-5195-4   396 p.
** from Greens Restaurant in Fort Mason, California.

V20   Nesbitt, Hilda. *Vegetarian recipes for good health and*

long life. Portland, OR: Nesbitt Enterprises, 1980.
ISBN: 0-6863-4439-1

V21   Null, Gary and Null, Shelly. *Vegetarian cooking for good health*. New York: Macmillan, 1991.
ISBN: 0-0201-0050-7

V22   Nutrition Education Collective. *Through the seasons: vegetarian cookery and nutrition*. North Amherst, MA: The Nutrition Education Collective, 1981.
ISBN: 0-9605-4501-8   2 v.   illustrated

V23   Pickle, Julianne. *100% vegetarian: eating naturally from your grocery store*. Seale, AL: Pickle Pub. Co., 1990.
ISBN: 0-9627-6450-7   120 p.

V24   Robertson, Laurel; Flinders, Carol; and Ruppenthal, Brian. *The New Laurel's kitchen: a handbook for vegetarian cookery and nutrition*. Berkeley, CA: Ten Speed Press, 1986.
ISBN: 0-8981-5166-X   511 p. illustrated, some color
**   vegetarian recipes with eggs and cheese

V25   Rose, Joel. *The Vegetarian connection*. New York: Facts on File Publications, 1985.
ISBN: 0-8160-1200-8   182 p. illustrated

V26   Satchidananda, Swami. *The Healthy vegetarian*. Yogaville, VA: Integral Yoga Publications, 1986.
ISBN: 0-9320-4032-2   115 p.

V27   Scott, David. *Protein-balanced vegetarian cookery.*
       Sebastopol, CA: CRCS Publications, 1987.
       ISBN: 0-9163-6039-3   174 p. illustrated

V28   Shandler, Nina. *How to make all the "meat" you eat
       from wheat: international gluten wheat "meat" cookbook.*
       New York: Rawson, Wade Publishers, 1980.
       ISBN: 0-8925-6131-9   241 p.

V29   Sharlin, Judith. *The Romantic vegetarian: a seasonal
       cookbook.* Chicago: Chicago Review Press, 1983.
       ISBN: 0-9140-9152-2   204 p. illustrated

V30   Spencer, Colin and Sanders, Tom. *The Vegetarian
       kitchen: a natural program for health and nutrition.*
       Tucson, AZ: Body Press, 1986.
       ISBN: 0-8958-6467-3   128 p. illustrated, color

V31   Tadej, Lorine. *Strict vegetarian cookbook.* Harrisville,
       NH: MMI Press, 1984.
       ISBN: 0-9121-4502-1   160 p.

V32   Thorpe, Susan. *The Four seasons vegetarian cookbook:
       nutritionally balanced recipes making the best use of
       seasonally available food.* New York: Thorsons, 1986.
       ISBN: 0-7225-1270-8   223 p. illustrated, some
       color

V33   Thrash, Agatha M. *Eat for strength: a vegetarian
       cookbook.* rev. ed. Seale, AL: Thrash Publications,
       1983.

222 p. illustrated

V34 Tracy, Lisa. *The Gradual vegetarian: for everyone finally ready to make the change.* New York: M. Evans, 1985.
ISBN: 07126-10561 300 p.

V35 Westcott, Alison. *Introducing vegetarian cookery.* Bath, Avon: Ashgrove, 1991.
ISBN: 1-8539-8025-0   184 p. illustrated
** originally published as *Basic vegetarian cookery*

FAST AND SIMPLE CUISINE

V36 Brown, Pamela. *Vegetarian cooker-top cookery: quick and easy meat-free meals.* rev. and reset. New York: Thorsons, published in co-operation with the Vegetarian Society of the United Kingdom, Ltd., 1985.
ISBN: 0-7225-1129-9   128 p. illustrated
** vegetarian recipes without using an oven

V37 Findlater, Evelyn. *Thorsons' vegetarian food processor: quick and easy recipes to make the most of your machines.* New York: Thorsons, 1987.
ISBN: 0-7225-1555-3   128 p. illustrated, some color

V38 Haynes, Linda. *The Vegetarian lunchbasket: 225 easy, nutritious recipes for the quality-conscious family on the go.* Willow Springs, MO: NUCLEUS Publications, 1990.

ISBN: 0-9459-3402-5   200 p. illustrated

V39   Mitchell, Paulette. *The 15 minute vegetarian gourmet.*
New York: Macmillan, 1987.
ISBN: 0-0258-5430-5   150 p. illustrated, some
color

V40   Praver, Asha and Gilchrist, Sheila; editors. *The Ananda
cookbook: easy-to-prepare recipes for the vegetarian
gourmet.* Nevada City, CA: Ananda Publications, 1985.
ISBN: 0-9161-2426-6   249 p. illustrated

V41   Shulman, Martha Rose. *Fast vegetarian feasts.* New
York: Doubleday, 1986.
ISBN: 0-3852-3330-2   356 p.
** recipes include the use of eggs, dairy products, and
fish

V42   Time-Life Books; editors of. *Meatless menus: great
meals in minutes.* Alexandria, VA: Time-Life Books,
1986.
ISBN: 0-8670-6301-7   105 p. illustrated, some
color
** ethnic recipes with eggs and cheese

V43   Wasserman, Debra and Stahler, Charles. *Meatless meals
for working people: quick and easy vegetarian recipes.*
Baltimore, MD: Vegetarian Resource Group, 1990.
ISBN: 0-9314-1106-8   96 p. illustrated
** features soy dishes, chinese cuisine, breakfast, main
dishes, and desserts

FESTIVE CUISINE

V44   Atlas, Nava. *Vegetarian celebrations: menus for holidays and other festive occasions.* Boston: Little, Brown, 1990.
ISBN: 0-3160-5744-4   276 p. illustrated
** ethnic recipes with eggs, dairy products, vegetables, and fruits

V45   Caviness, Cheryl Thomas. *Fabulous food for family and friends: healthy menus for entertaining with style.*
Hagerstown, MD: Review and Herald Pub. Association, 1990.
ISBN: 0-8280-0567-2   128 p. illustrated, color

V46   Lewis, Leon. *Vegetarian dinner parties.* New York: Thorsons, 1984.
ISBN: 0-7225-0766-6   192 p. illustrated

V47   Mangum, Karen. *Life's simple pleasures: fine vegetarian cooking for sharing and celebration.* Boise, ID: Pacific Press Pub. Association, 1990.
ISBN: 0-8163-0927-2   160 p. illustrated, color

V48   Mitchell, Paulette. *The New American vegetarian menu cookbook: from everyday dining to elegant entertaining.*
Emmaus, PA: Rodale Press, 1984.
ISBN: 0-8785-7494-8   214 p.

V49   Shaw, Diana. *Vegetarian entertaining.* New York: Harmony Books, 1991.

ISBN: 0-5175-7475-6

V50   Shulman, Martha Rose. *Gourmet vegetarian feasts.*
Rochester, VT: Healing Arts Press, 1990.
ISBN: 0-8928-1389-X
** vegetarian recipes using garlic, herbs, and honey

V51   Spencer, Colin. *Cordon Vert: 52 vegetarian gourmet
dinner party menus.* Chicago: Contemporary, 1985.
ISBN: 0-8092-4728-3   208 p. illustrated
** cookery arranged by seasons including the use of
cheese and eggs; menu complete with wine and liqueurs

FROM AROUND THE WORLD

V52   Hunt, Janet. *The Compassionate gourmet: the very best
of international vegan cuisine.* New York: Thorsons,
1986.
ISBN: 0-7225-1155-8   159 p. illustrated

V53   Moosewood Collective. *Sundays at Moosewood
Restaurant: ethnic and regional recipes from the cooks at
the legendary restaurant.* New York: Simon and
Schuster, 1990.
ISBN: 0-6716-7990-2   733 p. illustrated, color
** ethnic cuisine arranged by geographic locations or
countries; with menu planning

V54   Sacharoff, Shanta Nimbark. *The Ethnic vegetarian
kitchen: recipes with guidelines for nutrition.* San

Francisco, CA: 101 Productions, 1984.
ISBN: 0-8928-6227-0   190 p. illustrated
** includes the use of eggs and cheese

V55   Shulman, Martha Rose. *The Spice of vegetarian cooking: ethnic recipes from India, China, Mexico, Southeast Asia, the Middle East, and Europe: spicy vegetarian feasts.* Rochester, VT: Healing Arts Press, 1990.

V56   Skaarup, Kirsten. *The International vegetarian cookbook.* Translated by Bodii Wilson from *Vegtarisk Kokken.* Pownal, VT: Garden Way Pub., 1984.
ISBN: 0-8826-6362-3   184 p. illustrated

V57   Vegetarian Times, editors of; and Leavy, Herbert T. *The Vegetarian Times cookbook: 400 recipes that explore the best in vegetarian cuisine - ethnic specialties, wholesome desserts, and quick, balanced meals.* New York: Macmillan, 1984.
ISBN: 0-0262-1740-6   318 p.
** vegetarian variations; with eggs and dairy products; also includes holiday menu

FROM AMERICA, NORTH AND SOUTH

V58   Atlas, Nava. *American harvest: regional recipes for the vegetarian kitchen.* New York: Ballantine Books, 1987.
ISBN: 0-4499-0218-8   191 p. illustrated
** recipes for muffins, breads, soups, eggs, vegetables, rice, corn, beans, desserts, and southwestern tortilla

specialties; also includes regional menus for four seasons

V59   Diamond, Marilyn. *The American vegetarian cookbook from the fit for life kitchen.* New York: Warner, 1990.
ISBN: 0-4465-1561-2   422 p. illustrated
** vegan cookery with whole grains and no refined foods, from soups and desserts to main entrees

V60   Metcalfe de Plata, Edith. *Mexican vegetarian cooking: exotic and spicy recipes using wholefood ingredients.* New York: Thorsons, 1989.
ISBN: 0-8928-1341-5

FROM ASIA

V61   A. C. Bhaktivedanta Swami Prabhupada. *The Higher taste: a guide to gourmet vegetarian cooking and a karma-free diet.* Los Angeles: The Bhaktivedanta Book Trust, 1983.
ISBN: 0-8921-3128-4   161 p. illustrated

V62   Chapman, Pat. *Curry club vegetarian cookbook.* London: Piatkus, 1990.
ISBN: 0-8618-8965-7   190 p.

V63   Chuang, Lily. *Chinese vegetarian delights: sugar- and dairy-free cookbook.* Los Angeles, CA: Shrine of the Eternal Breath of Tao, College of Tao and Traditional Chinese Healing, 1987.
ISBN: 0-9370-6413-0   107 p. illustrated

V64   Dalal, Tarla. *Indian vegetarian cookbook.* New York: St. Martin's Press, 1985.
ISBN: 0-3124-1403-X

V65   Devi, Yamuna. *The Art of Indian vegetarian cooking: Lord Krishna's cuisine, more than 500 recipes with illustrations from India's great culinary tradition.* New York: Bala, 1987.
ISBN: 0-5252-4564-2   799 p. illustrated

V66   Downer, Lesley. *Japanese vegetarian cooking.* New York: Pantheon, 1986.
ISBN: 0-3947-5006-3   374 p. illustrated
** meals from vegetables, beans, soybean products, eggs, and grains

V67   Duff, Gail. *Oriental vegetarian cooking.* Rochester, VT: Healing Arts Press, distributed in USA by Harper and Row, 1989.
ISBN: 0-8928-1344-X   208 p. illustrated

V68   Fessler, Stella Lau. *Chinese meatless cooking: more than 180 recipes, a complete guide to mastering one of the world's most tempting and healthful cuisines.* revised and updated. New York: New American Library, 1983.
ISBN: 0-4522-5229-6   298 p. illustrated
** recipes from salads to sweets using soybean products, eggs, vegetables, rice and other Chinese ingredients; includes basics of Chinese cooking and how to plan a Chinese vegetarian meal; menus included

V69   Gee, Margaret and Goldin, Graeme. *The Longevity Chinese vegetarian cookbook: outstanding Pritikin-style recipes -- no added fat, salt, oil, sugar, or MSG.* rev. ed. New York: Thorsons, 1987.
ISBN: 0-7225-1459-X   128 p. illustrated, some color

V70   Hom, Ken. *Asian vegetarian feast: tempting vegetable and pasta recipes from the east.* New York: William Morrow and Co., Inc., 1988.
ISBN: 0-6880-7753-6   222 p.
** Chinese, Japanese, and Southeast Asian cooking with eggs, vegetables, grains, and fruits from appetizers to desserts, without using MSG

V71   Jaffrey, Madhur. *Eastern vegetarian cooking.* London: J. Cape, 1983.
ISBN: 0-2240-2955-X   531 p. illustrated

V72   Lo, Kenneth. *New Chinese vegetarian cooking.* New York: Pantheon, 1986.
ISBN: 0-3947-5005-5   211 p. illustrated
** cuisine with soybeans, eggs, vegetables, rice, soup, noodles, steamed buns, dumplings, pancakes, sweet rice gruels, and sweet soups

V73   Pandya, Michael. *Indian vegetarian cooking.* New York: Thorsons, distributed by Inner Traditions International, 1985.
ISBN: 0-7225-0950-2   208 p. illustrated

V74   Sahni, Julie. *Classic Indian vegetarian and grain cooking*. New York: Morrow, 1985.
ISBN: 0-6880-4995-8   511 p. illustrated

V75   Singh, Manju Shivraj. *The Spice Box: vegetarian Indian cookbook*. Trumansburg, NY: Crossing Press, 1981.
ISBN: 0-8959-4053-1   221 p.
** vegetarian recipes using eggs and cheese

V76   Stidham, Martin. *The Fragrant vegetable: simple vegetarian delicacies from the Chinese*. Los Angeles: J.P. Tarcher, 1986.
ISBN: 0-8747-7378-4   224 p. illustrated
** a vegetable and tofu cookbook

V77   Vatcharin Bhumichitr. *Thai vegetarian cooking*. New York: C.N. Potter, 1991.
ISBN: 0-5175-8167-1

FROM EUROPE

V78   Antreassian, Alice. *The 40 days of Lent: selected Armenian recipes*. New York: Ashod Press, 1985.
ISBN: 0-9351-0216-7   130 p. illustrated
** includes Armenian vegetarian recipes

V79   Antreassian, Alice and Jebejian, Mariam. *Classic Armenian recipes: cooking without meat*. 2nd ed. New York: Ashod Press, 1983.
ISBN: 0-9351-0211-6   308 p. illustrated

V80   Canter, David; Canter, Kay; and Swann, Daphne. *The Cranks recipe book: traditional vegetarian cooking: recipes from Europe's famous Cranks restaurants.* Rochester, VT: Healing Arts Press, 1991.
ISBN: 0-8928-1425-X   204 p. illustrated, some color
** recipes from Cranks Restaurant use 100% whole-grain flour, raw sugar, free-range eggs, fresh fruit and dairy produce for all types of dishes from soups to desserts; originally published as *Cranks recipe book*, 1982

V81   Chaitow, Alkmini. *Greek vegetarian cooking: colourful dishes from the eastern shores of the Mediterranean.* rev. ed. New York: Thorsons, 1991.
ISBN: 0-7225-2496-X   160 p.

V82   Gavin, Paola. *Italian vegetarian cooking.* New York: M. Evans, 1990.
ISBN: 0-8713-1575-0   285 p.
** includes eggs and dairy products

V83   Marcangelo, Jo. *Italian vegetarian cooking: a wealth of traditional Italian dishes using all the goodness of natural whole food ingredients.* Rochester, VT: Healing Arts Press, 1989.
ISBN: 0-8928-1343-1

V84   Santa Maria, Jack. *Greek vegetarian cookery.* Boston: Shambhala, distributed by Random House, 1985.
ISBN: 0-8777-3332-5   160 p. illustrated

V85   Scaravelli, Paola and Cohen, Jon. *Cooking from an Italian garden: over 300 classic meatless recipes, from antipasti to desserts*. New York: Holt, Rinehart, and Winston, 1985.
ISBN: 0-1562-2592-1   354 p.
** a vegetarian cookbook using cheese and eggs

V86   Spencer, Colin. *Mediterranean vegetarian cooking*. New York: Thorsons, distributed by Inner Traditions International, 1986.
ISBN: 0-7225-0979-0   256 p. illustrated

FROM THE MIDDLE EAST

V87   Friedman, Rose. *Jewish vegetarian cooking: the finest traditional recipes made exciting and original by the use of healthy, natural ingredients*. New York: Thorsons, distributed by the Inner Traditions International, 1985.
ISBN: 0-7225-0910-3   128 p. illustrated
** the official cookbook of the International Jewish Vegetarian Society; appetizer, main dish, salad, dessert, and Passover recipes

V88   Karaoglan, Aida. *Food for the vegetarian: traditional Lebanese recipes*. New York: Interlink Books, 1988.
ISBN: 0-9407-9315-6   167 p. illustrated

WITH MICROWAVE OVEN

V89   Baird, Pat. *Quick harvest: a vegetarian's guide to microwave cooking.* New York: Prentice Hall Press, 1991.
ISBN: 0-1394-5718-6   272 p.

V90   Kafka, Barbara. *The Microwave gourmet healthstyle cookbook.* New York: Barrie and Jenkins, 1990.
ISBN: 0-7126-3928-4   512 p.
** natural-food cookery

V91   Paun, Aruna. *Microwave goes vegetarian: a complete practical guide to vegetarian cooking.* Mississauga, ON: A. Paun, 1990.
ISBN: 0-9695-1300-3   302 p. illustrated

WITH NATURAL INGREDIENTS

V92   Arentzen, Shelly; Mills, Georgina; and Malin, Sue. *Nature's pantry cookbook.* Bellevue, WA: Nature's Pantry, 1990.
131 p.
** vegetarian meals using natural foods

V93   Brown, Edward Espe. *The Tassajara cooking.* Boston: Shambhala, 1986.
ISBN: 0-8777-3344-9   255 p. illustrated
** a lacto-ovo-vegetarian cookbook; recipes use organic, natural, unrefined, unprocessed, and unadulterated fruits, vegetables, eggs, cheeses, flours, nuts, legumes, and fish, among others

V94 Brown, Judy. *Judy Brown's Guide to natural foods cooking.* Summertown, TN: Book Publishing Co., 1989. ISBN: 0-9139-9062-0   159 p. illustrated, color ** includes some macrobiotic diet recipes; natural cooking without eggs, meats, or dairy products

V95 Colbin, Annemarie. *The Natural gourmet: delicious recipes for healthy, balanced eating.* New York: Ballantine Books, 1989. ISBN: 0-3453-2771-3   322 p. illustrated ** vegetarian cuisine using natural ingredients including whole grains, beans, vegetables, and fish; foods grouped into Chinese phases: wood, fire, earth, metal, and water; five-phase theory cooking makes sure all phases are represented in meals

V96 Dalsass, Diana. *Cashews and lentils, apples and oats: from the basics to the fine points of natural foods cooking with 233 superlative recipes.* Chicago: Contemporary Books, 1981. ISBN: 0-8092-5934-6   301 p. illustrated ** a lacto-ovo-vegetarian cookbook

V97 Dribin, Lois and Ivankovich, Susan. *The Not-strictly vegetarian cookbook.* Tucson, AZ: Fisher Books, 1982. ISBN: 0-1556-1029-3   242 p. illustrated ** vegetarian dishes using natural foods including seafood and chicken

V98 Estella, Mary. *Natural foods cookbook: vegetarian dairy-free cuisine.* Tokyo: Japan Publications, distributed

through Harper and Row, USA, 1985.
ISBN: 0-8704-0583-7   250 p. illustrated, some
color

V99   Meyer, Barbara Friedlander. *Earth water fire air: a
       vegetarian cookbook for the 90s.* New York: Allied
       Books, 1990.
       ISBN: 0-8022-2578-0   192 p. illustrated
       ** low-fat, high-fiber, ethnic, and all-Kosher recipes
using natural ingredients that are free of sugar, additives,
or preservatives

V100   Moosewood Collective. *New recipes from Moosewood
       Restaurant.* Berkeley, CA: Ten Speed Press, 1987.
       ISBN: 0-8981-5208-9   302 p. illustrated, color
       ** natural-ingredient vegetarian cookery for appetizers,
main dishes, desserts, and condiments

V101   Nearing, Helen. *Simple food for the good life: an
       alternative cookbook: with a collection of easy recipes
       that have evolved from necessity or available garden
       produce intended for the use of people of moderate
       fortune who do not affect magnificence in their style of
       living.* Walpole, NH: Stillpoint Publishing, 1985.
       ISBN: 0-9132-9924-3   309 p.
       ** a strict vegetarian (vegan) cookbook using natural
ingredients

V102   Null, Gary. *The Vegetarian handbook: eating right for
       total health.* New York: St. Martin's Press, 1987.
       ISBN: 0-3120-1107-5   266 p.

V103 Pickarski, Ron. *Friendly foods: gourmet vegetarian cuisine.* Berkeley, CA: Ten Speed Press, 1991.
ISBN: 0-8981-5377-8   277 p.

V104 Quigley, Delia and Pitchford, Polly. *Starting over: learning to cook with natural foods.* Summertown, TN: Book Publishing Co., 1988.
ISBN: 0-9139-9055-8   143 p. illustrated, color
** vegetarian recipes calling for natural foods, including eggs and cheese

V105 Watson, Gail C. *Cooking naturally for pleasure and health.* Davie, FL: Falkynor Books, 1982.
ISBN: 0-9168-7816-3   242 p. illustrated
** vegetarian meals of natural foods

V106 Williamson, Darcy. *The All natural international vegetarian entree cookbook.* Bend, OR: Maverick Publications, 1987.
ISBN: 0-8928-8155-0   133 p.

YOGA VEGETARIAN DIET

V107 Ballentine, Martha; compiler. *Himalayan Mountain cookery: a vegetarian cookbook.* Honesdale, PA: Himalayan International Institute of Yoga Science and Philosophy of the U.S.A., 1985.
ISBN: 0-8938-9015-4   203 p. illustrated
** an Indic Yoga cookbook

V108 Buxbaum, Larry. *The Yoga food book: a guide to vegetarian eating and cooking.* St. Louis, MO: Universal Great Brotherhood, 1974.
115 p. illustrated

V109 Himalayan International Institute of Yoga Science and Philosophy. *Yoga way cookbook: natural vegetarian recipes.* 4th ed. Honesdale, PA: Himalayan International Institute of Yoga Science and Philosophy (Honesdale, PA 18431), 1980.
ISBN: 0-8938-9067-7   249 p. illustrated
** lacto-ovo-vegetarian Yoga cookbook utilizing natural food ingredients

V110 Hittleman, Richard L. *Yoga for health.* New York: Ballantine Books, 1983.
ISBN: 0-3453-2798-5   209 p. illustrated
** vegetarian recipes

V111 Kripalu Yoga Ashram. *Food for the soul: a guide to Yogic cooking.* Sumneytown, PA: Kripalu Yoga Ashram, 1976.
82 p.   illustrated
** a vegetarian cookbook

ZEN VEGETARIAN DIET

V112 Abehsera, Michel. *Zen macrobiotic cooking: book of Oriental and traditional recipes.* New York: Citadel Press, 1971.

ISBN: 0-8065-0254-1   205 p.

V113   Nishimoto, Miyoko. *The Now and Zen epicure: gourmet cuisine for the enlightened palate*. Summertown, TN: Book Pub. Co., 1991.
ISBN: 0-9139-9078-7
** Japanese cuisine

V114   Yoneda, Soei; Hoshino, Koei; and Schuefftan, Kim. *The Heart of Zen cuisine*. New York: Ballantine Books, 1989.
ISBN: 0-3453-5988-7   280 p. illustrated
** Japanese vegetarian meals

SELECTED ASSOCIATIONS AND FOUNDATIONS

American Vegan Society
P.O. Box H, Malaga, New Jersey 08328
609-694-2887

International Vegetarian Union
10 Kings Drive, Marple, Stockport, Cheshire SK6 6NQ, England

Jewish Vegetarian Society - America
P.O. Box 5722, Baltimore, Maryland 21208-0722
301-486-4948

North American Vegetarian Society
P.O. Box 72, Dolgeville, New York 13329
518-568-7970

AUTHOR INDEX

Fisher, Hans C53
Fisher, Helen V. C88
Fishman, Joan CA1
Fitzgerald, Geraldine MS16
Fitzgerald, Peter H14
FitzGibbon, Theodora D18
Flack, Dora D. CA40
Flaste, Richard W81
Fleetwood, Jenni CA32
Fletcher, Anne M. C17
Fletcher, Janet Kessel CA75
Flinders, Carol V24
Flynn-Esquivel, Sheila L25
Fobel, Jim W80
Foreyt, John P. C124
Forsythe, Elizabeth CA33
Fowler, Rosalind D14
Fox, Arnold C20
France, Richard CA15
Franey, Pierre C129, W81
Franz, Marion C181, D19
Fraser, Margaret CA34
Frazier, Claude Albee F11
Fredal, Judy MS20
Fredericks, Carlton
    CA35, D20, MS6
Freifeld, Karen L21
Friday, Sandra K. N21
Friedlander, Barbara L68
Friedman, Rose V87
Friesen, Joyce F53

Fromer, Jacki L41

-G -

Gallagher, Kathy W170
Galland, Leo H15
Gan, Sheila L66
Garden Way Publishing C35
Gaskin, Kathy CA69
Gates, Ronda W9
Gaunt, LaRene W132
Gavin, Paola V82
Gazella, Jacqueline G. L6
Gee, Margaret V69
Gelles, Carol CA76
Gentle World V11
George Ohsawa Macrobiotic
    Foundation M1, M2, M4,
    M11-M13
George, Phyllis W10
Germann, Judy Dvorak D12
Gernhofer, Niki L. C45, C46
Gerras, Charles N22
Gerstenzang, Sharon M.
    Dregne D103
Gibbons, Barbara W40,
    W116, W171
Gibson, Robin F69
Gibson, Sheila F69
Gilchrist, Sheila V40

- K -

Kafka, Barbara C126, V90
Kagemori, Teruha M14
Kahn, Ada P. D26
Kaiser Permanente Medical
   Ctr., Cleveland, OH W40
Kallison, Jeri C200
Kamen, Betty L8
Kamen, Si L8
Kane, Tyra C. R8
Kaplan, Dorothy J. D27
Karaoglan, Aida V88
Karmel, Annabel L27
Katahn, Martin W65, W86
Katahn, Terri W86
Kaufman, William I. W121
Kaufmann, Doug A. F19
Keenan, Emma W. C6, R13
Kenda, Margaret E. L39
Kendig, Joan V16
Kendig, Keith V16
Kent, Amnon H45
Kenyon, Judy L35
Kerr, Mimi H. L48
Kidder, Beth F90
Kidder, Lew CA69
Kidney Foundation of Iowa
   R9, R10

Kidushim-Allen, Deborah
   C117, W161
Kilham, Christopher S. N25
Kimmel, David L28
Kimmel, Martha L28
Kindel, Beverly C11
King, Elizabeth A. W1, W2
King, Joy D. CA2
King, Mary Ellen C61
Kirkpatrick, Joy C138, C193
Kirsta, Alix H22
Kishi, Asako N51
Kisslinger, Juanita F56
Klaper, Michael L22
Klein, Diane L9
Klein, Erica Levy H46
Klinger, Judith L. L73
Knight, Gerri C93
Knight, Karin L29
Koblin, Seymour A. M15
Koch, Lee M13
Koh, Frances M. CA51
Kokoska, Vera D28
Kowalski, Robert E. C62,
   C80, W70
Kraus, Barbara C63
Krawitt, Laura P. R21
Kreitzman, Sue W137, W156
Krimmel, Edward A.
   C64, D66

313

Morningstar, Amadea H37
Morris, Edwin Lee C19
Morrissey, Kevin W151
Morse, Barbara H27
Moses, Antoinette W18
Mosimann, Anton N28
Mother Earth News N29
Mount Sinai Hospital,
    Minneapolis, MN D48
Mozzer, Patricia D117
Murkoff, Heidi E. L4
Murray, Frank CA26
Myers, Jill D55
Myerson, Bess W91

- N -

Nash, Bruce W34
National Kidney Foundation
    of Illinois R18
National Kidney Foundation
    of Massachusetts R14
Nearing, Helen V101
Nelson, Ralph A. R25
Nesbitt, Hilda V20
Ness, Joanne MS23
New Hampshire Dental
    Society OR3
New York University Medical
    Center L73

Newport, Cristine C128
Nicholson, Susan C13
Nidetch, Jean W19-W21
Niedermayer, Flo W92
Nilson, Bee H31
Nishimoto, Miyoko V113
Niven, Penelope OR9, OR10
Noh, Chin-Hwa W141
Nonken, Pamela P. F80
Nori, Angela F84
Norris, Rosalie N. OR11
Norwak, Mary CA66
Norwich Inn and Spa W111
Null, Gary F22, F23,
    V21, V102
Null, Shelly V21
Nussbaum, Elaine CA18
Nutrition and Dental Health
    Consortium OR4
Nutrition Education
    Collective V22

- O -

O'Brien, Jane N47
Ochsner Medical Inst. C125
Oexmann, Mary Jean D37
Ohsawa, Lima M24
Ojakangas, Beatrice CA62
Oliver, Margo L77
Olivo, Rey C14

One Thousand and Six
Summit Avenue Society
CA63
Ontario Dietetic Assoc. D10
Oppenheimer, Frances C.
C45, C46
Oregon Health Sciences
University C194
Orenstein, Neil S. C47
Orleans, Valerie L25
Ornish, Dean C7
O'Rorke, Maureen MS15
Orr, Suezanne T. CA53
Orton, Ellen CA81
Orton, Vrest CA81
Oxford Dietetic Group D70
Oxley, Veronica D86

- P -

Paananen, Donna L15
Paine, Harriett W177
Paino, John N48
Palumbo, P. J. D31, D38
Pandya, Michael V73
Paone, Marion W75
Parent, Edward A. W144
Paris-Turner, Becky L32
Park Nicollet Medical
Foundation D39
Parker, Valerie W142

Parsley, Terry Martin C157
Parsonage, Sally CA82
Patten, Marguerite W122
Patton, Tim W168
Paul, Aileen W36
Paun, Aruna V91
Pay, Joanna L49
Payne, Alma L33
Peavy, Linda S. L16
Pelican, Suzanne D40
Pepin, Jacques C122
Perkins, Eric W37, W93
Perry, Paul C5
Petersen, Marilyn L63, L68
Pickarski, Ron V103
Pickle, Julianne V23
Pierce, Gail CA58
Pinion Press W124
Pinker, Jennifer D86
Piscatella, Joseph C8, C97
Pitchford, Polly V104
Pitzer, Sara CA83
Polak, Jeanne C108
Polunin, Miriam CA84
Postley, John E. F24
Powell, Janet C. OR11
Powers, Margaret F58
Prabhupada, A.C.
Bhaktivedanta Swami *see*
A.C. Bhaktivedanta Swami
Prabhupada

TITLE INDEX

- A -

323

Bircher-Benner Nutrition plan for headache and migraine patients H9

Bircher-Benner Nutrition plan for liver and gallbladder problems G4

Bircher-Benner Nutrition plan for prostate problems H20

Bircher-Benner Nutrition plan for skin problems H21

Bland-diet cookbook G11

Bless your heart C61

Bloomingdale's Eat healthy diet W98

Body type diet and lifetime nutrition plan, Dr. Abravanel's W2

Book of elegant everyday cooking, Time-Life C123

Book of kudzu H34

Book of soybeans N51

Book of tempeh N49

Book of tofu N50

Book of whole meals V6

Bragg Gourmet health recipes N9

Bread and Circus Whole food bible N25

Breads, grains and pastas, Cooking light W76

Breakfast, lunch, and dinner of champions L62

Brewer Medical diet for normal and high-risk pregnancy L1

Brilliant Bean CA68

Bristol recipe book CA4

Brown rice cookbook CA58

Brown rice cookbook CA59

Bypass patients' wellness diet C6

- C -

Cabbagetown Cafe cookbook V15

Calcium-requirement cookbook MS23
Calendar cookbook M1
California Dental Association Low-sugar cookbook OR1
Canada cooks! L32
Candida albicans yeast-free cookbook H4
Candida control cookbook H3
Canning and Preserving without sugar D91
Carbohydrate addict's diet W120
Carbohydrate and sodium controlled recipes R16
Carbohydrate craver's diet cookbook W43
Cardiac cuisine C104
Caring and cooking for the allergic child F38
Caring and cooking for the hyperactive child F42
Caring for the healing heart C3
Carlson Wade's Factbook on arthritis, nutrition, and natural
    therapy MS13
Carlton Fredericks' New low blood sugar and you D20
Carlton Fredericks' High-fiber way to total health CA35
Cashews and lentils, apples and oats V96
Celiac disease needs a diet for life F50
Change of heart: steps to healthy eating C52
Changing seasons macrobiotic cookbook M16
Cheap and nutritious (and delicious) cookbook L69
Chico-san cookbook M3
Chinese American food practices, customs, and holidays D3
Chinese meatless cooking V68
Chinese salt-free diet cookbook C203
Chinese vegetarian delights V63
Cholesterol and children C80
Cholesterol count down C59
Cholesterol lowering and controlling C64

- E -

Earth water fire air V99
Eastern vegetarian cooking V71
Easy livin' low-calorie microwave cooking W114
Easy-to-chew and easy-on-salt OR11
Eat and lose weight, Betty Crocker's W158
Eat and stay slim, Better Homes and Gardens W72
Eat fish, live better C17
Eat for strength V33
Eat light and love it! C106
Eat light W78
Eat right, eat well--the Italian way C89
Eat smart for a healthy heart cookbook C2
Eat well, be well cookbook C137
Eater's choice C55
Eating alive G2
Eating and competing L66
Eating for a healthy baby, Good Housekeeping L7
Eating for a healthy heart, Good Housekeeping C54
Eating for A's L58
Eating for the eighties V13
Eating for two L2
Eating healthy in the fast lane W172
Eating hints: recipes and tips for better nutrition during
    cancer treatment CA9
Eating naturally: recipes for food with fibre CA27
Eating right for two L9
Eating right W46
Eating well in a busy world C27
Eating well when you just can't eat the way you used to L78

- F -

- H -

- I -

- J -

Jane Brody's Good food gourmet W6
Japanese vegetarian cooking V66
Jeanne Rose's Herbal guide to food H48
Jenifer Lang Cooks for kids L47
Jewish low-cholesterol cookbook C66
Jewish vegetarian cooking V87
Jim Fobel's Diet feasts W80
Joy of gluten-free cooking F56
Joy of living salt-free C179
Judy Beck's Gourmet cookbook for a slimmer you W118
Judy Brown's Guide to natural foods cooking V94
Juel Andersen's Tempeh primer N40
Juel Andersen's Tofu kitchen N37
Juicing book H40
Just what the doctor ordered H27

- K -

K factor: reversing and preventing high blood pressure
    without drugs C180
Kamen Plan for total nutrition during pregnancy L8
Kathy cooks--vegetarian, low cholesterol C140
Kay Spicer's Light and easy choices D42
Kidfood L51
Kidney patients' wellness diet--tasty recipes R13
Kid's diet cookbook W36
Kids dish it up--sugar-free L52
Kids, food and diabetes D52
Kitchen crew L57
Kitchen herbal H47

- L -

Lunchbox book L45

- M -

Macro-nutrient diet for quick permanent weight loss,
    Dr. Homola's W58
Macrobiotic cancer prevention cookbook CA16
Macrobiotic community cookbook M20
Macrobiotic cooking for everyone M9
Macrobiotic cuisine M24
Macrobiotic dessert book M27
Macrobiotic family favorites M17
Macrobiotic kitchen M3
Macrobiotics and beyond M26
Magic of tofu and other soybean products N47
Magic of wheat cookery CA45
Main courses for the microwave-convection oven F27
Make it easy, make it light W154
Making do without salt C171
Making your own baby food L34
Making your own home proteins N18
Margo Oliver's Cookbook for seniors L77
Mayo Clinic Renal diet cookbook R23
McDougall Health-supporting cookbook W52
McDougall Plan for super health and life-long
    weight loss W54
McDougall program W53
Meals in minutes cookbook W30
Meals without squeals L41
Mealtime manual for people with disabilities and the
    aging L73

Not-strictly vegetarian cookbook V97
Nourishing your unborn child L19
Now and Zen epicure V113
Nutri/System Flavor Set-Point weight loss cookbook W24
Nutrition and eating problems of oral and head-neck
    surgeries OR7
Nutrition and the cancer patient CA10
Nutrition: for patients receiving chemotherapy and
    radiation treatment CA8
Nutrition for the childbearing year L6
Nutrition nuggets recipes W9
Nutrition plan for digestive problems, Bircher-Benner G1
Nutrition plan for liver and gallbladder problems,
    Bircher-Benner G4
Nutrition, the cancer answer CA14
Nutritional cooking with tofu N45

- O -

Oat and wheat bran health plan C37
Oat bran baking book C31
Oat bran cookbook C38
Oat bran cookbook C40
Oat bran recipes C42
Oat bran way C44
Oat cookbook C32
Oat cuisine C36
Oat cuisine C43
Off the shelf N20
Official eating to win cookbook L61
Older Americans cookbook L76

Pregnancy, children and the vegan diet L22
Pritikin Permanent weight-loss manual W49
Pritikin promise W95
Protein-balanced vegetarian cookery V27
Protein restricted recipes R20
Pure and simple N11

- Q -

Quick and delicious low-fat low-salt cookbook C195
Quick and easy menu cookbook, Weight Watchers W106
Quick and easy recipes to lower your cholesterol C67
Quick and natural macrobiotic cookbook M18
Quick and organized healthy cuisine for busy people C114
Quick cholesterol clean-out C50
Quick harvest V89
Quick 'n natural, no salt, low cholesterol cooking C142
Quick Start Plus Program cookbook, Weight Watchers W21
Quick Success Program cookbook, Weight Watchers W20

- R -

Real food cookbook N30
Recipe for health H14
Recipes for allergics F78
Recipes for better bones MS20
Recipes for diabetics D75
Recipes for life C147
Recipes for the heart C197
Recipes for the patient with diabetes D23
Recipes to lower your fat thermostat W132

Recovery: from cancer to health through macrobiotics CA18
Reducing cholesterol C98
Regenerative diet H24
Reluctant cook L70
Renal diet cookbook, Mayo Clinic R25
Renal family cookbook R25
Renal lifestyles manual and diet guide, 1989 R6
Renal patient's guide to good eating R12
Renny Darling's Cooking great! looking great! feeling great! W166
Reversing diabetes D47
Revolutionary 7-unit low fat diet W128
Rice flour cookbook F56
Richard Simmons' Never-say-diet cookbook W26
Richard Simmons' Better body book W25
Rodale's Basic natural foods cookbook N22
Romantic vegetarian V29
Rosemary Conley's Hip and thigh diet cookbook W130
Rotation diet cookbook W86
Rutgers Guide to lowering your cholesterol C53

- S -

Salt-free baking at home C154
Salt-free cooking C155
Salt-free diet book C177
Salt-free herb cookery C190
Salt-free recipes: to save your life! C175
Salt: the role of sodium in your diet C169
Save your heart with Susan C13
Savory soups F95

Superimmunity for kids H15
Suzanne's Natural food cookbook M21
Sweet and natural D112
Sweet and natural desserts D99
Sweet and sugarfree D94
Sweets without sugar D98
Switchover! CA38

- T -

T-factor diet W65
TAG: a diabetic food system D37
Taming of the C.A.N.D.Y.* monster L53
Taming of tofu N52
Target recipes W125
Tassajara cooking V93
Taste for health C103
Taste of life C111
Taste of tofu N46
Tasting good: the international salt-free diet cookbook C188
Teen cuisine OR10
Teenage surefire diet cookbook W38
Tempeh Cookbook N38
Tempeh primer, Juel Andersen's N40
Thai vegetarian cooking V77
There is a cure for arthritis MS1
There is a way F14
Thin so fast W8
30-day cholesterol program, Barbara Kraus C63
30-day way to the born-again body W42
30-minute light gourmet W159

- U -

- Y -

- Z -

KEYWORD INDEX

low-carbohydrate C81,
D72-D73, H5, R16, W70,
W119-W124
low-cholesterol C4, C8,
C21, C22-C27, C31, C33,
C44-C150, D69, D75,
D76, H27, L64, L67, L71,
MS22, MS23, N45, W59,
W109, W117, W151,
W160, W162, W163,
W166, W167, W169,
W182
low-fat CA47-CA53,
CA90-CA91, C2, C8, C23-
C29, C31, C82-C141,
C151-C153, C193-C206,
D34, D69-D71, D74-D77,
D96, D116, F57, H27,
L67, L71, L78, MS17,
MS18, MS20, MS22, R13,
V99, W32, W44, W51,
W63-W68, W109, W123,
W125-W182
low-milk D73
low-phenylalanine H18-H19
low-phosphorus R12
low-potassium R12, R13,
R22, R23
low-protein C111, H18-H19,
R12, R13, R19-R23, W45
low-red-meat W167

low-residue CA5
low-salt C2, C4, C8, C26,
C112-C139, C142-C148,
C154-C206, D34, D69,
D76, H27, L67, L71, L78,
MS22, N11, N45, R12,
R13, R16, R22-R25, W32,
W45-W46, W50, W52,
W63, W116-W118, W124,
W158-W169, W172-W177
low-saturated-fat C96, C105
low-starch W63
low-sugar C8, C27,
C128-C140, C146-C148,
C198-C206, D69-D71,
D73, D78-D113, D116,
F57, F75, L78, MS20,
OR1, OR3, W45, W63,
W68, W109, W118,
W163-W171, W174-W182
low-sweetener C201
lunchbasket V38
lunchbox L45

- M -

macro-nutrient W58
macrobiotic CA15-CA18,
CA57, C207-C208, D114-
D115, H37, H49-H51, M1-
M28, MS8, V94, V112

REFERENCES

Aihara, Herman. *Basic macrobiotics*. Tokyo: Japan Publications; Distributed through New York: Harper and Row, 1985.

American Diabetes Association Task Force on Nutrition and Exchange Lists. "Nutritional recommendations and principles for individuals with diabetes mellitus: 1986". *Diabetes Care* 1987 V.10: 126-132.

American Dietetic Association Reports. "Position paper on the vegetarian approach to eating". *Journal of American Dietetic Association* 1980 V.77: 61-69.

Anderson, J.W.; Chen, W.L.; and Sieling, B. "Hypolipidemic effects of high-carbohydrate, high-fiber diets". *Metabolism* 1980 V.29: 551-558.

Anderson, J.W.; Gustafson, N.J.; Bryant, C.A.; and Tietyen-Clark, J. "Dietary fiber and diabetes: a comprehensive review and practical application". *Journal of the American Dietetic Association* 1987 V.87: 1189-1197.

Anderson, J.W.; Story, L.; Sieling, B.; Chen, W.J.L.; Petro, M.S.; and Story, J. "Hypocholesterolemic effects of oat-bran or bean intake for hypercholesterolemic men". *American Journal of Clinical Nutrition* 1984 V.40: 1146-1155.

Armstrong, B. and Doll, R. "Environmental factors and cancer incidence and mortality in different countries, with special reference to dietary practices". *International Journal of Cancer*

1975 V.15: 617-631.

Atkins, F.M. "The basis of immediate hypersensitivity reactions to food". *Nutrition Reviews* 1983 V.41(8): 229-234.

Barillas, C. and Solomons, N.W. "Effective reduction of lactose maldigestion in preschool children by direct addition of beta-galactosidases to milk at mealtime". *Pediatrics* 1987 V.79: 766-772.

Bates, D. "Dietary lipids and multiple sclerosis". *Upsala Journal of Medical Sciences Supplements* 1990 V.48: 173-187.

Bertram, J.S.; Kolonel, L.N.; and Meyskens, F.L. "Rationale and strategies for chemoprevention of cancer in humans". *Cancer Research* 1987 V.47: 3012-3031.

Bierman, E.L. "Nutritional management of adult and juvenile diabetics". In Winick, M. ed. *Nutritional management of genetic disorders.* New York: Wiley, 1979, pp. 107-117.

Browner, W. "Preventable complications of diabetes mellitus". *Western Journal of Medicine* 1986 V.145: 701-703.

Brunzell, J.D.; Lerner, R.L.; Hazzard, W.R.; Porte, D.; and Bierman, E.L. "Improved glucose tolerance with high carbohydrate feeding in mild diabetes". *New England Journal of Medicine* 1971 V.284: 521-524.

Brunzell, J.D.; Lerner, R.L.; Porte, D.; and Bierman, E.L. "Effect of a fat free high carbohydrate diet on diabetic subjects with fasting hyperglycemia". *Diabetes* 1974 V.23: 138-142.

Bulpitt, C.J.; Broughton, P.M.; Markowe, H.L.J.; Marmot, M.G.; Rose, G.; Semmence A.; and Shipley, M.J. "The relationship between both sodium and potassium intake and blood pressure in London civil servants". *Journal of Chronic Diseases* 1986 V.39: 211-219.

Butrum, R.R.; Clifford, C.K.; and Lanza, E. "NCI dietary guideline: rationale". *American Journal of Clinical Nutrition* 1988 V.48 supplements.

Carroll, K.K. and Khor, H.T. "Dietary fat in relation to tumorigenesis". *Progress in Biochemical Pharmacology* 1975 V.10: 308-353.

Cathcart, E.S.; Gonnerman, W.A.; Leslie, C.A.; and Hayes, K.C. "Dietary n-3 fatty acids and arthritis". *Journal of Internal Medicine Supplement* 1989 V.225(731): 217-223.

Chandra, R.K. and Sahni, S. "Immunological aspects of gluten intolerance". *Nutrition Reviews* 1981 V.39: 117-120.

Corbin, S.B.; Kleinman, D.V.; and Lane, J.M. "New opportunities for enhancing oral health: moving toward the 1990 objectives for the nation". *Public Health Reports* 1985 V.100: 515-524.

Dagnelie, P.C.; van Staveren, W.A.; Vergote, F.J.; Burema, J.; vant Hof, M.A.; van Klaveren, J.D.; and Hautvast, J.G. "Nutritional status of infants aged 4 to 18 months on macrobiotic diets and matched omnivorous control infants: a population-based mixed-longitudinal study. II. Growth and psychomotor development". *European Journal of Clinical Nutrition* 1989 V.43(5): 325-338.

Dagnelie, P.C.; van Staveren, W.A.; Vergote, F.J.; Dingjan, P.G.; van den Berg, H.; and Hautvast, J.G. "Increased risk of vitamin B-12 and iron deficiency in infants on macrobiotic diets". *American Journal of Clinical Nutrition* 1989 V.50(4): 818-824.

Dagnelie, P.C.; van Staveren, W.A.; Verschuren, S.A.; and Hautvast, J.G. "Nutritional status of infants aged 4 to 18 months on macrobiotic diets and matched omnivorous control infants: a population-based mixed-longitudinal study. I. Weaning pattern, energy and nutrient intake". *European Journal of Clinical Nutrition* 1989 V.43(5): 311-323.

Dagnelie, P.C.; Vergote, F.J.; van Staveren, W.A.; ven den Berg, H.; Dingjan, P.G.; and Hautvast, J.G. "High prevalence of rickets in infants on macrobiotic diets". *American Journal of Clinical Nutrition* 1990 V.51(2): 202-208.

Department of Health and Human Services. Public Health Service. *The Surgeon General's report on nutrition and health.* Washington, DC: Dept. of Health and Human Services, 1988.

Dornbrand, Laurie; Hoole, Axalla J.; Fletcher, Robert H.; and Pickard, C. Glenn; editors. *Manual of clinical problems in adult ambulatory care with annotated key references.* Boston, MA: Little, Brown and Co., 1985.

Encyclopedia of associations, 1991. 25th ed. Detroit, MI: Gale, 1990.

Encyclopedia of associations: international organizations, 1990. 24th ed. Detroit, MI: Gale, 1990

Encyclopedia of governmental advisory organizations, 1990-1991. 7th ed. Detroit, MI: Gale, 1989.

Farris, R.P.; Cresanta, J.; Croft, J.; Weber, L.; Frank, G.; and Berenson, G. "Macronutrient intakes of 10-year-old children, 1973-1982". *Journal of the American Dietetic Association* 1986 V.86: 765-770.

Garfinkel L. *Presentation before the American Cancer Society 2nd National Conference on Diet, Nutrition and Cancer.* Houston, TX, 1985.

Gibson, R.A. "The effect of diets containing fish and fish oils on disease risk factors in humans". *Australian and New Zealand Journal of Medicine* 1988 V.18(5): 713-722.

Gluten Intolerance Group. *Fact sheet on celiac sprue.* Seattle, WA.

Goodnight, S.H.; Harris, W.S.; Connor, W.E.; and Illingworth, R.D. "Polyunsaturated fatty acids, hyperlipidemia, and thrombosis". *Arteriosclerosis* 1982 V.2: 87-113.

Graham, S.; Dayal, H.; Swanson, M.; Mittelman, A.; and Wilkinson, G. "Diet in the epidemiology of cancer of the colon and rectum". *Journal of the National Cancer Institute* 1978 V.61: 709-714.

Gussow, J.D. and Thomas, P.R. "Health, natural, and organic: foods or frauds?" In Gussow, J.D. and Thomas, P.R. *The Nutrition debate: sorting out some answers.* Palo Alto, CA: Bull Publishing Co., 1986, pp. 208-267.

Gustafsson, B.E.; Quensel, C.E.; Lanke, L.S.; Lundquist, C.; Grahnen, H.; Bonow, B.E.; and Krasse, B. "The Vipeholm dental caries study: the effect of different levels of carbohydrate intake on caries activity in 436 individuals observed for five years". *Acta Odontologica Scandinavica* 1954 V.11: 232-364.

Hornstra, G. "Dietary prevention of coronary heart disease: effect of dietary fats on arterial thrombosis". *Postgraduate Medical Journal* 1980 V.56: 563-570.

Hubert, H.B.; Feinleib, M.; McNamara, P.M.; and Castelli, W.P. "Obesity as an independent risk factor for cardiovascular disease: a 26-year follow-up of participants in the Framingham Heart Study". *Circulation* 1983 V.67: 968-977.

Jenkins, D.J.A.; Leeds, A.R.; Newton, C.; and Cummings, J.H. "Effect of pectin, guar gum, and wheat fiber on serum cholesterol". *Lancet* 1975 V.i: 1116-1117.

Jenkins, D.J.A.; Wolever, T.M.S.; Jenkins, A.L.; Lee, R.; Wong, G.S.; and Josse, R. "Glycemic response to wheat products: reduced response to pasta but no effect of fiber". *Diabetes Care* 1983 V.6: 155-159.

REFERENCES

Jenkins, D.J.A.; Wolever, T.M.S.; Taylor, R.H.; Barker, H.; and Fielden, H. "Exceptionally low blood glucose response to dried beans: comparison with other carbohydrate foods". *British Medical Journal* 1980 V.281: 578-80.

Kannel, W. B. and Thom, T.J. "Declining cardiovascular mortality". *Circulation* 1984 V.70: 3, 331-336.

Kawasaki, T.; Delea, C.S.; Bartter, F.C.; and Smith, H. "The effect of high-sodium and low-sodium intakes on blood pressure and other related variables in human subjects with idiopathic hypertension". *American Journal of Medicine* 1978 V.64: 193-198.

Kirby, R.W.; Anderson, J.W.; Sieling, B.; Rees, E.C.; Chen, W.-J. L; Miller, R.E.; and Kay, R.M. "Oat-bran intake selectively lowers serum low-density lipoprotein cholesterol concentrations of hypercholesterolemic men". *American Journal of Clinical Nutrition* 1981 V.34: 824-829.

Kolars, J.C.; Levitt, M.S.; Aouji, M.; and Savaiano, D.A. "Yogurt - an autodigesting source of lactose". *New England Journal of Medicine* 1984 V.310: 1-3.

Kotzsch, Ronald E. *Macrobiotics, yesterday and today.* Tokyo: Japan Publications; Distributed through New York: Harper and Row, 1985.

Kromhout, D.; Bosschieter, E.B.; and Coulander, C. de L. "The inverse relation between fish consumption and 20 year mortality from coronary heart disease". *New England Journal of Medicine* 1985 V.312: 1205-1224.

Krotkiewski, M.; Bjorntorp, P.; Sjostrom, L.; and Smith, U. "Impact of obesity on metabolism in men and women: importance of regional adipose tissue distribution". *Journal of Clinical Investigation* 1983 V.72: 1150-1162.

Kummet, T.; Moon, T.E.; and Meyskens, F.L., Jr. "Vitamin A: evidence for its preventive role in human cancer". *Nutrition and Cancer* 1983 V.5(2): 96-106.

Lenfant, C. "Advancements in meeting the 1990 hypertension objectives". *Journal of the American Medical Association* 1987 V.257: 2709-2718.

Leslie, C.A.; Conte, J.M.; Hayes, K.C. and Cathcart, E.S. "A fish oil diet reduces the severity of collagen induced arthritis after onset of the disease". *Clinical Experimental Immunology* 1988 V.73(2): 328-332.

Lew, E.A. and Garfinkel, L. "Variations in mortality by weight among 750,000 men and women". *Journal of Chronic Diseases* 1979 V.32: 563-576.

MacMahon, S.W. "Alcohol consumption and hypertension". *Hypertension* 1987 V.9: 111-121.

Metcalfe, D.D. "Food Allergens". *Clinical Reviews in Allergy* 1985 V.3: 331-349.

Metllin, C. "Epidemiologic studies on vitamin A and cancer". *Advances in Nutrition Research* 1984 V.6:47-65.

Miller, D.R.; Specker, B.L.; Ho, M.L.; and Norman, E.J. "Vitamin B-12 status in a macrobiotic community". *American Journal of Clinical Nutrition* 1991 V.53(2): 524-529.

Morley, J.E. "Nutritional status of the elderly". *American Journal of Medicine* 1986 V.81: 679-698.

Navia, J.M. "Research advances and needs in nutrition in oral health and disease". In Pollack, R.L. and Kravitz, E.; eds. *Nutrition in oral health and disease.* New York: Lea and Febiger, 1985, pp. 426-467.

1988 Joint National Committee. "The 1988 report of the Joint National Committee on Detection, evaluation, and treatment of high blood pressure". *Archives of Internal Medicine* 1988 V.148: 36-69.

Paige, David M. *Clinical nutrition.* 2nd ed. St. Louis, MO: C.V. Mosby Co., 1988.

Palgi, A. "Vitamin A and lung cancer: a perspective". *Nutrition and Cancer* 1984 V.6(2): 105-120.

Pemberton, Cecilia M.; Moxness, Karen E.; German, Mary J.; Nelson, Jennifer K.; and Gastineau, Clifford F. *Mayo clinic diet manual: a handbook of dietary practices.* 6th ed. Philadelphia, PA: B.C. Decker Inc., 1988.

REFERENCES

Richards, A.M.; Nicholls, M.G.; Espiner, E.A.; Ikram, K.; Maslowski, A.H.; Hamilton, E.J.; and Wells, J.E. "Blood-pressure response to moderate sodium restriction and to potassium supplementation in mild essential hypertension". *Lancet* 1984 V.i: 757-761.

Riggs, B.L. and Melton, L.J. "Involutional osteoporosis". *New England Journal of Medicine* 1986 V.314: 1676-1686.

Rose, D.P.; Boyar, A.P.; and Wynder, E.L. "International comparisons of mortality rates for cancer of the breast, ovary, prostate, and colon, and per capita food consumption". *Cancer* 1986 V.58: 2363-2371.

Sampson, H.A.; Buckley, R.H.; and Metcalfe, D.D. "Food allergy". *Journal of the American Medical Association* 1987 V.258(20): 2886-2890.

Sinnett, P.F. and Whyte, H.M. "Epidemiological studies in a total highland population, Tukisenta, New Guinea. Cardiovascular disease and relevant clinical, electrocardiographic, radiological, and biochemical findings". *Journal of Chronic Diseases* 1973 V. 26: 265-290.

Southgate, D.A.T. "Natural or unnatural foods?" *British Medical Journal* 1984 V288: 881-882.

Swank, R.L. and Dugan, B.B. "Effect of low saturated fat diet in early and late cases of multiple sclerosis". *Lancet* 1990 V.336(8706): 37-39.

Tyroler, H. A.; Heyden, S.; and Hames, C.G. "Weight and hypertension: Evans County studies of blacks and whites". In Paul, O. ed. *Epidemiology and control of hypertension.* New York: Stratton, 1975, pp. 177-205.

Walser, Mackenzie; Imbembo, Anthony L.; Margolis, Simeon; and Elfert, Gloria A. *Nutritional management: the John Hopkins handbook.* Philadelphia, PA: W.B. Saunders Co., 1984.

Williams, Sue Rodwell. *Mowry's basic nutrition and diet therapy.* 7th ed. St. Louis, MO: Times Mirror/Mosby College Publishing, 1984.

Yetiv, Jack Zeev. *Popular nutritional practices: a scientific appraisal.* Toledo, OH: Popular Medicine Press, 1986.

Ziegler, R.G.; Mason, T.J.; Stemhagen, A.; Hoover, R.; Schoenberg, J.B.; Gridley, G.; Virgo, P.W.; and Fraumeni, J.F. "Carotenoid intake, vegetables, and the risk of lung cancer among white men in New Jersey". *American Journal of Epidemiology* 1986 V.123: 1080-1093.

APPENDIX 1:
DIRECTORY OF
SELECTED PUBLISHERS

Alaska Northwest Pub. Co.
 Box 4-EEE, Anchorage, AK 99509
Allergy Publications
 P.O. Box 640, Menlo Park, CA 94026
Allied Books
 31 W. 21st Street, New York, NY 10010
American Cancer Society
 National Office, 1599 Clifton Road, N.E., Atlanta, GA 30329
American Digestive Disease Society
 60 E. 42nd Street, Room 411, New York, NY 10165
American Institute for Cancer Research
 P.O. Box 76216, Washington, DC 20013
Andrews and McMeel
 4900 Main Street, Kansas City, MO 64112
Apple Press
 5536 S. E. Harlow, Milwaukie, OR 97222
Appleton-Century-Crofts
 292 Madison Ave., New York, NY 10017
Ashgrove Press
 26 Gay Street, Bath, Avon, England BA1 2PD
Bala
 268 West 23rd Street, New York, NY 10011
Barrie and Jenkins
 29 W. 35th St., New York, NY 10001
Betterway Publications
 White Hall, VA 22987

Blue Poppy Press
    212-2678 West Broadway, Vancouver, BC, Canada V6K 2G3
Body Press
    P.O. Box 5367, Tucson, AZ 85703
Book Peddlers
    18326 Minnetonka Blvd., Deephaven, MN 55391
Book Publishing Company
    P.O. Box 99, Summertown, TN 38483
Bristol Publishing Enterprises, Inc.
    P.O. Box 1737, San Leandro, CA 94577
British Diabetic Association
    10 Queen Anne Street, London, England W1M 0BD
C. C. Thomas
    2600 S. 1st Street, Springfield, IL 62794
C. L. Lorimer
    128 E. Drummond Ave., Glendale Heights, IL 60139
Capitol Neighborhood Press
    2420 So. Columbia, Olympia, WA 98501
Cedar Creek Publishers
    2310 Sawmill Rd., Fort Wayne, IN 46825
Central Vermont Publishers
    P.O. Box 700, Morrisville, VT 05661
Century Hutchinson Ltd.
    Brookmount House, 62-65 Chandos Place, Covent Garden,
    London, England WC2N 4NW
Commercial Writing Service
    P.O. Box 3074, Iowa City, IA 52244
Cornwall Books
    4 Cornwall Drive, East Brunswick, NJ 08816
Creative Arts Communications
    833 Bancroft Way, Berkeley, CA 94701

Creative Cuisine, Inc.
 P.O. Box 518, Naples, FL 33939
Cromlech Books
 175 Nobska Rd., Woods Hole, MA 02543
Crossing Press
 Trumansburg, NY 14886
Cy DeCosse
 5900 Green Oak Drive, Minnetonka, MN 55343
DCI Pub.
 P.O. Box 47945, Minneapolis, MN 55447
Dell
 1 Dag Hammarskjold Plaza, New York, NY 10017
Dial Press
 1 Dag Hammarskjold Plaza, New York, NY 10017
Diabetes Center
 P.O. Box 739, Wayzata, MN 55391
Earthtones Press
 P.O. Box 2341, Grass Valley, CA 95945
East-West Press
 P.O. Box 4204, Minneapolis, MN 55414
Elfin Cove Press
 P.O. Box 924, Redmond, WA 98073-0924
Elins Laboratories
 Box 90, West Chester, PA 19381
F. Whalen
 P.O. Box 5981, Lake Charles, LA 70606
FC&A Publishing
 103 Clover Green, Peachtree City, CA 30269
Fisher Books
 P.O. Box 38040, Tucson, AZ 85740

Fitness Publications
  1991 Country Place, Ojai, CA 93023
Fleming H. Revell Co.
  Old Tappan, NJ 07675
Forbes
  60 5th Ave., New York, NY 10020
Franklin Publishers
  P.O. Box 1338, Bryn Mawr, PA 19010
Frederick Fell Publishers
  386 Park Ave. South, New York, NY 10016
George F. Stickley
  210 West Washington Square, Philadelphia, PA 19106
Globe Pequot Press
  Chester, CT 06412
Golden Press
  850 Third Ave., New York, NY 10022
Good Housekeeping
  120 Park Ave., New York, NY 10017
Grafton
  145 Palisades, Dobbs Ferry, NY 10522
Graphique Publishing
  P.O. Box 1332, Ann Arbor, MI 48106
Grunwald and Radcliff
  5049 Admiral Wright Rd., Suite 344, Virginia Beach, VA
  23462
Gulf & Western
  1230 Avenue of the Americas, New York, NY 10020
Hamlyn
  31 Pamaren Way, Nevato, CA 94949
Healing Kitchen
  P.O. Box 331, Graton, CA 95444

Health Saver Press
   Route 3, Box 972, Troup, TX 75789
Henry Regnery Co.
   180 N. Michigan Ave., Chicago, IL 60601
Himalayan International Institute of Yoga Science and
   Philosophy
   Honesdale, PA 18431
Hippocrene Books
   171 Madison Ave., New York, NY 10016
Hollym International Corp.
   18 Donald Place, Elizabeth, NJ 07208
International Diabetes Center
   P.O. Box 739, Wayzata, MN 55391
International Diabetes Center, Park Nicollet Medical
   Foundation
   5000 W. 39th Street, Minneapolis, MN 55416
J.P. Guenther
   P.O. Box 453, Palatine, IL 60078-0453
Keats Publishing
   27 Pine Street, Box 876 New Canaan, CT 06840
Kerry and Christy Briggs
   2649 Cypress Way, Salt Lake City, UT 84121
Larousse
   572 Fifth Ave., New York, NY
Life, Mind, & Body
   1515 Scott Street, San Francisco, CA 94115
Lowfat Publications
   52 Condolea Court, Lake Oswego, OR 97035
M. Evans
   216 E. 49th Street, New York, NY 10017

Meadowbrook, Inc.
   18318 Minnetonka Blvd., Deephaven, MN 55391
Medi-Ed Press
   P.O. Box 957, East Lansing, MI 48823
Melius & Peterson Publishing Corp.
   Aberdeen, SD 57401
National Cancer Institute
   Building 31, Room 10A24, Bethesda, MD 20892
Nature's Pantry
   10200 NE 10th Street, Bellevue, WA 98004
Nutrition Publications
   P.O. Box 313, Hinsdale, IL 60521
Omega Books
   42 Bloomsbury St., London, WC18 3QJ
101 Productions
   834 Mission Street, San Francisco, CA 94103
Optima
   251-33 Anza Dr., St. Clarita, CA 91355
Oregon Health Sciences University Bookstore
   3181 S. W. Sam Jackson Park Rd., Portland, OR 97201
Ortho Information Services
   Box 5047, San Ramon, CA 94583
Pawson Books
   Hall Farm Cottage, Hooton Lane, Ravenfield, Rotherham,
   South Yorkshire S65 4NH
Pelican Publishing Co.
   1101 Monroe Street, Gretna, LA 70053
Piatkus Books
   5 Windmill St., London W1P 1HF
Price Stern Sloan, Inc.
   360 N. La Cienega Boulevard, Los Angeles, CA 90048

Prima Publishing & Communications
P.O. Box 1260JZ, Rocklin, CA 95677
R.M. Baskin
P.O. Box 717, Oneonta, NY 13820
Robert J. Brady Co.
Bowie, MD 20715
Routledge & Kegan Paul
29 W. 35th Street, New York, NY 10001
Royal House Publishing Co., Inc.
9456 Wilshire Boulevard, Beverly Hills, CA 90212
Rutledge Hill Press
513 3rd Ave. South, Nashville, TN 37210
St. Joseph Hospital
Community Health Education Department, 1110 W. Stewart
Drive, Orange, CA 92668
Shambhala
314 Dartmouth Street, Boston, MA 02116
Smuggler's Cove Publishing
107 W. John Street, Seattle, WA 98119
Stein & Day
Scarborough House, Briarcliff Manor, New York, NY 10510
Straight Status Press
P.O. Box 315, New Castle, IN 47354
Surrey Books
101 E. Erie Street, Suite 900, Chicago, IL 60611
Ten Speed Press
P.O. Box 7123, Berkeley, CA 94707
Thorsons Publishers
377 Park Ave. South, New York, NY 10016
Tudor
P.O. Box 3443, Greensboro, NC 27402

Turning Point Publications
   1122 M Street, Eureka, CA 95501
Vitality House International
   3707 North Canyon Rd., # 8-C, Provo, UT 84604
Warner Books
   75 Rockefeller Plaza, New York, NY 10019
Wheat Bin, Inc.,
   R.R. #1, Box 64, Halstead, KS 67056
Woodbridge Press
   P.O. Box 6189, Santa Barbara, CA 93160
Wordscope Associates
   P.O. Box 1594, Skokie, IL 60077
Workman Publishing Inc.
   1 West 39th Street, New York, NY 10018

APPENDIX 2:
NUMBERS OF DEATHS AND RANKS OF SELECTED CAUSES OF DEATH, ALL RACES, UNITED STATES, 1985-88

Rank	Cause of Death	1985	1986	1987	1988
	all causes	2,086,440	2,105,361	2,123,323	2,167,999
1	heart diseases	771,169	765,490	760,353	765,156
2	cancer	461,563	469,376	476,927	485,048
3	stroke	153,050	149,643	149,835	150,517
4	accidents & adverse effects	93,457	95,277	95,020	97,100
5	chronic obstructive pulmonary diseases	74,662	76,559	78,380	82,852
6	pneumonia & influenza	67,615	69,812	69,225	77,662
7	diabetes mellitus	36,969	37,184	38,532	40,368
8	suicide	29,453	30,904	30,796	30,407
9	chronic liver disease & cirrhosis	26,767	26,159	26,201	26,409

Source: National Center for Health Statistics. *Health, United States, 1990.* Hyattsville, Maryland, 1991.

APPENDIX 3:
1990 DIETARY GUIDELINES AND
ADVICE FOR AMERICANS

1. *Eat a variety of foods, choosing different foods from each group.* Get the many nutrients your body needs by choosing different foods you enjoy eating from these five groups daily: vegetables, fruits, grain products, milk and milk products, and meats and meat alternatives.

2. *Maintain healthy weight.* If you are too fat or too thin, your chances of developing health problems are increased. Check to see if you are at a healthy weight. If not, set reasonable weight goals and try for long-term success through better habits of eating and exercise. Have children's heights and weights checked regularly by a doctor.

3. *Choose a diet low in fat, saturated fat, and cholesterol.* Have your blood-cholesterol level checked, preferably by a doctor. If it is high, follow the doctor's advice about diet and, if necessary, medication. If it is at the desirable level, help keep it that way with a diet low in fat, saturated fat, and cholesterol: eat plenty of vegetables, fruits, and grain products; choose lean meats, fish, poultry without skin, and lowfat dairy products most of the time; and use fats and oils sparingly.

4. *Choose a diet with plenty of vegetables, fruits and grain products.* Eat more vegetables, including dry beans and peas; fruits; and breads, cereals, pasta, and rice. Increase your fiber intake by eating more of a variety of foods that contain fiber

naturally.

5. *Use sugars only in moderation*--sparingly if your calorie needs are low. Avoid excessive snacking and brush and floss your teeth regularly.

6. *Use salt and sodium only in moderation.* Have your blood pressure checked. If it is high, consult a doctor about diet and medication. If it is normal, help keep it that way; maintain a healthy weight, exercise regularly, and try to use less salt and sodium. (Normal blood pressure for adults: systolic less than 140 mmHg and diastolic less than 85 mmHg.)

7. *If you drink alcoholic beverages, do so in moderation.* The definition for moderation for women is no more than one drink a day and for men, no more than two drinks a day. The following are counted as one drink: one 12 ounces of regular beer, one 5 ounces of wine, or one 1-1/2 ounces of distilled spirits (80 proof).

Source:
Department of Agriculture and Department of Health and Human Services, U.S. *Nutrition and your health: dietary guidelines for Americans.* 3rd. ed. Washington, DC: Government Printing Office, 1990.